The
Imitation
of
Christ

"Write, read, sing, sigh, keep silence, pray, bear thy crosses manfully; eternal life is worthy of all these, and greater combats."

—*Bk. III, chap. 47*

The Imitation of Christ

by

Thomas à Kempis

Translated from the Original Latin
by the Right Rev.
Richard Challoner, D.D.

To which are added
Practical Reflections and a Prayer
after Each Chapter

TAN BOOKS AND PUBLISHERS

Imprimatur: ✚ Michael Augustine
                  Archbishop of New York
                  New York
                  May 3, 1895

Nihil Obstat: Arthur J. Scanlan, S.T.D.
                  Censor Librorum

Imprimatur: ✚ Patrick Cardinal Hayes
                  Archbishop of New York
                  New York
                  September 14, 1926

Published by Benziger Brothers, New York.

Retypeset and republished in 1989 by TAN Books and Publishers, Inc.

Library of Congress Catalog Card No.: 88-51073

ISBN: 978-0-89555-348-5

Printed and bound in the United States of America.

TAN BOOKS AND PUBLISHERS
1989

"Are not all painful labors to be endured for everlasting life?

"It is no small matter to lose or gain the Kingdom of God.

"Lift up therefore thy face to Heaven. Behold, I, and all My saints with Me, who in this world have had a great conflict, do now rejoice, are now comforted, are now secure, are now at rest, and they shall for all eternity abide with Me in the Kingdom of My Father."

—*Bk. III, chap. 47*

CONTENTS

BOOK I
Useful Admonitions for a Spiritual Life

BOOK II

Admonitions Concerning Interior Things

BOOK III

Of Internal Consolation

Book IV

Of the Blessed Sacrament

Book I

Useful Admonitions
for a
Spiritual Life

Chapter 1

Of the Imitation of Christ, and the Contempt of All the Vanities of the World

"HE THAT followeth me, walketh not in darkness," saith Our Lord. (*John* 8:12). These are the words of Christ, by which we are admonished, that we must imitate His life and manners, if we would be truly enlightened, and delivered from all blindness of heart.

Let it then be our chief study to meditate on the life of Jesus Christ.

2. The doctrine of Christ surpasseth all the doctrines of the saints, and whosoever hath the spirit will find therein a hidden manna. (*Apoc.* 2:17).

But it happeneth that many, by frequent hearing of the Gospel, are very little affected: because they have not the spirit of Christ.

But he who would fully and feelingly understand the words of Christ, must study to make his whole life conformable to that of Christ.

3. What doth it avail thee to discourse profoundly of the Trinity if thou be void of humility, and consequently, displeasing to the Trinity?

In truth, sublime words make not a man holy and just: but a virtuous life maketh him dear to God.

I would rather feel compunction, than know its definition.

If thou didst know the whole Bible by heart, and the sayings of all the philosophers, what would it all profit thee

3

without the love of God and His grace?

"Vanity of vanities, and all is vanity" (*Eccles.* 1:2), besides loving God and serving Him alone.

This is the highest wisdom, by despising the world to tend to heavenly kingdoms.

4. It is vanity, therefore, to seek after riches which must perish, and to trust in them.

It is vanity also to be ambitious of honors, and to raise one's self to a high station.

It is vanity to follow the lusts of the flesh, and to desire that for which thou must afterwards be grievously punished.

It is vanity to wish for a long life, and to take little care of leading a good life.

It is vanity also to mind this present life, and not to look forward unto those things which are to come.

It is vanity to love that which passeth with all speed, and not to hasten thither where everlasting joy remaineth.

5. Often remember that proverb: "The eye is not satisfied with seeing, nor is the ear filled with hearing." (*Eccles.* 1:8).

Study, therefore, to withdraw thy heart from the love of visible things, and to turn thyself to things invisible. For they that follow their sensuality, defile their conscience, and lose the grace of God.

Practical Reflections

If we would really honor Jesus Christ, we must apply ourselves to know Him, to love Him, and to follow Him in the practice of every Christian virtue. This is absolutely necessary for salvation, as we cannot become true Christians, but by knowing, loving, and following Christ. To pretend to please our Blessed

Saviour by a profound knowledge of His divinity, without endeavoring to follow His example, without living as He lived, would be most dangerously to delude ourselves.

Prayer

What will it avail me, O Jesus, to study and to know in part Thy supreme greatness, and the most sublime of Thy mysteries, if I endeavor not to derive advantage and merit from them, by cherishing Thy disposition and copying Thy virtues, since, to save my soul, I must not only know, but practice what Thou hast taught me by Thy word, and manifested in Thy life for my imitation—I must know and practice my religion? This, my Saviour, is the grace which I now ask of Thee, with a firm hope that Thou wilt grant my petition. Amen.

Chapter 2

Of Having an Humble Opinion of One's Self

ALL MEN naturally desire to know, but what does knowledge avail without the fear of God?

Indeed an humble husbandman, that serves God, is better than a proud philosopher, who neglecting himself, considers the course of the heavens. (*Ecclus.* 19:21).

He who knows himself well, is mean in his own eyes, and is not delighted with being praised by men.

If I should know all things that are in the world, and should not be in charity (*Rom.* 13:8; *1 Cor.* 13:2), what would it avail me in the sight of God, who will judge me by my deeds?

2. Leave off that excessive desire of knowing: because

there is found therein much distraction and deceit.

They who are learned, are desirous to appear, and to be called wise.

There are many things, the knowledge of which is of little or no profit to the soul.

And he is very unwise who attends to other things than what may serve to his salvation.

Many words do not satisfy the soul; but a good life gives ease to the mind; and a pure conscience affords a great confidence in God. (*1 Tim.* 3:9).

3. The more and better thou knowest, the more heavy will be thy judgment unless thy life be also more holy.

Be not, therefore, puffed up with any art or science: but rather fear upon account of the knowledge which is given thee.

If it seem to thee that thou knowest many things, and understandest them well enough, know at the same time, that there are many more things of which thou art ignorant.

Be not high-minded, but rather acknowledge thine ignorance. Why wouldst thou prefer thyself to anyone, since there are many more learned and skillful in the law than thyself?

If thou wouldst know and learn anything to the purpose, love to be unknown and esteemed as nothing.

4. This is the highest science and most profitable lesson, truly to know and despise ourselves.

To have no opinion of ourselves, and to think always well and commendably of others, is great wisdom and high perfection.

If thou shouldst see another openly sin, or commit some

heinous crime, yet thou oughtst not to esteem thyself better: because thou knowest not how long thou mayest remain in a good state.

We are all frail: but see thou think no one more frail than thyself.

Practical Reflections

The thoughts of man, says the Scripture, are vain and useless, if, in them, he does not apply his mind to know and to love God, to forget and to hate himself. The simple and lively faith of a soul which believes all that God teaches, without examination or hesitation, and performs all that He requires for the attainment of salvation, is preferable to all divine and human sciences, which, of themselves, without such a faith, only fill the mind with pride, leave the heart dry, and avail naught for salvation.

Prayer

Moderate, O Jesus, my eagerness to know so much, and correct my negligence in doing so little for salvation, since Thou wilt not judge me according to what I have known, but by what I have done, or neglected to do, to obtain it. Can I apply my thoughts to know Thee thoroughly, and not admire and love Thee? and can I truly know myself, and not despise and hate myself? O life unknown! life hidden in Jesus Christ, in God! what an excellent means art thou of sanctification and salvation, yet how little art thou practiced amongst Christians! Grant, O Lord, that all may know, esteem, and love it, and be directed by it. Amen.

Chapter 3

Of the Doctrine of Truth

HAPPY is he whom Truth teacheth by itself, not by figures and words that pass, but as it is in itself. (*Ps.* 17:36; *Is.* 28:26). Our opinion and our sense often deceive us, and discover but little.

What availeth a great dispute about abstruse and obscure matters, for not knowing which we shall not be questioned at the Day of Judgment?

It is a great folly for us to neglect things profitable and necessary, and willingly to busy ourselves about those which are curious and hurtful. We have eyes and see not. (*Ps.* 115:5).

2. And what need we concern ourselves about terms of philosophy?

He to whom the eternal Word speaketh, is set at liberty from a multitude of opinions.

From one word are all things, and this one all things speak; and this is the beginning which also speaketh to us.

Without this word, no one understands or judges rightly.

He to whom all things are one, and who draws all things to one, and who sees all things in one, may be steady in heart, and peaceably repose in God. (*1 Cor.* 2:2).

O Truth! my God, make me one with Thee in eternal love. (*John* 17:21).

I am wearied with often reading and hearing many things; in Thee is all that I will or desire.

Let all teachers hold their peace; let all creatures be silent in Thy sight; speak Thou alone to me.

3. The more a man is united within himself and interiorly simple, the more and higher things doth he understand without labor, because he receiveth the light of understanding from above.

A pure, simple, and steady spirit is not dissipated by a multitude of affairs, because he performs them all to the honor of God, and endeavors to be at rest within himself, and free from all self-seeking.

What is a greater hindrance and trouble to thee than thine own unmortified affection of heart?

A good and devout man first disposes his works inwardly which he is to do outwardly.

Neither do they draw him to the desires of an inordinate inclination, but he bends them to the rule of right reason. Who hath a stronger conflict than he who striveth to overcome himself?

And this must be our business, to strive to overcome ourselves, and daily to gain strength over ourselves, and to grow better and better.

4. All perfections in this life are attended with some imperfections, and all our speculations with a certain obscurity.

The humble knowledge of thyself is a surer way to God than the deepest search after science.

Learning is not to be blamed, nor the mere knowledge of anything, which is good in itself, and ordained by God; but a good conscience, and a virtuous life, are always to be preferred before it.

But because many make it more their study to know than to live well, therefore are they often deceived, and bring forth none, or very little fruit.

5. Oh, if men would use as much diligence in rooting out vices and planting virtues, as they do in proposing questions, there would not be so great evils committed, nor scandals among the people, nor so much relaxation in monasteries.

Verily, when the Day of Judgment comes, we shall not be examined on what we have read, but what we have done; nor how learnedly we have spoken, but how religiously we have lived.

Tell me where are now all those great doctors, with whom thou wast well acquainted, whilst they were living and flourished in learning?

Now others fill their places, and I know not whether they ever think of them.

In their lifetime they seemed to be something, and now they are not spoken of.

6. Oh, how quickly doth the glory of the world pass away! (*1 John* 2:17). Would that their lives had been answerable to their learning! then would they have studied and read well.

How many perish in the world through vain learning, who little care for the service of God!

And because they chose rather to be great than to be humble, therefore they are lost in their own imaginations.

He is truly great, who is great in charity.

He is truly great, who is little in his own eyes, and holdeth as naught the pinnacle of honor.

He is truly prudent who looks upon all earthly things as nothing, that he may gain Christ. (*Phil.* 3:8).

And he is very learned indeed, who does the will of God, and renounces his own will.

Practical Reflections

To study the truths of religion, not so much to know as to practice them; to listen to the Divine Word, which speaks more to the heart than to the understanding; to know and to do what is necessary for salvation, is the true science of a Christian. I am weary of speculative knowledge, which does not change nor move my heart, but only flatters the curiosity of my mind; I am tired of knowing and saying so much concerning eternal truths and salvation, and yet doing so little to obtain it.

Prayer

O Jesus! Who hast taught us that not all those who say Lord, Lord, shall enter into the Kingdom of Heaven, but only such as do the will of Thy Father, whose lives correspond with their belief, grant us a truly Christian spirit, a Christian heart, and guide us in the paths of a Christian life. Grant that I may become detached from all things, and in all things seek Thee alone. Grant that I may direct all my knowledge, my whole capacity, all my happiness, and all my exertions, to please Thee, to love Thee, and to obtain Thy love for time and eternity. Amen.

Chapter 4

Of Prudence in Our Undertakings

WE MUST not be easy in giving credit to every word and suggestion; but carefully and leisurely weigh the matter according to God.

Alas, such is our weakness, that we often more readily believe and speak of another that which is evil than that which is good!

But perfect men do not easily give credit to every report, because they know a man's weakness, which is very prone to evil, and very subject to fail in words.

2. It is great wisdom not to be rash in our doings, nor to maintain too obstinately our own opinion:

Nor should we believe every man's word, nor presently tell others the things which we have heard or believed.

Consult with a wise and conscientious man (*Tobias* 4:19), and seek rather to be instructed by one who is better, than to follow thine own inventions.

A good life makes a man wise according to God, and expert in many things. The more humble a man is in himself, and more subject to God, the more wise will he be in all things, and the more at peace.

Practical Reflections

Nothing is more opposite to charity, or more fatal to salvation, than the evil reports we make of one another, whether they be true or false; because they irritate the mind, disorder the heart, foment divisions, and embitter hatreds, and because we cannot obtain God's pardon for them, unless we resolve, in our confessions, to repair the evil we have done, and to reconcile those we may have set at variance. We should therefore neither spread evil reports of others, nor listen to them; and if we do hear anything against our neighbor, we should be careful not to repeat it.

Prayer

Grant, O my Saviour, that I may observe, with the greatest care, Thy precept of charity towards my neighbor, to love him as Thou hast loved us, since this is absolutely necessary for salvation. Give me also that tenderness of charity which may prevent me from wounding it in any way: for Thou hast said that to offend our neighbor is to wound the apple of Thine eye. Grant, therefore, that I may avoid Thy displeasure by not incurring the displeasure of my neighbor. Amen.

Chapter 5

Of Reading the Holy Scriptures

TRUTH is to be sought for in Holy Scripture, not eloquence. All Holy Scripture ought to be read with that spirit with which it was made.

We must rather seek for profit in the Scriptures than for subtlety of speech.

We ought as willingly to read devout and simple books, as those that are high and profound.

Let not the authority of the writer offend thee, whether he was of little or of great learning; but let the love of pure truth lead thee to read.

Inquire not who said this; but attend to what is said.

2. Men pass away; "but the truth of the Lord remaineth forever." (*Ps.* 116:2).

God speaks many ways to us, without respect of persons.

Our curiosity often hinders us in reading the Scriptures, when we attempt to understand and discuss that which should be simply passed over.

If thou wilt receive profit, read with humility, simplicity and faith; and seek not at any time the fame of being learned.

Willingly inquire after, and hear with silence the words of the saints; and be pleased with the parables of the ancients, for they are not spoken without cause. (*Ecclus.* 32:9).

Practical Reflections

Read the Sacred Scriptures and books of piety with the same spirit in which they were written, that is, read them in quest of truth, for instruction, for edification, and to bring thee to a truly Christian way of life. Read the Holy Scriptures with faith, humility, respect, and docility, praying the Holy Ghost, who dictated it, to enable thee to understand it, to relish it, and to practice it.

Prayer

Speak, my God, speak to my heart and change it, while the truths which I read strike and convince my mind. Grant that, being instructed in Thy law and in Thy holy will, by the reading of good books, I may follow them in all things, so that what Thou teachest may ever be the rule of my conduct. Amen.

Chapter 6

Of Inordinate Affections

WHENSOEVER a man desires any thing inordinately, he is presently disquieted within himself.

The proud and covetous are never easy.

The poor and humble of spirit live in much peace.

The man that is not yet perfectly dead to himself, is soon tempted and overcome with small and trifling things.

He that is weak in spirit, and in a manner yet carnal and inclined to sensible things, can hardly withdraw himself wholly from earthly desires.

And therefore he is often sad, when he withdraws himself from them, and is easily moved to anger if anyone thwarts him.

2. And if he has pursued his inclination, he is immediately tormented with the guilt of his conscience, because he has followed his passion, which helps him not at all toward the peace he sought for.

It is then by resisting our passions, that we are to find true peace of heart, and not by being slaves to them.

There is no peace, therefore, in the heart of a carnal man, nor in a man that is addicted to outward things; but only in a fervent spiritual man.

Practical Reflections

The peace of the soul, next to the grace of God, is the greatest of blessings, and we should spare no pains to maintain it within us. But we can neither obtain nor preserve this peace of the soul but by resisting our passions and irregular desires; for the more we endeavor to satisfy them, the more restless do they make us; the more we fight against them, the less trouble do they give us; the more we resist them, the more do they leave us in peace.

Prayer

Give us, O Lord, this interior peace, this repose of conscience, this tranquillity which raises our confidence in Thy goodness, and makes us faithful in corresponding with it: this peace of God which surpasseth all understanding, which keeps our minds and our hearts in Thy love, and which Thou alone canst give. Calm the storms and emotions of our passions by giving us courage to overcome them. Grant that our desires may become submissive to reason, our reason to faith, and the whole man to God. Amen.

Chapter 7

Of Flying Vain Hope and Pride

HE is vain who puts his trust in men, or in creatures. (*Jer.* 17:5; *Ps.* 114:24).

Be not ashamed to serve others, and to appear poor in this world, for the love of Jesus Christ. (*2 Cor.* 4:5).

Confide not in thyself; but place thy hope in God. (*Ps.* 72:28).

Do what is in thy power, and God will be with thy good will.

Trust not in thine own knowledge, nor in the cunning of any man living; but rather in the grace of God, who helps the humble, and humbles those who presume on themselves.

2. Glory not in riches, if thou hast them, nor in friends, because they are powerful; but in God, who gives all things, and desires to give Himself above all things. (*1 Cor.* 1:31).

Boast not of the stature nor beauty of thy body, which is

spoiled and disfigured by a little sickness.

Do not take a pride in thine ability or talent, lest thou displease God, to whom apperthaineth every natural good quality and talent which thou hast.

3. Esteem not thyself better than others, lest, perhaps, thou be accounted worse in the sight of God, who knows what is in man.

Be not proud of thine own works; for the judgments of God are different from the judgments of men; and often times, that displeaseth Him which pleaseth men.

If thou hast anything of good, believe better things of others, that thou mayest preserve humility.

It will do thee no harm to esteem thyself the worst of all; but it will hurt thee very much to prefer thyself before anyone.

Continual peace is with the humble; but in the heart of the proud is frequent envy and indignation.

Practical Reflections

Depend only upon God, whom nothing can move, on whom alone thou oughtest to rely; for nothing is weaker, more uncertain, and more inconstant than man, who is made up of error, malice, and lies. Hope all things of God, and nothing from thyself, nor from others. Do not glory in thy good works or ability, but in all things, and by all things give glory to God, to whom alone glory is due.

Prayer

As, O Jesus, Thou hatest and despisest those who through a secret self-complacency exalt themselves before Thee, but lovest and honorest those who attribute nothing to themselves but evil, and refer all good to Thee, impart to us, we beseech Thee, interior humility of heart, which brings us nigh to Thee, and makes us worthy of Thy love: heal the pride and vanity of our high and haughty minds, which remove us to a distance from Thee, and excite Thy hatred against us: and make our hearts humble, submissive, and docile to Thy holy will, that so we may bring down Thy mercies upon us. Amen.

Chapter 8

Of Shunning Too Much Familiarity

"**O**PEN not thy heart to every man" (*Ecclus.* 8:22), but treat of thine affairs with a man that is wise and feareth God.

Keep not much company with young people and strangers.

Be not a flatterer with the rich, nor willingly appear before the great.

Associate thyself with the humble and simple, with the devout and virtuous; and treat of those things which edify. (*Rom.* 14:19).

Be not familiar with any woman; but recommend all good women in general to God.

Desire to be familiar only with God and His angels, and fly the acquaintance of men.

2. We must have charity for all, but familiarity is not expedient.

It sometimes happens that a person, when not known, shines by a good reputation, who, when he is present, is disagreeable to them that see him.

We think sometimes to please others by being with them, and we begin rather to disgust them, by the evil behavior which they discover in us.

Practical Reflections

Avoid worldly company, useless conversations, and those overflowings and attachments of the heart which are neither regulated nor governed by the love of God. For all these things dissipate the soul, withdraw it from God, hinder it from being recollected, and deprive it of that interior spirit which is so necessary for salvation; they expose it to many dangers, and insensibly subvert all interior discipline. Let your friends be persons of piety, whose lives are regular and irreproachable, that their good example may withdraw you from sin, and lead you to virtue. Happy the Christian who is attached only to Jesus Christ, to his duties, and to his salvation, who lives in God and for God, and thus commences in time that which shall be his continual occupation for eternity.

Prayer

Grant, O Jesus, that I may love Thee more than my parents, relations, or friends, more than I love myself. Grant that I may earnestly endeavor to know Thee, to love Thee, and to follow Thee, that so, having been accustomed and conformed to Thee, I may not be exposed as many Christians are, to the danger of appearing, after my departure hence, before a God whom I know not, whom I have never loved; for not to love Thee in time, is not to love Thee for eternity; whereas, if I endeavor to love Thee now, I shall have reason to hope that I shall love Thee forever. O most amiable God! O most loving

God! Grant that I may love Thee with my whole heart, with my whole soul, with all my strength and with all my mind. Amen.

Chapter 9

Of Obedience and Subjection

IT IS a very great thing to stand in obedience, to live under a superior, and not be at our own disposal.

It is much more secure to be in a state of subjection than in authority.

Many are under obedience, more out of necessity than for the love of God; and such as these are in pain, and easily repine.

Nor will they gain freedom of mind, unless they submit themselves, with their whole heart, for God's sake.

Run here or there, thou wilt find no rest, but in an humble subjection under the government of a superior.

The imagination and changing of places has deceived many.

2. It is true, everyone is desirous of acting according to his own liking, and is more inclined to such as are of his own mind.

But if God be amongst us, we must sometimes give up our own opinion for the sake of peace.

Who is so wise as to be able fully to know all things?

Therefore trust not too much to thine own thoughts, but be willing also to hear the sentiments of others.

Although thine opinion be good, yet if for God's sake

thou leave it to follow that of another, it will be more profitable to thee.

3. For I have often heard, that it is more safe to hear and to take counsel than to give it.

It may also happen that each one's thought may be good, but to refuse to yield to others, when reason or a just cause requires it, is a sign of pride and willfulness.

Practical Reflections

How delightful to depend solely on God in the persons of our superiors, who hold His place, and how very meritorious is the constant practice of obedience, which is a perpetual exercise of abnegation, of self-renunciation, and of the most perfect love of God! Obedience constitutes the excellence, the happiness, and the merit of a Christian and religious life, and makes God the absolute master and proprietor of our hearts.

But for this, our minds, our hearts, and all our actions must combine in the practice of obedience: the mind by approving it, the heart by loving it, and our actions by exercising it promptly, generously, and constantly.

Prayer

Is it possible, O my Saviour, to behold Thee sacrifice the independence of a God to obedience, and I not love and practice it? Can I behold Thee, for thirty years, punctually obedient to Thy blessed Mother and St. Joseph, and not endeavor faithfully to observe what Thou ordainest me by Thine inspiration, by my rules, and by my superiors? How can I listen to the repugnance and difficulty which I experience in obedience, when I behold Thee obedient even to the very executioners who nailed Thee to the Cross? Grant, O Jesus, that in imitation of

Thee, I may subject myself to obedience, and thus evince my desire of pleasing Thee, and of doing in all things, and at all times, Thy holy will. Amen.

Chapter 10

Of Avoiding Superfluity of Words

FLY THE tumult of men as much as thou canst, for treating of worldly affairs hinders very much, although they be discoursed of with a simple intention.

For we are quickly defiled and ensnared with vanity.

I could wish I had oftener been silent, and that I had not been in company.

But why are we so willing to talk and discourse with one another, since we seldom return to silence without prejudice to our conscience.

The reason why we are so willing to talk is, because by discoursing together we seek comfort from one another, and would gladly ease the heart, wearied by various thoughts.

And we very willingly talk and think of such things as we most love and desire, or which we imagine contrary to us.

2. But, alas, it is often in vain and to no purpose, for this outward consolation is no small hindrance to interior and divine comfort!

Therefore we must watch and pray (*Matt.* 26:41), that our time may not pass away without fruit.

If it be lawful and expedient to speak, speak those things which may edify.

A bad custom, and the neglect of our spiritual advancement, is a great cause of our keeping so little guard upon our mouth.

But devout conferences, concerning spiritual things, help very much to spiritual progress, especially where persons of the same mind and spirit are associated together in God.

Practical Reflections

"Watch and pray" is the simple means which Jesus Christ prescribes to enable a Christian to resist temptation, to avoid sin, and secure his salvation. To speak little to creatures and much to God, to renounce useless and curious conversations, to speak only what is good or necessary, is an excellent method of becoming an interior man, of preserving purity of heart and peace of conscience, and of becoming entirely united to God. A soul which gives itself through the senses to creatures, and lives not an interior life, but amuses itself with trifles, is not at all in a state to relish the things of God, or to apply to prayer or recollection, which are so useful and so necessary for salvation. Why, says St. Austin, dost thou, O dissipated and wandering soul, seek content in created objects, in the goods and pleasures of life? Seek within thyself, by recollection, the only true and sovereign Good, who is there, and who alone can satisfy thy desires.

Prayer

Give me, O God, that spirit of interior recollection which will make me attentive to Thy holy will and faithful to Thy graces. Grant that the remembrance of Thine awful presence may remind me continually of Thy blessed life and conversation, and effectually control me during my earthly pilgrimage. I am weary, O God, of living an exile from Thy presence, and of being so little affected by the consideration of Thy majesty as to do nothing to please Thee. What can I find in Heaven or on earth that is comparable to Thee? Thou art the God of my heart: grant I may be ever sensible of Thy presence, and desire only the happiness of pleasing Thee, in time, that Thou mayest be my portion for eternity. Amen.

Chapter 11

Of Acquiring Peace and Zeal for Spiritual Progress

WE MIGHT have much peace if we would not busy ourselves with the sayings and doings of others, and with things which belong not to us.

How can he remain long in peace who entangles himself with other people's cares: who seeks occasions abroad, and who is little or seldom inwardly recollected?

Blessed are the single-hearted, for they shall enjoy much peace.

2. What was the reason why some of the saints were so perfect and contemplative?

Because they made it their study wholly to mortify in themselves all earthly desires; and thus they were enabled, with every fiber of the heart, to cleave to God, and freely to attend to themselves.

We are too much taken up with our own passions; and too solicitous about transitory things.

And seldom do we perfectly overcome so much as one

vice, nor are we earnestly bent upon our daily progress; and therefore we remain cold and tepid.

3. If we were perfectly dead to ourselves, and no ways entangled in our interior, then might we be able to relish things divine, and experience something of heavenly contemplation.

The whole and greatest hindrance is, that we are not free from passions and lusts, and strive not to walk in the perfect way of the saints.

And when we meet with any small adversity, we are too quickly dejected, and turn away to seek after human consolation.

4. If we strove like valiant men to stand up in the battle, doubtless we should see Our Lord help us from Heaven.

For He is ready to help them that fight and trust in His grace: who furnishes us with occasions of combat that we may overcome.

If we place our progress in religion in these outward observances only, our devotion will quickly be at an end.

But let us lay the axe to the root, that, being purged from passions, we may possess a quiet mind.

5. If every year we rooted out one vice, we should soon become perfect men.

But now we often find it quite otherwise: that we were better and more pure in the beginning of our conversion, than after many years of our profession.

Our fervor and progress ought to be every day greater; but now it is esteemed a great matter if a man can retain some part of his first fervor.

If we would use but a little violence upon ourselves in

the beginning, we might afterwards do all things with ease and joy.

6. It is hard to leave off our old customs; but harder to go against our own will.

But if thou dost not overcome things that are small and light, when wilt thou overcome greater difficulties?

Resist thine inclination in the beginning, and break off thine evil habit, lest perhaps by little and little the difficulty increase upon thee.

Oh, if thou wert sensible how much peace thou shouldst procure to thyself, and joy to others, by behaving thyself well, thou wouldst be more solicitous for thy spiritual progress.

Practical Reflections

As nothing is more opposite to true peace, to the happiness and comfort of this life, and to an assured hope of salvation hereafter, than to abandon ourselves to our passions, and submit to be their slaves and victims, so nothing is more capable of establishing within us true repose of conscience, and of obtaining merit and happiness in this life, and eternal salvation in the next, than ever to resist and conquer our evil inclinations, and to refuse our hearts, on all occasions, the gratification of their irregular desires. Endeavor, therefore, seriously to die to thyself, to overcome thy repugnance to do good, to subdue the ardor of thy desires, and to renounce thine own will in all things, for this alone will make thee happy in time and eternity. There is no true peace of conscience, nor hope of future reward, but in doing all for God, and in opposition to thyself.

Prayer

How happy should I be, my Saviour, how content and how sure of salvation, did I but strive as much to satisfy Thy justice by penance, and Thy love by fidelity, as I do to satisfy my passions and the demands of self-love! Suffer me not, O Lord, to serve any other master than Thee. Break my chains asunder, deliver me from the unjust and cruel servitude of my passions. My heart is made for Thee. Permit not vanity, self-love, sensuality, idleness, and anger, like strange gods, to divide it, or rather rob it, of the empire of Thy love. Not to give Thee my whole heart is to withdraw it from Thee, Who wilt have all or none. O my God and my all! O God of my heart! be Thou my portion forever. Amen.

Chapter 12

Of the Utility of Adversity

IT IS good for us to have sometimes troubles and adversities, for they make a man enter into himself, that he may know that he is in a state of banishment, and may not place his hopes in anything of this world.

It is good that we sometimes suffer contradictions, and that men have an evil or imperfect opinion of us, even when we do and intend well. These things are often helps to humility, and defend us from vainglory.

For then we better run to God, our inward witness, when outwardly we are despised by men, and little credit is given to us.

2. Therefore should a man so establish himself in God, as to have no need of seeking many comforts from men.

When a man of good will is troubled, or tempted, or afflicted with evil thoughts, then he better understands what need he has of God, without whom he finds he can do no good. (*John* 15:5).

Then also he laments, he sighs, and prays, by reason of the miseries which he suffers.

Then he is weary of living longer, and he wishes death to come, that he may be "dissolved and be with Christ." (*Phil.* 1:23).

Then also he will perceive that perfect security and full peace cannot be found in this world.

Practical Reflections

We should regard contradictions as the trials by which God would prove and purify our charity. If all persons had the consideration and regard for us which our self-love desires, and which it often induces us to believe we deserve, we should entertain only a natural regard for our neighbor, subject to the caprices of humor, a species of gratitude purely human, and a secret complacency in ourselves. But God would have us everywhere meet with and suffer contradictions, disappointments, and opposition to our designs, from those with whom we live, that so we may love them solely for His sake, and because He so ordained. Happy the soul which tribulation tries, and temptation purifies, as gold is tried and purified in the fire! It thus becomes worthy of acceptance with God, for it is after God's own heart.

Prayer

Support me, O Lord, under all the troubles and contradictions which Thou permittest to befall me and willest I should suffer; that they may not weaken my charity for my neighbor, nor my fidelity towards Thee. Grant that temptations, far from separating me from Thee, may unite me more closely to Thee, by obliging me to experience a continual and pressing need of Thy powerful assistance. Amen.

Chapter 13

Of Resisting Temptations

AS LONG as we live in this world we cannot be without tribulation and temptation.

Hence it is written in Job: "The life of man upon earth is a warfare." (*Job* 7:1).

Therefore ought everyone to be solicitous about his temptations, and to watch in prayer, lest the devil, who never sleeps, but "goeth about seeking whom he may devour," find room to deceive him. (*1 Ptr.* 5:8).

No man is so perfect and holy as not to have sometimes temptations, and we cannot be wholly without them.

2. Yet temptations are often very profitable to a man, although they be troublesome and grievous, for in them a man is humbled, purified, and instructed.

All the saints have passed through many tribulations and temptations, and have profited by them; and they who could not support temptations, have become reprobates, and fallen away.

There is no order so holy, nor place so retired, where there are not temptations and adversities.

3. A man is never entirely secure from temptations as long as he lives, because we have within us the source of

temptation, having been born in concupiscence.

When one temptation or tribulation is over, another comes on; and we shall have always something to suffer, because we have lost the good of our original happiness.

Many seek to fly temptations, and fall more grievously into them.

By flight alone we cannot overcome; but by patience and true humility we are made stronger than our enemies.

He who only declines them outwardly, and does not pluck out the root, will profit little; nay, temptations will sooner return to him, and he will find himself in a worse condition.

By degrees, and by patience, with longanimity, thou shalt by God's grace better overcome them than by harshness and thine own importunity.

In temptation often take counsel, and deal not roughly with one that is tempted; but comfort him as thou wouldst wish to be done to thyself.

4. Inconstancy of mind, and small confidence in God, is the beginning of all evil temptations.

For as a ship without a rudder is tossed to and fro by the waves, so the man who is remiss, and who quits his resolution, is many ways tempted.

Fire tries iron, and temptation tries a just man.

We often know not what we can do; but temptation discovers what we are.

However, we must be watchful, especially in the beginning of temptation, because then the enemy is easier overcome, if he is not suffered to come in at all at the door of the soul, but is kept out and resisted at his first knock.

Whence a certain man said: "Withstand the beginning, after-remedies come too late."

For first a bare thought comes to the mind; then a strong imagination; afterwards delight, and evil motion and consent.

And thus, by little and little, the wicked enemy gets full entrance, when he is not resisted in the beginning.

And the longer a man is negligent in resisting, so much the weaker does he daily become in himself, and the enemy becomes stronger against him.

5. Some suffer great temptations in the beginning of their conversion, and some in the end.

And some there are who are much troubled, in a manner, all their lifetime.

Some are but lightly tempted, according to the wisdom and equity of the ordinance of God, who weighs the state and merits of men, and pre-ordains all for the salvation of the elect.

6. We must not, therefore, despair when we are tempted, but pray to God with so much the more fervor that He may vouchsafe to help us in all tribulations; who, no doubt, according to the saying of St. Paul, will "make such issue with the temptation, that you may be able to bear it." (*1 Cor.* 10:13).

Let us, therefore, humble our souls under the hand of God in all temptations and tribulations: for the humble in spirit He will save and exalt.

7. In temptations and tribulations a man is proved as to what progress he has made; and in them there is a greater merit, and his virtue appears more conspicuous.

Nor is it much if a man be devout and fervent when he feels no trouble; but if in the time of adversity he bears up with patience, there will be hope of a great advancement.

Some are preserved from great temptations, and are often overcome in little daily ones; that, being humbled, they may never presume on themselves in great things, who are weak in such small occurrences.

Practical Reflections

Temptations serve to free us from all lurking inclinations to vanity or self-love, and from at all depending upon ourselves, because they make us feel the weight of our own miseries, give us a disgust for all earthly gratifications, and oblige us to rely solely upon God. They serve also to humble us by the experience they afford us of our own weakness, and of the depth of our natural corruption. They serve, in a word, to convince us of our inability to do the least good, or to avoid the smallest sin, without the assistance of God.

Prayer

I am sensible, O Jesus, that in the time of temptation, of myself, I cannot but offend Thee, and that, carried along by my natural inclination for evil, I am in danger of ruining myself. But I know, also, that Thou canst, and Thine Apostle assures me Thou wilt, defend me against the most violent assaults of my passions. Wherefore, mistrusting myself, and relying upon Thee, I will exclaim, "Lord, save me, or I perish"; I will stretch out my hand to Thee as St. Peter did, and confidently hope that Thou wilt not let me perish. Amen.

Chapter 14

Of Avoiding Rash Judgment

TURN thine eyes back upon thyself, and see thou judge not the doings of others. In judging others, a man labors in vain, often errs, and easily sins; but in judging and looking into himself, he always labors with fruit.

We frequently judge of a thing according as we have it at heart: for we easily lose true judgment through a private affection.

If God were always the only object of our desire, we would not so easily be disturbed at the resistance of our opinions.

2. But often something lies hid within, or occurs without, which draws us along with it.

Many secretly seek themselves in what they do, and are not sensible of it.

They seem also to continue in good peace, when things are done according to their will and judgment; but if it fall out contrary to their desires, they are soon moved, and become sad.

Difference of thoughts and opinions is too frequently the source of dissensions amongst friends and neighbors, amongst religious and devout persons.

3. An old custom is with difficulty relinquished; and no man is led willingly farther than he himself sees or likes.

If thou reliest more upon thine own reason or industry than upon the virtue that subjects to Jesus Christ, thou wilt seldom and hardly be an enlightened man, for God will have us to be perfectly subject to Himself, and to transcend all reason by inflamed love.

Practical Reflections

We frequently allow ourselves to be biased in our judgments by the inclinations of the heart, instead of being guided by the light of the understanding.

Through self-love we ordinarily approve in ourselves what in others we frequently condemn, and are as much alive to the defects of our neighbor as we are blind to our own. A soul recollected in the presence of God, and faithful to the motions of His grace, being thus engaged with God, and united to Him, is solely occupied with God in itself and itself in God; and, endeavoring to keep a strict guard over its own heart, it forgives nothing in itself, and everything in others.

Prayer

O my God! When shall I be so free from all attachment to creatures, and from all self-seeking, as to keep my mind and my heart solely upon Thee, attentive to my duties and to securing my salvation? Grant, O Jesus, that I may forget or be wholly ignorant of everything which I ought neither to know nor observe; and thus live only for Thee, with Thee, and in Thee. Vanities, pleasures, news, amusements, and curiosities, how little, or how really nothing are ye, to a soul for whom its God is its all! Suffer me not, O my Saviour, to seek, to know, to love, or to possess anything but Thee, Who art more to me than all things else. Inflame my heart with an ardent desire of pleasing Thee, and an humble acquiescence in all things to Thy good pleasure. Amen.

Chapter 15

Of Works Done out of Charity

E VIL ought not to be done, either for anything in the world, or for the love of any man, but for the profit of one that stands in need a good work is sometimes freely to be omitted, or rather to be changed for a better.

For by so doing a good work is not lost, but is changed into a better.

Without charity the outward work profiteth nothing; but whatever is done out of charity, be it ever so little and contemptible, all becomes fruitful. (*1 Cor.* 13:3).

For God regards more with how much affection and love a person performs a work, than how much he does. (*Luke* 7:47).

2. He does much who loves much.

He does much, that does well what he does.

He does well who regards rather the common good than his own will.

That seems often to be charity which is rather natural affection; because our own natural inclination, self-will, hope of reward, desire of our own interest, will seldom be wanting.

3. He that has true and perfect charity, seeks himself in no one thing, but desires only the glory of God, in all things.

He envies no man, because he loves no private joy; nor does he desire to rejoice in himself: but above all things, he wishes to be made happy in God.

He attributes nothing good to any man, but refers it

totally to God, from whom all things proceed as from their fountain, in the enjoyment of whom all the saints repose as in their last end.

Ah, if a man had but one spark of perfect charity, he would doubtless perceive that all earthly things are full of vanity!

Practical Reflections

We cannot dwell too much upon these words of the author: "God regards more with how much love and affection a person performs a work than how much he does, and he does much who loves much"; that is, our actions are really pleasing to God, only in proportion as they are influenced by a desire of pleasing Him, and, as it were, stamped with the seal of His love. Whatsoever you do, says St. Paul, do all for the honor and glory of God. It is a lively, active and often renewed love which constitutes the merit of our good actions; faith itself becomes weak and languishing, if not animated by charity and by a pious and affectionate tendency towards the Author of these truths which it unfolds to us.

Let us, therefore, endeavor to love God in all we do, and to do all for the love of Him. All for Thee, O Jesus, all with Thee, all in Thee! Behold, my soul, what thou shouldst say and do incessantly in order to lead a supernatural and meritorious life, and to commence in time what thou hopest to continue throughout eternity.

Prayer

How wearied am I, O my God, with being so often forgetful of Thy presence and devoid of Thy love! What confusion for me to think so little of a God whose thoughts are always upon me, and to be so frequently indifferent about Thee, my Jesus, Who art ever burning with the love of me! Suffer me not to live one moment without loving Thee; and as Thou art the center of my heart, inflame me with such a continual affection for Thee, such a lively and ardent desire of pleasing Thee and of seeking Thee in and before all things, that I may find no repose nor true happiness but in Thee. Amen.

Chapter 16

Of Bearing the Defects of Others

WHAT a man cannot amend in himself or others, he must bear with patience, till God ordains otherwise. Think that perhaps it is better so, for thy trial and patience, without which our merits are little worth.

Thou must, nevertheless, under such impediments, earnestly pray that God may vouchsafe to help thee, and that thou mayest bear them well.

2. If anyone being once or twice admonished, does not comply, contend not with him, but commit all to God, that His will may be done, and He be honored in all His servants, who knows well how to convert evil into good.

Endeavor to be patient in supporting the defects and infirmities of others, of what kind soever; because thou also hast many things which others must bear withal.

If thou canst not make thyself such a one as thou wouldst, how canst thou expect to have another according to thy liking?

We would willingly have others perfect, and yet we mend not our own defects.

3. We would have others strictly corrected, but are not willing to be corrected ourselves.

The large liberty of others displeases us, and yet we would not be denied anything we asked for.

We are willing that others should be bound up by laws, and we suffer not ourselves by any means to be restrained.

Thus it is evident how seldom we weigh our neighbor in the same balance with ourselves.

If all were perfect, what then should we have to suffer from others, for God's sake?

4. But now God has so disposed things that we may learn to bear one another's burdens (*Gal.* 6:2); for there is no man without defect, no man without his burden, no man sufficient for himself, no man wise enough for himself; but we must support one another, comfort one another, assist, instruct, and admonish one another.

But how great each one's virtue is best appears by occasions of adversity; for occasions do not make a man frail, but show what he is.

Practical Reflections

How excellent a means of sanctifying us and of fitting us for Heaven, is the exercise of that charity by which we support in ourselves and in others those weaknesses which we cannot correct! For nothing can humble and confound us before God more than a sense of our own miseries; and nothing can be more just than that we should bear in others, those things which we would have them support in ourselves. We should, therefore, bear with the tempers of others, and endeavor to give no cause of uneasiness to anyone on account of our own.

It is thus, according to St. Paul, we shall carry one another's burdens, and fulfill the law of Jesus Christ, which is a law of charity, meekness and patience.

Prayer

How true it is, O Lord, that contradictions are most advantageous to a Christian who endeavors to support them with patience and resignation! for they prove and purify his virtue and bring it to perfection. But Thou knowest what difficulty we experience in supporting these trials, and how sensible we are to everything that opposes our desires. Permit us not, O God, to yield to our feelings; but grant we may sacrifice them for the happiness of pleasing Thee; since to feel much, and not to follow the bent of our feelings, to keep silence when the heart is moved, and to withhold ourselves when we are all but overcome, is the most essential practice, and the surest mark for that truly Christian virtue which is to gain for us eternal happiness. This, O Jesus, we hope to obtain from Thine infinite bounty. Amen.

Chapter 17

Of a Monastic Life

THOU must learn to renounce thine own will in many things, if thou wilt keep peace and concord with others.

It is no small matter to live in a monastery, or in a congregation, and to converse therein without reproof, and to persevere faithful till death. (*Matt.* 10:22).

Blessed is he who has there lived well, and made a happy end.

If thou wilt stand as thou oughtest, and make a due progress, look upon thyself as a banished man, and a stranger upon earth. (*Heb.* 11:13).

Thou must be content to be made a fool for Christ, if thou wilt lead a religious life.

2. The habit and the tonsure contribute little; but a change of manners, and an entire mortification of the passions, make a truly religious man.

He that seeks here any other thing, than purely God and the salvation of his soul, will find nothing but trouble and sorrow.

Neither can he long remain in peace, who does not strive to be the least, and subject to all.

3. Thou camest hither to serve, not to govern; know that thou art called to suffer and to labor, not to idle and to talk.

Here, then, men are tried, as gold in the furnace.

Here no man can stand, unless he be willing, with all his heart to humble himself, for the love of God.

Practical Reflections

In order to live happily and contented in a community or religious house, and to labor effectually for the attainment of perfection and salvation, we must endure much, and restrain and conquer ourselves upon many occasions. As the dispositions of those with whom we live are often contrary to our own, grace must preserve peace and charity, by enabling us to suffer and to bear with a contrariety of tempers and nature preserves the order of the universe by reconciling a contrariety of elements. We shall never find true repose of conscience, nor acquire an assured hope of salvation, but by the practice of interior mortification and true humility of heart, by which we bear all things, and refuse the soul its desires.

Prayer

As Thou hast commanded me, O Jesus, to seek peace, and to keep it with all men, and as I cannot enjoy this advantage but by humbly bearing with others, and by giving them no cause of uneasiness on my own account, command in this respect what Thou pleasest, and give me what Thou commandest; for how can I bring the pride and haughtiness of my mind to bear and accept willingly the repulses, contempt, and humiliations which so frequently befall me, if Thou assist me not, O Lord, with the all-powerful aid of Thy grace? And how shall I stifle the feelings, and sallies of my heart under contradictions, if Thou arrest them not? Grant therefore, O God, that on occasions of repulses or contradictions, influenced by the respect that is due to Thy holy presence, and by the submission which I ought to render to Thy blessed will, I may calm all troubles within me, and bring all to give place to Thy love. Amen.

Chapter 18

Of the Examples of the Holy Fathers

LOOK upon the lively examples of the holy Fathers, in whom true perfection and religion were most shining, and thou wilt see how little, and almost nothing, that is which we do.

Alas, what is our life, if compared to theirs?

The saints and friends of Christ served the Lord in

hunger and thirst, in cold and nakedness, in labor and weariness, in watchings and fastings, in prayers and holy meditations, in persecutions and many reproaches. (*Heb.* 11:3–7).

2. Ah, how many and how grievous tribulations have the Apostles, martyrs, confessors, virgins, and all the rest undergone, who have been willing to follow Christ's footsteps!

For they hated their lives in this world, that they might possess them for eternity. (*John* 12:25).

Oh, how strict and mortified a life did the holy Fathers lead in the desert! What long and grievous temptations did they endure! How often were they molested by the enemy! What frequent and fervent prayers did they offer to God! What rigorous abstinence did they go through! What great zeal and fervor had they for their spiritual progress! How strong a war did they wage for overcoming vice! How pure and upright was their intention to God!

They labored all the day, and in the night they gave themselves to prayer: though even whilst they were at work they ceased not from mental prayer.

3. They spent all their time profitably: every hour seemed short which they spent with God, and through the great sweetness of divine contemplation they forgot even the necessity of their bodily refreshment.

They renounced all riches, dignities, honors, friends, and kindred; they desired to have nothing of this world; they scarcely allowed themselves the necessaries of life; the serving the body, even in necessity, was irksome to them.

They were poor, therefore, as to earthly things, but very rich in grace and virtue.

Outwardly they were in want, but inwardly they were

refreshed with divine graces and consolations.

4. They were strangers to the world, but near and familiar friends to God.

They seemed to themselves as nothing, and were despised by this world; but in the eyes of God they were very precious and beloved.

They stood in true humility, they lived in simple obedience, they walked in charity and patience; and therefore they daily advanced in spirit, and obtained great favor with God.

They were given as an example for all religious, and ought more to excite us to make good progress, than the number of the lukewarm to grow slack.

5. Oh, how great was the fervor of all religious in the beginning of their holy institution!

Oh, how great was their devotion in prayer! How great their zeal for virtue! What great discipline was in force among them! What great reverence and obedience in all, flourished under the rule of a superior!

The footsteps remaining, still bear witness that they were truly perfect and holy men, who, waging war so stoutly, trod the world under their feet.

Now he is thought great who is not a transgressor, and who can with patience endure what he hath undertaken.

6. Ah, the lukewarmness and negligence of our state, that we so quickly fall away from our former fervor, and are now even weary of living through sloth and tepidity.

Would to God that advancement in virtues was not wholly asleep in thee who hast so often seen many examples of the devout!

Practical Reflections

Nothing can so powerfully excite us to live holily as the example of those who are holy. Example convinces us of the possibility of virtue, makes it practicable and easy, and offers it to us already illustrated in others, and, as it were, prepared for our exercise. For, when we read the lives or witness the examples of the saints, we naturally say to ourselves: See what men like ourselves have done, and suffered, and forsaken, for the Kingdom of Heaven, which is equally the object of our hopes. But what have we done to obtain it? Why do we not exert ourselves as they did to become worthy of the same recompense? Alas! I have reason to apprehend that when I shall appear before God, He will compare my life with my faith, with my religion, and with the examples of holy men who have lived in the same state of life as myself, and confronting me with these witnesses, will say to me: See what thou shouldst have done, and how thou hast neglected it; judge thou thyself: what dost thou deserve?

Prayer

Enter not, O Lord, into judgment with Thy servant; for my life, when compared with the conduct of the saints, can never justify me. Grant me the grace which Thou, my Saviour, didst merit for me, of attending to the discharge of my duties, of entering into the spirit of religion, of observing its rules and maxims, and of conforming my life to my faith, that so, when I appear before Thee, I may be clothed in the robes of Thy justice, supported by Thy mercy, and animated with Thy love. Amen.

Chapter 19

Of the Exercises of a Good Religious

THE LIFE of a good religious man ought to be eminent in all virtues, that he may be such interiorly as he appears to men in his exterior.

And with good reason ought he to be much more in his interior than he exteriorly appears; because He who beholds us is God, of whom we ought exceedingly to stand in awe, wherever we are, and like angels walk pure in His sight.

We ought every day to renew our resolution, and excite ourselves to fervor as if this were the first day of our conversion, and to say:

Help me, O Lord God, in my good resolution and in Thy holy service, and give me grace now this day perfectly to begin, for what I have hitherto done is nothing.

2. According as our resolution is will the progress of our advancement be; and he hath need of much diligence who would advance much.

Now, if he that makes a strong resolution often fails, what will he do who seldom or but weakly resolves?

The falling off from our resolution happens divers ways, and a small omission in our exercises seldom passeth without some loss.

The resolutions of the just depend on the grace of God, rather than on their own wisdom; and in Him they always put their trust, whatever they take in hands:

For man proposes, but God disposes, nor is the way of man in his own hands. (*Prov.* 14:12).

3. If for piety's sake, or with a design to the profit of our

brother, we sometimes omit our accustomed exercises it may afterwards be easily recovered.

But if, through a loathing of mind, or negligence, it be lightly passed over it is no small fault and will prove hurtful. With our utmost endeavors we will still be apt to fail in many things.

But we must always resolve on something certain, and in particular against those things which hinder us most.

We must examine and order well both our exterior and interior; because both conduce to our advancement.

4. If thou canst not continually recollect thyself do it sometimes, and at least once a day, that is, at morning or evening.

In the morning resolve, in the evening examine thy performances, how thou hast behaved this day in word, work, or thought; because in these, perhaps, thou hast often offended God and thy neighbor.

Prepare thyself like a man to resist the wicked attacks of the devil; bridle gluttony, and thou shalt the easier restrain all carnal inclinations.

Be never altogether idle, but either reading or writing, or praying or meditating, or laboring in something that may be for the common good.

Yet in bodily exercises a discretion is to be used; nor are they equally to be undertaken by all.

5. Those things which are not common are not to be done in public, for particular things are more safely done in private.

But take care thou be not backward in common exercises and more forward in things of thine own particular devotion; but having fully and faithfully performed what thou art bound to, and what is enjoined thee, if thou hast any time remaining, give thyself to thyself according as thy devotion shall incline thee.

All cannot have the self-same exercise; but this is more proper for one and that for another.

Moreover, according to the diversity of times, divers exercises are more pleasing; for some relish better on festival days, others on common days.

We stand in need of one kind in time of temptation, and of another in time of peace and rest.

Some we willingly think on when we are sad, others when we are joyful in the Lord.

6. About the time of the principal festivals we must renew our good exercises and more fervently implore the prayers of the saints.

We ought to make our resolution from festival to festival, as if we were then to depart out of this world, and to come to the everlasting festival.

Therefore we ought carefully to prepare ourselves at times of devotion, and to converse more devoutly, and to keep all observances more strictly, as being shortly to receive the reward of our labor from God.

7. And if it be deferred, let us believe that we are not well prepared and that we are as yet unworthy of the great glory which shall be revealed to us at the appointed time *(Rom.* 7:18); and let us endeavor to prepare ourselves better for our departure.

Blessed is that servant, says the Evangelist St. Luke *(Luke* 12:57), whom, when his Lord shall come he shall find watching. Amen, I say to you, he shall set him over all his possessions.

Practical Reflections

To engage us to die to ourselves, and to live to God and for God, how efficacious are lively desires when constantly directed to that object! for we ever accomplish what we earnestly desire: but our misfortune is, that oftentimes our desires of pleasing God are weak and feeble, while the desires of gratifying ourselves are strong and active. Hence proceeds the inefficacy of our good purposes, which is a great obstacle to perfection and salvation. We wish to give ourselves to God, and we wish it not; we desire to do so in time of prayer and the Holy Communion, and at other times we desire it not. We in part, and for a time only, would acquit ourselves of our duties; hence our lives become a succession of good desires and evil effects, of promises and infidelities. Is this to labor effectually for salvation?

Prayer

Weary, O Lord, of the inefficacy of our desires, and of offering Thee only thoughts which we reduce not to practice, and promises which we never fulfill, we earnestly supplicate Thee to grant us the grace of adding effect to our desires, and of uniting the practice with the knowledge of virtue; for we well know, as Thou teachest in the Gospel, that not everyone who says, "Lord, Lord," shall enter into the Kingdom of Heaven, but only those who do the will of Thy Father; grant, therefore, O my Saviour, that I may not only think of and desire, but ever accomplish Thy blessed will. Amen.

Chapter 20

Of the Love of Solitude and Silence

SEEK a proper time to retire into thyself, and often think of the benefits of God.

Let curiosities alone.

Read such matters as may rather move thee to compunction than give thee occupation.

If thou wilt withdraw thyself from superfluous talk and idle visits, as also from giving ear to news and to reports, thou wilt find time sufficient and proper to employ thyself in good meditations.

The greatest saints avoided the company of men as much as they could and chose to live to God in secret.

2. "As often as I have been amongst men," said a philosopher, "I have returned less a man"; this we often experience when we talk long.

It is easier to be altogether silent than not to exceed in words.

It is easier to keep retired at home than to be able to be sufficiently upon one's guard abroad.

Whosoever, therefore, aims at arriving at internal and spiritual things, must, with Jesus, go aside from the crowd. (*John* 5:13).

No man is secure in appearing abroad, but he who would willingly lie hid at home.

No man securely speaks but he who loves to hold his peace.

No man securely governs but he who would willingly live in subjection.

No man securely commands but he who has learned well to obey.

3. No man securely rejoiceth unless he hath within him the testimony of a good conscience. (*2 Cor.* 1:12).

Yet the security of the saints was always full of the fear of God.

Neither were they less careful or humble in themselves, because they were shining with great virtues and graces.

But the security of the wicked arises from pride and presumption, and will end in deceiving themselves.

Never promise thyself security in this life, though thou seem to be a good religious man, or a devout hermit.

4. Oftentimes they that were better in the judgment of men have been in greater danger by reason of their too great confidence.

So that it is better for many not to be altogether free from temptations but to be often assaulted; that they may not be too secure lest, perhaps, they be lifted up with pride, or take more liberty to go aside after exterior comforts.

Oh, how good a conscience would that man preserve, who would never seek after transitory joy, nor ever busy himself with the world!

Oh, how great peace and tranquillity would he possess, who would cut off all vain solicitude, and only think of the things of God, and his salvation, and place his whole hope in God!

5. No man is worthy of heavenly comfort who has not diligently exercised himself in holy compunction.

If thou wouldst find compunction in thy heart retire into thy chamber and shut out the tumult of the world, as it is written: "Have compunction in your chambers." (*Ps.* 4:5). Thou shalt find in thy cell what thou shalt often lose abroad.

Thy cell, if thou continue in it, grows sweet; but if thou keep not to it, it becomes tedious and distasteful. If in the beginning of thy conversion thou accustom thyself to remain in thy cell and keep it well, it will be to thee afterwards a dear friend and a most agreeable delight.

6. In silence and quiet the devout soul goes forward and learns the secrets of the Scriptures.

There she finds floods of tears, with which she may wash and cleanse herself every night, that she may become the more familiar with her Maker, by the farther she lives from all worldly tumult. (*Ps.* 6).

For God with His holy angels will draw nigh to him who withdraws himself from his acquaintances and friends.

It is better to lie hidden and take care of one's self than neglecting one's self to work even miracles.

It is commendable for a religious man to go seldom abroad, to fly being seen, and not desire to see men.

7. Why wilt thou see what thou must not have? "The world passeth away, and the concupiscence thereof." (*1 John* 2:17).

The desires of sensuality draw thee abroad, but when the hour is past what dost thou bring home but a weight upon thy conscience and a dissipation of heart.

A joyful going abroad often brings forth a sorrowful coming home; and a merry evening makes a sad morning.

So all carnal joys enter pleasantly but in the end bring remorse and death.

What canst thou see elsewhere which thou seest not

here? Behold the heavens and the earth, and all the elements; for of these are all things made.

8. What canst thou see anywhere which can continue long under the sun?

Thou thinkest perhaps to be satisfied, but thou canst not attain to it.

If thou couldst see all things at once before thee what would it be but a vain sight? (*Eccles.* 1:14).

Lift up thine eyes to God on high and pray for thy sins and negligences. (*Eccles.* 3:4; *Ps.* 122:1).

Leave vain things to vain people, but mind thou the things which God hath commanded thee.

Shut thy door upon thee, and call to thee Jesus thy beloved.

Stay with Him in thy cell, for thou shalt not find such great peace anywhere else.

If thou hadst not gone abroad, nor hearkened to rumors, thou hadst kept thyself better in good peace; but since thou art delighted sometimes to hear news thou must thence suffer a disturbance of heart.

Practical Reflections

Exterior retirement is not sufficient to engage and satisfy a heart which would really withdraw itself from creatures to be occupied on itself alone, but interior retirement is likewise necessary, which is a spirit of recollection and prayer. A soul which is separated from all the amusements of the senses, seeks and finds in God that pure satisfaction which it can never meet with in creatures. A respectful and frequent remembrance of the presence of God occupies the mind, and an ardent desire of pleasing Him and of becoming worthy of His love engages the heart. It is absorbed in Him alone: all things else dwindle into nothing. It buries itself in its dear solitude, and dies to itself and all things in God: it breathes only His love, it forgets all to remember only Him; penetrated with grief for its infidelities it mourns incessantly in His pressure, it sighs continually for the pleasure of seeing and possessing Him in Heaven, it nourishes itself with reading good books, and with the exercise of prayer, it is never tired of treating with God on the affairs of salvation, at least it humbly supports the irksomeness it may experience, and with a view of honoring His sovereign dominion by the complete destruction of sin in itself, it renounces all desire of finding any other satisfaction than that of pleasing Him.

Prayer

O my God, when will silence, retirement, and prayer, become the occupations of my soul, as they are now frequently the objects of my desires? How am I wearied with saying so much and yet doing so little for Thee! Come, Jesus, come, Thou the only object of my love, the center and supreme happiness of my soul! Come, and impress my mind with such a lively conviction of Thy presence that all within me may yield to its influence. Come, Lord, and speak to my heart, communicate to it Thy holy will, and mercifully work within it both to will and to do according to Thy good pleasure. Alas, how long shall my exile be prolonged? When shall the veil be removed which separates time from eternity? When shall I see that which I now believe? When shall I find what I seek? When shall I possess what I love, which is Thyself, O my God! Grant, O Jesus, that these holy desires with which Thou now inspirest me may be followed by that eternal happiness which I hope for from Thine infinite mercy. Amen.

Chapter 21

Of Compunction of Heart

IF THOU wilt make any progress keep thyself in the fear of God (*Prov.* 23:17), and be not too free, but restrain all thy senses under discipline, and give not thyself up to foolish mirth.

Give thyself to compunction of heart and thou shalt find devotion.

Compunction opens the way to much good, which dissolution is wont quickly to lose.

It is wonderful that any man can heartily rejoice in this life who weighs and considers his banishment and the many dangers of his soul.

2. Through levity of heart and the little thought we have of our defects we feel not the sorrows of our soul, but often vainly laugh when in all reason we ought to weep.

There is no true liberty, nor solid joy, but in the fear of God with a good conscience.

Happy is he who can cast away all impediments of distractions and recollect himself to the union of holy compunction.

Happy is he who separates himself from all that may burden or defile his conscience.

Strive manfully; custom is overcome by custom.

If thou canst let men alone they will let thee do what thou hast to do.

3. Busy not thyself with other men's affairs, nor entangle thyself with the causes of great people.

Have always an eye upon thyself in the first place and

take special care to admonish thyself preferably to all thy dearest friends.

If thou hast not the favor of men be not grieved thereat: but let thy concern be that thou dost not carry thyself so well and so circumspectly as it becomes a servant of God, and a devout religious mean to demean himself.

It is oftentimes more profitable and more secure for a man not to have many comforts in this life, especially according to the flesh.

Yet, that we have not divine comforts, or seldomer experience them, is our own fault, because we do not seek compunction of heart, nor cast off altogether vain and outward satisfactions.

4. Acknowledge thyself unworthy of divine consolation, and rather worthy of much tribulation.

When a man has perfect compunction then the whole world is to him burdensome and distasteful.

A good man always finds subjects enough for mourning and weeping.

For whether he considers himself, or thinks of his neighbor, he knows that no man lives here without tribulation; and the more thoroughly he considers himself, the more he grieves.

The subjects for just grief and interior compunction are our vices and sins, in which we lie entangled in such a manner as seldom to be able to contemplate heavenly things.

5. If thou wouldst oftener think of thy death than of a long life, no doubt thou wouldst more fervently amend thyself.

And if thou didst seriously consider in thy heart the future punishment of Hell or Purgatory, I believe thou wouldst willingly endure labor and pain, and fear no kind of austerity.

But because these things reach not the heart, and we still love the things which flatter us, therefore we remain cold and very sluggish.

6. It is oftentimes a want of spirit which makes the wretched body so easily complain.

Pray, therefore, humbly to Our Lord, that He may give thee the spirit of compunction, and say with the Prophet, "Feed me, O Lord, with the bread of tears and give me drink of tears in measure." (*Ps.* 79:6).

Practical Reflections

Can we be sensible of our miseries and not deplore them, and humble ourselves under them before God, and have continual recourse to Him to support and keep us from offending Him? It is this humble diffidence in ourselves, and firm confidence in God, which constitute the spirit of compunction of which the author speaks in this chapter. How is it possible that we should taste true joy for one moment in this life, in which we are beset with miseries and sin—are continually in danger of being lost forever, and are exiles from Paradise, our true country? Well might St. Augustine say that a true Christian suffereth life, and sigheth after death, which will put an end to sin, and unite him forever to his God. How afflicting to feel ever prone to offend God—always in danger of forfeiting salvation! O life! how burdensome art thou to a soul that truly loves God and is grieved at being separated at a distance from Him—an exile from Heaven! O death, how sweet art thou to a soul that breathes only God and can no longer exist without possessing Him!

Prayer

Grant, O God, that my heart may become detached from all things, and, being wholly recollected in Thee, relish no other pleasure than that of loving Thee, of acting and suffering for Thy sake. I willingly consent to the sweet portion Thou allottest me to do by patiently receiving all the pains Thou sendest me, that Thou mayest become my happiness for eternity. What should I not do and suffer for such a reward? Keep me, O Lord, in the holy desire with which Thou now inspirest me, of sparing no pains to obtain it. Amen.

Chapter 22

Of the Consideration of the Misery of Man

THOU art miserable wherever thou art, and which way soever thou turnest thyself, unless thou dost turn thyself to God.

Why art thou troubled because things do not succeed with thee according to thy will and desire? Who is there that has all things according to his will! Neither I, nor thou, nor any man upon earth.

There is no man in the world without some trouble or affliction, though he be a king or a pope.

Who is it that is most at ease? Doubtless he who is willing to suffer something for God's sake.

2. Many unstable and weak men are apt to say: Behold how well such a man lives; how rich, how great, how mighty and powerful.

But attend to heavenly goods and thou wilt see that all

these temporal things are nothing but very uncertain and rather burdensome, because they are never possessed without care and fear.

The happiness of a man consisteth not in having temporal things in abundance, but a moderate competency sufficeth.

It is truly a misery to live upon earth.

The more a man desireth to be spiritual, the more this present life becomes distasteful to him, because he the better understands and more clearly sees the defects of human corruption.

For to eat, drink, watch, sleep, rest, labor, and to be subject to other necessities of nature, is truly a great misery and affliction to a devout man who desires to be released and free from all sin.

3. For the inward man is very much burdened with the necessities of the body in this world.

And, therefore, the Prophet devoutly prays to be freed from them, saying, "From my necessities deliver me, O Lord." (*Ps.* 24:17).

But woe to them that know not their own misery, and more woe to them that love this miserable and corruptible life.

For some there are that love it to that degree, although they can scarce get necessaries by laboring or begging, that if they could live always here they would not care at all for the Kingdom of God.

4. O senseless people, and infidels in heart, who lie buried so deep in earthly things as to relish nothing but the things of the flesh.

Miserable wretches, they will in the end find to their cost

how vile a nothing that was which they so much loved!

But the saints of God and all the devout friends of Christ made no account of what pleased the flesh or flourished in this life; but their whole hope and intention aspired to eternal goods.

Their whole desire tended upwards to things everlasting and invisible, lest the love of visible things should draw them down to things below.

5. Lose not, brother, thy confidence of going forward to spiritual things; there is yet time, the hour is not yet past.

Why wilt thou put off thy resolutions from day to day? Arise, and begin this very moment, and say: now is the time for doing, and now is the time to fight; now is the proper time to amend my life.

When thou art troubled and afflicted then is the time to merit.

Thou must pass through fire and water before thou comest to refreshment. *(Ps.* 65:12).

Unless thou do violence to thyself thou wilt not overcome vice.

As long as we carry about us this frail body we cannot be without sin nor live without uneasiness and sorrow.

We would fain be at rest from all misery, but because we have lost innocence by sin we have also lost true happiness.

We must, therefore, have patience and wait for the mercy of God till iniquity pass away and this mortality be swallowed up by life. (*2 Cor.* 5:4).

6. Oh, how great is human frailty, which is always prone to vice!

Today thou confessest thy sins, and tomorrow thou

again committest what thou hast confessed.

Now thou resolvest to take care, and an hour after thou dost as if thou hadst never resolved.

We have reason, therefore, to humble ourselves and never to think much of ourselves since we are so frail and inconstant.

That may also be quickly lost through negligence, which, with much labor and time, was hardly gotten by grace.

7. What will become of us yet in the end who grow luke-warm so very soon?

Woe be to us if we are for giving ourselves to rest, as if we had already met with peace and security, when there does not as yet appear any mark of true sanctity in our con-versation. (*1 Thess.* 5:3).

It would be very needful that we should again, like good novices, be instructed in all good behavior and if so, per-haps there would be some hopes of future amendment and greater spiritual progress.

Practical Reflections

What a happiness and what a gain to see and to find God, in whom we may forget all our cares and end all our miseries! And how happy are we in knowing and feeling that it is really true happiness, a heaven upon earth, to suffer all for God's sake, even such things as are most humiliating and repugnant to our nature, for this can proceed only from the true love of God! How miserable are we if we are not sensible of or love the mis-eries of this life, and sigh not incessantly for the enjoyments of the life to come! How justly does St. Gregory observe that to act thus is to love hunger and misery, and not to love nourishment and happiness! Can we experience every hour, as we do the inconstancy and frailty of our hearts, how soon we forget our good resolutions, and how light we make of our promises to God, and not humble ourselves in His presence, and implore Him, with holy Judith, to fortify us and make us faithful?

Prayer

We beseech Thee, O Father of mercies, and God of all consolation, to support us in the perpetual combats we are summoned to maintain against our passions, our self-love, and our whole self, which is so opposed to Thee; for alas! O God, what can we do of ourselves if Thou support us not but fall into sin and offend Thee? Leave us not, therefore, to ourselves, but strengthen us in the inward man, that so we may at all times and in all things renounce our evil inclinations, which are incessantly endeavoring to withdraw our hearts from Thee. Complete Thy conquest, and make us all Thine own both now and forever. Amen.

Chapter 23

Of the Thoughts of Death

VERY quickly must thou be gone from hence, see then how matters stand with thee; a man is here today and tomorrow he is vanished. (*1 Mach.* 2:63).

And when he is taken away from the sight he is quickly also out of mind.

Oh, the dullness and hardness of man's heart, which only thinks of what is present, and looks not forward to things to come.

Thou oughtst in every action and thought so to order thyself as if thou wert immediately to die.

If thou hadst a good conscience thou wouldst not much fear death.

It were better for thee to fly sin than to be afraid of death. (*Dan.* 13:23).

If thou art not prepared today how shalt thou be tomorrow?

Tomorrow is an uncertain day; and how dost thou know that thou shalt be alive tomorrow? (*James* 4:14).

2. What benefit is it to live long when we advance so little?

Ah, long life does not always make us better, but often adds to our guilt!

Would to God we had behaved ourselves well in this world even for one day!

Many count the years of their conversion; but oftentimes the fruit of amendment is but small.

If it be frightful to die, perhaps it will be more dangerous to live longer.

Blessed is he that has always the hour of death before his eyes and every day disposes himself to die. *(Ecclus.* 7:40).

If thou hast at any time seen a man die think that thou must also pass the same way.

3. In the morning imagine that thou shalt not live till night; and when evening comes presume not to promise thyself the next morning.

Be therefore always prepared, and live in such a manner that death may never find thee unprovided.

Many die suddenly and when they little think of it:

"Because at what hour you know not the Son of man will come." (*Matt.* 24:44).

When that last hour shall come thou wilt begin to have quite other thoughts of thy whole past life; and thou wilt be exceedingly grieved that thou hast been so negligent and remiss. (*Wis.* 5:6).

4. How happy and prudent is he who strives to be such now in this life as he desires to be found at his death.

For it will give a man a great confidence of dying happily if he has a perfect contempt of the world, a fervent desire of advancing in virtue, a love for discipline, the spirit of penance, a ready obedience, self-denial, and patience in bearing all adversities for the love of Christ.

Thou mayest do many good things whilst thou art well, but when thou art sick I know not what thou wilt be able to do.

Few are improved by sickness; so too they that travel much abroad seldom become holy.

5. Trust not in thy friends and relations, nor put off the welfare of thy soul to hereafter; for men will sooner forget thee than thou imaginest.

It is better now to provide in time, and send some good before thee, than to trust to the help of others after thy death. (*Matt.* 6:20).

If thou art not now careful for thyself who will be careful for thee hereafter?

The present time is very precious; "Now is the acceptable time: now is the day of salvation." (*2 Cor.* 6:2).

But it is greatly to be lamented that thou dost not spend this time more profitably in which thou mayest acquire wherewith to live forever.

The time will come when thou wilt wish for one day or hour to amend, and I know not whether thou shalt obtain it.

6. O my dearly beloved, from how great a danger mayest thou deliver thyself! from how great a fear mayest thou be freed if thou wilt but now be always fearful and looking for death!

Strive now so to live that in the hour of thy death thou mayest rather rejoice than fear.

Learn now to die to the world that then thou mayest begin to live with Christ. (*Rom.* 6:8).

Learn now to despise all things that then thou mayest freely go to Christ.

Chastise thy body now by penance that thou mayest then have an assured confidence. (*1 Cor.* 9:27).

7. Ah fool, why dost thou think to live long when thou art not sure of one day? (*Luke* 12:20).

How many thinking to live long have been deceived and unexpectedly snatched away!

How often hast thou heard related that such a man was slain by the sword; another drowned; another falling from on high broke his neck; this man died at the table; that other came to his end when he was at play.

Some have perished by fire, some by the sword, some by pestilence, some by robbers: and thus death is the end of all, and man's life passeth suddenly like a shadow. (*Eccles.* 7:1).

8. Who will remember thee when thou art dead, and who will pray for thee?

Do now, beloved, do now all thou canst, because thou knowest not when thou shalt die; nor dost thou know what shall befall thee after death.

Whilst thou hast time heap to thyself riches that will never die! (*Matt.* 6:20).

Think of nothing but thy salvation, care for nothing but the things of God.

Make now to thyself friends, by honoring the saints of God, and imitating their actions, that when thou shalt fail in this life they may receive thee into everlasting dwellings. (*Luke* 16:9).

9. Keep thyself as a pilgrim, and a stranger upon earth, to whom the affairs of this world do not in the least belong. (*1 Ptr.* 2:11).

Keep thy heart free and raised upwards to God, because thou hast not here a lasting abode.

Send thither thy daily prayers, with sighs and tears, that after death thy spirit may be worthy to pass happily to Our Lord. Amen.

Practical Reflections

To fear death, and not to avoid sin, which alone can make it really terrible, is to fear it unavailably for salvation; for, as Christians, we ought to dread it so as to make the fear of it the motive and rule of a good life. The great secret of dying happily is to live always in the same state in which we hope to die, and in which we desire that God may find us when our last hour shall have arrived. We should therefore do all the good and practice all the virtues now which we shall then wish to have done and practiced. Endeavor to die daily to some one of all those things which, when thou departest hence, thou must leave forever. Happy the Christian who dies often in spirit ere he quits the flesh. His death shall be holy and precious in the sight of God.

Prayer

Knowing that I shall certainly die, but ignorant of the day, of the hour, and of the state of my soul, in which I shall depart hence, I beseech Thee, most blessed Saviour, by the merits of Thy sacred Passion, to prepare me for that awful moment. Assist me to become diligent in my employments, faithful to Thy graces, attentive at my prayers, regular in frequenting the Sacraments, and constant in the performance of those good works, and in the practice of those virtues which are proper for my state: that so, through Thy merits, I may experience consolation in my last moments, and leave this valley of tears in the assured hope of salvation. Grant that I may ever persevere in Thy grace, seek in all things to please Thee, and breathe only Thy love: for living thus, my Jesus, by Thee, for Thee, and like unto Thee, it will be at all times most advantageous for me to die, that I may never offend Thee more, but see, love, and enjoy Thee for all eternity. Amen.

Chapter 24

Of Judgment, and the Punishment of Our Sins

IN ALL things look to thine end (*Ecclus.* 7:40), and how thou shalt be able to stand before a severe Judge, from whom nothing is hidden, who takes no bribes, nor receives excuses, but will judge that which is just.

O most wretched and foolish sinner, what answer wilt thou make to God, who knows all thine evils? thou who art sometimes afraid of the looks of an angry man.

Why dost thou not provide for thyself against the Day of Judgment, when no man can be excused or defended by another, but everyone shall have enough to do to answer for himself?

At present thy labor is profitable; thy tears are acceptable, thy sighs will be heard, thy sorrow is satisfactory, and may purge away thy sins.

2. A patient man hath a great and wholesome purgatory, who, receiving injuries, is more concerned at the person's sin than his own wrong; who willingly prays for his adversaries, and from his heart forgives offenses; who delays not to ask forgiveness of others; who is easier moved to compassion than to anger; who frequently useth violence to himself, and labors to bring the flesh wholly under subjection to the spirit.

It is better now to purge away our sins and to cut up our vices than to reserve them to be purged hereafter.

Truly we deceive ourselves through the inordinate love we bear to our flesh.

3. What other things shall the fire feed on but thy sins?

The more thou sparest thyself now and followest the flesh the more grievously shalt thou suffer hereafter and the more fuel dost thou lay up for that fire.

In those things which a man has more sinned shall he be more heavily punished.

There the slothful shall be pricked forward with burning goads, and the glutton will be tormented with extreme hunger and thirst.

There the luxurious and the lovers of pleasure shall be covered all over with burning pitch and stinking brimstone, and the envious like mad dogs shall howl for grief.

4. There is no vice which will not there have its proper torment.

There the proud shall be filled with all confusion, and the covetous be straitened with most miserable want.

There one hour of suffering will be more sharp than a hundred years here spent in the most rigid penance.

There is no rest, no comfort for the damned; but here there is sometimes intermission of labor, and we receive comfort from our friends.

Be careful at present and sorrowful for thy sins, that in the Day of Judgment thou mayest be secure with the blessed.

"For then shall the just stand with great constancy against those that have afflicted and oppressed them." (*Wis.* 5:1).

Then will he stand to judge who now humbly submits himself to the judgment of men.

Then the poor and the humble shall have great confidence and the proud shall fear on every side.

5. Then will it appear that he was wise in this word who learned for Christ's sake to be a fool and despised.

Then all tribulation suffered with patience will be pleasing "and all iniquity shall stop her mouth." (*Ps.* 106:42).

Then every devout person shall rejoice and the irreligious shall be sad.

Then the flesh that has been mortified shall triumph more than if it had always been pampered in delights.

Then shall the mean habit shine and fine clothing appear contemptible.

Then shall the poor cottage be more commended than the gilded palace.

Then constant patience shall more avail than all the power of the world.

Then simple obedience shall be more prized than all

worldly craftiness.

6. Then a pure and good conscience shall be a greater subject of joy than learned philosophy.

Then the contempt of riches shall weigh more than all the treasures of worldlings.

Then wilt thou be more comforted that thou hast prayed devoutly than that thou hast fared daintily.

Then wilt thou rejoice more that thou hast kept silence than that thou hast made long discourses or talked much.

Then will holy works be of greater value than many fair words.

Then will a strict life and hard penance be more pleasing than all the delights of the earth.

Learn, at present, to suffer in little things, that then thou mayest be delivered from more grievous sufferings.

Try first here what thou canst suffer hereafter.

If thou canst now endure so little how wilt thou be able to bear everlasting torments?

If a little suffering now makes thee so impatient what will hellfire do hereafter?

Surely thou canst not have both joys—take thy pleasure in this world and afterwards reign with Christ.

7. If to this day thou hadst always lived in honors and pleasures what would it avail thee if thou wert now in a moment to die?

All then is vanity but to love God and to serve Him alone. (*Eccles.* 1:2; *Deut.* 10:20).

For he that loves God with his whole heart neither fears death, nor punishment, nor judgment, nor Hell; because perfect love gives secure access to God.

But he that is yet delighted with sin no wonder if he be afraid of death and judgment.

It is good, however, that if love, as yet, reclaim thee not from evil, at least the fear of Hell restrain thee.

But he that lays aside the fear of God will not be able to continue long in good, but will quickly fall into the snares of the devil.

Practical Reflections

How powerfully do the fear of God's judgments and the dread of a miserable eternity act as a restraint upon our passions, arrest the sallies of temper, and oblige us to withdraw from the allurements and pleasures of sin! To what end (let us say to ourselves in time of temptation) is the criminal pleasure of this sin of revenge, impurity, anger, injustice, or lying? To afford myself a momentary gratification. And should I die immediately after having yielded, without repentance, without the Sacraments (which may happen, and which does happen to thousands), where will this sinful enjoyment terminate? In a miserable eternity. A momentary pleasure, an eternity of pain! No, I will not expose myself to the danger of being miserable forever for the sake of a moment of pleasure. How true it is, according to the Wise Man, that to avoid sin, at least habitual sin, we must remember our last end. Did we frequently and seriously reflect that we must one day give an exact account of our consciences, of the conduct of our whole lives, of all our sins, to a Judge who knoweth and remembereth all things, who would not be terrified at the apprehension of Judgment, and of the terrible account we are then to give, and would not watch over himself, and endeavor to correct all his faults? Let us be convinced that the sure way to avoid condemnation in the next life is to condemn and punish ourselves in this.

Prayer

O Sovereign Judge of the living and the dead! Who, at the moment of our death, will decide our eternal doom, remember that Thou art our Saviour as well as our Judge, and that as much as our sins have provoked Thee to wrath, Thy sacred Wounds have inclined Thee to mercy. Look, therefore, on those Wounds inflicted on Thee for our sins, and on the Blood which Thou hast shed for their expiation, and by those precious pledges of salvation we conjure Thee to pardon our manifold transgressions. Amen.

Chapter 25

Of the Fervent Amendment Of Our Whole Life

B E VIGILANT and diligent in God's service, and often think with thyself to what end thou camest hither, and why thou didst leave the world: Was it not that thou mightest live in God and become a spiritual man?

Be fervent, therefore, in thy spiritual progress, for thou shalt shortly receive the reward of thy labors; and then grief and fear shall no more come near thee.

Thou shalt labor now a little and thou shalt find great rest; yea, everlasting joy.

If thou continue faithful and fervent in working, God will doubtless be faithful and liberal in rewarding.

Thou must preserve a good and firm hope of winning the victory; but must not think thyself secure, lest thou grow negligent or proud.

2. When a certain person in anxiety of mind was often wavering between hope and fear, and, on a time, being overwhelmed with grief, had prostrated himself in prayer in the church before a certain altar, he revolved these things within himself saying: "If I did but know that I should still persevere"; and presently he heard within himself this answer from God: "And if thou didst know this what wouldst thou do? Do now what thou wouldst then do, and thou shalt be very secure."

And immediately, being comforted and strengthened, he committed himself to the divine will, and his anxious wavering ceased.

Neither had he a mind anymore to search curiously, to know what should befall him hereafter; but rather studied to inquire what was the will of God, "well pleasing and perfect" (*Rom.* 12:2), for the beginning and accomplishment of every good work.

3. "Trust in the Lord, and do good," saith the Prophet, "and dwell in the land, and thou shalt be fed with its riches." (*Ps.* 36:3).

There is one thing which keeps many back from spiritual progress and fervent amendment of life: and that is, dread of difficulty, or the labor which must be gone through in the conflict.

And they indeed advance most of all others in virtue, who strive manfully to overcome those things which they find more troublesome or contrary to them.

For there a man makes greater progress and merits greater grace where he overcomes himself more and mortifies himself in spirit.

4. But all men have not equal difficulties to overcome and mortify.

Yet he that is diligent and zealous, although he may have more passions to fight against, will be able to make a greater progress than another who has fewer passions but is withal less fervent in the pursuit of virtue.

Two things particularly conduce to a great amendment: these are, forcibly to withdraw one's self from that to which nature is viciously inclined, and earnestly to labor for that good which one wants most.

Study likewise to fly more carefully and to overcome those faults which most frequently displease thee in others.

5. Turn all occasions to thy spiritual profit: so that if thou see or hear any good examples thou mayest be spurred on to imitate them.

But if thou observe anything that is reprehensible take heed thou commit not the same; or if thou at any time hast done it, labor to amend it quickly.

As thine eye observeth others so art thou also observed by others.

Oh, how sweet and comfortable is it to see brethren fervent and devout, regular and well disciplined! *(Ps.* 132:1).

How sad a thing and how afflicting to see them walk disorderly, and practice nothing of what they are called to!

How hurtful it is to neglect the intent of our vocation and turn our minds to things that are not our business.

6. Be mindful of the resolution thou hast taken, and set before thee the image of the crucifix.

Well mayest thou be ashamed if thou hast looked upon the life of Jesus Christ, that thou hast not yet studied to conform thyself more to His pattern, although thou hast been long in the way of God.

A religious man, who exercises himself seriously and devoutly in the most holy life and Passion of Our Lord, shall find there abundantly all things profitable and necessary for him; nor need he seek any better model than that of Jesus.

Oh, if our crucified Jesus did but come into our heart, how quickly and sufficiently learned should we be!

7. A fervent religious man bears and takes all things well that are commanded him.

A negligent and lukewarm religious man has trouble upon trouble, and on every side suffers anguish, because he has no comfort within and is hindered from seeking any without.

A religious man that lives not in discipline lies open to dreadful ruin.

He that seeks to be more loose and remiss will always be uneasy, for one thing or other will always displease him.

8. How do so many other religious do who live under strict monastic discipline?

They seldom go abroad, they live very retired, their diet is very poor, their habit coarse, they labor much, they speak little, they watch long, they rise early, they spend much time in prayer, they read often and keep themselves in all discipline.

Consider the Carthusians, the Cistercians, and the monks and nuns of divers Orders, how every night they rise to sing psalms to the Lord.

It would, therefore, be a shame for thee to be sluggish

at so holy a time, when such multitudes of religious begin with joy to give praise to God.

9. Oh, that we had nothing else to do but to praise the Lord our God with our whole heart and mouth!

Oh, that thou didst never want to eat, nor drink, nor sleep, but couldst always praise God and be employed solely in spiritual exercises!

Thou wouldst then be much more happy than now whilst thou art under the necessity of serving the flesh.

Would there were no such necessities, but only the spiritual refreshments of the soul, which, alas, we taste too seldom.

10. When a man is come to this, that he seeks comfort from nothing created, then he begins perfectly to relish God; then likewise will he be well content, however matters happen to him.

Then will he neither rejoice for much, nor be sorrowful for little, but will commit himself wholly and confidently to God, who is to him all in all; to whom nothing perishes or dies, but all things live to Him and serve Him at a nod without delay.

11. Always remember thine end and that time once lost never returns. Without care and diligence thou shalt never acquire virtues.

If thou begin to grow lukewarm thou wilt begin to be uneasy.

But if thou give thyself to fervor thou shalt find great peace, and the grace of God and love of virtue will make thee feel less labor.

A fervent and diligent man is ready for all things.

It is a greater task to resist vices and passions than to toil at bodily labors.

He that does not shun small defects by little and little falls into greater. (*Ecclus.* 19:1).

Thou shalt always rejoice in the evening if thou spend the day profitably.

Watch over thyself, stir up thyself, admonish thyself, and whatever becometh of others neglect not thyself.

The greater violence thou offerest to thyself the greater progress thou shalt make.

Practical Reflections

According to our zeal for advancement, we take advantage of the good we see to practice it, and carry us to God. To advance in virtue we must overcome and renounce ourselves in all things and die to the insatiable desires of our heart. It is certain that we can merit in the service of God only in proportion as we do violence to ourselves. Wherefore, let us fight against and subdue the irregular inclinations which allure us to sin or to relaxation of our fervor: by this means we shall secure our salvation. A vigorous, constant, and generous effort to overcome ourselves, forwards us more in the ways of perfection and salvation than all those fruitless desires by which we would give ourselves to God, yet we do not what we would. The more we die to ourselves, the more do we live to God; and the more we refuse to gratify ourselves, so much the more do we please Him. How delightful must the life of that Christian be whose desires are so regulated that his chief happiness is in denying himself, and pleasing God! How sure a means of obtaining a happy eternity!

Prayer

Thou knowest, O Jesus, the extreme difficulty we experience in subduing and subjecting ourselves to Thee: suffer not this difficulty to hinder us from accomplishing it. It is just we should prefer Thy glory, and Thy holy will, to our own will and gratification, and hence we are resolved to do so. Strengthen us in this resolution, and make us faithful; grant that all in us may yield to Thee, that, advancing daily in virtue, and leading a supernatural and through Thy merits an acceptable life, we may become worthy of Thy grace here, and of Thine eternal glory hereafter. Amen.

Book II

Admonitions
Concerning
Interior Things

Chapter 1

Of Interior Conversation

T HE KINGDOM of God is within you *(Luke* 17:21), saith the Lord. Convert thyself with thy whole heart to the Lord *(Joel* 2:12), and quit this miserable world, and thy soul shall find rest.

Learn to despise exterior things, and give thyself to the interior, and thou shalt see the Kingdom of God will come into thee.

For the Kingdom of God is peace and joy in the Holy Ghost, which is not given to the wicked. *(Rom.* 14:17).

Christ will come to thee, discovering to thee His consolation, if thou wilt prepare Him a fit dwelling within thee.

All His glory and beauty is in the interior *(Ps.* 44:14), and there He pleaseth Himself.

Frequently doth He visit the internal man, sweet in His communication with him, delightful His consolation, much peace, and a familiarity exceedingly to be admired.

2. O faithful soul, prepare thy heart for this thy spouse, that He may vouchsafe to come to thee, and dwell in thee!

For so He saith: "If any man love me he will keep my word, and my Father will love him, and we will come to him, and we will make our abode with him." *(John* 14:23).

Make room then for Christ within thee and deny entrance to all others.

When thou hast Christ thou art rich and He is sufficient for thee; He will provide for thee, and will be thy faithful procurator in all things, so that thou needst not trust to men.

For men quickly change and presently fail: but Christ remains forever and stands by us firmly to the end.

3. There is no great confidence to be put in a frail mortal man, though he be profitable and beloved (*Ps.* 145:2); nor much grief to be taken if sometimes he be against thee and cross thee.

They that are with thee today may be against thee tomorrow; and on the other hand often changed like the wind.

Place thy whole confidence in God and let Him be thy fear and thy love; He will answer for thee and do for thee what is for the best. (*Jer.* 17:7).

Thou hast not here a lasting city and wherever thou art thou art a stranger and a pilgrim (*1 Ptr.* 2:11); nor wilt thou ever have rest unless thou be interiorly united to Christ.

4. Why dost thou stand looking about thee here, since this is not thy resting place?

Thy dwelling must be in Heaven, and all things of the earth are only to be looked upon as passing by.

All things pass away and thou along with them. (*Wis.* 5:9).

See that thou cleave not to them, lest thou be ensnared and be lost.

Let thy thought be with the Most High, and thy prayer directed to Christ without intermission.

If thou knowest not how to meditate on high and heavenly things, rest on the Passion of Christ, and willingly dwell in His sacred Wounds.

For if thou flee devoutly to the Wounds and precious stigmas of Jesus, thou shalt feel great comfort in tribulation; neither wilt thou much regard being despised by men, but wilt easily bear up against detracting tongues.

5. Christ was also in this world despised by men, and in His greatest necessity forsaken by His acquaintance and friends in the midst of reproaches.

Christ would suffer and be despised, and dost thou dare to complain of anyone?

Christ had adversaries and backbiters, and wouldst thou have all to be thy friends and benefactors?

Whence shall thy patience be crowned if thou meet with no adversity?

If thou wilt suffer no opposition, how wilt thou be a friend of Christ?

Suffer with Christ and for Christ if thou desirest to reign with Christ. (*2 Tim.* 2:12).

6. If thou hadst once perfectly entered into the interior of Jesus and experienced a little of His burning love, then wouldst thou not care at all for thine own convenience or inconvenience, but wouldst rather rejoice at reproach, because the love of Jesus makes a man despise himself.

A lover of Jesus and of truth, and a true internal man, that is free from inordinate affections, can freely turn himself to God and in spirit elevate himself above himself, and rest in enjoyment.

7. He to whom all things relish as they are, not as they are esteemed or said to be, is wise indeed, and taught rather by God than men.

He who knows how to walk internally, and to make little account of external things, is not at a loss for proper places or times for performing devout exercises.

An internal man quickly recollects himself, because he

never pours forth his whole self upon outward things.

Exterior labor is no prejudice to him, or any employment which for a time is necessary; but as things fall out, he accommodates himself to them.

He that is well-disposed and orderly in his interior heeds not the strange and perverse carriages of men.

As much as a man draws things to himself, so much is he hindered and distracted by them.

8. If thou hadst a right spirit within thee, and wert well purified from earthly affections, all things would turn to thy good and to thy profit.

For this reason do many things displease and often trouble thee, because thou art not as yet perfectly dead to thyself, nor separated from all earthly things.

Nothing so defiles and entangles the heart of man as impure love to created things.

If thou reject exterior comfort thou wilt be able to contemplate heavenly things, and frequently to feel excessive joy interiorly.

Practical Reflections

"Convert thyself with thy whole heart to the Lord. Learn to despise exterior things, and give thyself to the interior." These words teach us that the true happiness and only merit of this life consist in retirement and recollection in God, which are maintained by means of a respectful remembrance of His presence, and a continual turning of souls towards Him. A recollected mind and a faithful heart form the character of an interior man who adores God in spirit and in truth, that is, who pays Him that interior homage which becometh His sovereign greatness, and is so necessary for a soul whose sole business is to live in God and for God. It is this abiding of God in the soul, this establishment of the soul in God, by raising itself up to Him in sighs and lamentations, and by casting its whole self upon Him, which enables it to live an interior life, a life of merit, and above nature, which is Heaven upon earth, and an anticipated possession of the felicity of God. I am resolved therefore to mortify my senses, to banish from my mind all vain and useless reflections, and to keep a strict guard over my heart, that nothing may enter therein but what will promote the fear and love of Jesus Christ. Everything else shall be to me as though it were not; and I will endeavor above all things, to know, love, and imitate my Redeemer, content to suffer all for Him and in Him, that I may one day reign with Him. O my soul! breathe only His love, live only to please Him, sigh only for the happiness of possessing Him.

Prayer

O my most amiable Saviour! the life of my soul! the only object of my hope, and the assurance of my salvation! Come, take possession of my heart, which is already Thine, infuse into it the spirit of Thy mysteries. Thine interior dispositions, and the virtues which Thou didst practice. Grant that, animated by Thy Spirit, living in and by Thee, and, as it were, clothed with Thy justice, I may become more Thine than my own. Mayest thou live in me; and may I, by a happy transmutation, yielding myself entirely to Thee, act only from the influences of Thy love. Amen.

Chapter 2

Of Humble Submission

MAKE no great account who is for thee or against thee, but let it be thy business and thy care that God may be with thee in everything thou dost. (*Rom.* 8:31).

Have a good conscience, and God will sufficiently defend thee.

For he whom God will help no man's malice can hurt.

If thou canst but hold thy peace and suffer, thou shalt see, without doubt, that the Lord will help thee.

He knows the time and manner of delivering thee and therefore thou must resign thyself to Him.

It belongs to God to help and to deliver us from all confusion.

Oftentimes it is very profitable for keeping us in greater humility that others know and reprehend our faults.

2. When a man humbles himself for his defects he then easily appeases others, and quickly satisfies those that are angry with him.

The humble man God protects and delivers; the humble He loves and comforts; to the humble He inclines Himself; to the humble He gives grace (*Prov.* 29:23), and after he has been depressed, raises him to glory.

To the humble He reveals His secrets, and sweetly draws and invites him to Himself.

The humble man having received reproach maintains himself well enough in peace, because he is fixed on God, and not on the world.

Never think thou hast made any progress till thou lookest upon thyself as inferior to all.

Practical Reflections

How easy it is, when we are approved of, esteemed and praised by others, to say we are unworthy of such honor, and deserve only contempt. To know whether we speak the truth, let us see if we should say the same under contempt. Upon this point I am resolved to accept, as from the hands of God, all the evil that may be said or done against me, as my due; and, far from murmuring, I will bless the Lord for permitting others to do me justice, that He may show me mercy; esteeming it too great a happiness to die, and to be extinguished in the minds of men, that I may live only in the mind of God by the love of contempt, and the practice of true humility.

Prayer

Thou knowest, O God, how sensible I am to contradictions, calumnies, and contempt. Everything revolts within me when I have occasion to suffer them. But I know also that what is impossible to me is easy to Thee, and that, supported and fortified by the help of Thy grace, I can patiently endure humiliations, which of myself, I should receive with murmurs and vexation. Grant then, O my Saviour, that, imbued with Thy maxims, and animated with Thy spirit, I may regard with horror the glory, esteem, and praise which so often render me contemptible in Thy sight; and, on the contrary, receive injuries and affronts with submission and gratitude, that so I may hope to become the object of Thy love and the possessor of eternal glory. Amen.

Chapter 3

Of a Good Peaceable Man

KEEP thyself first in peace and then thou wilt be able to bring others to peace.

A peaceable man does more good than one that is very learned.

A passionate man turns every good to evil and easily believes evil.

A good peaceable man turns all things to good.

He that is in perfect peace suspects no man, but he that is discontented and disturbed is tossed about with various suspicions; he is neither quiet himself nor does he suffer others to be quiet.

He often says that which he should not say, and omits that which would be better for him to do.

He considers what others are obliged to do, and neglects that to which he himself is obliged.

Have, therefore, a zeal in the first place over thyself, and then thou mayest justly exercise thy zeal towards thy neighbor.

2. Thou knowest well enough how to excuse and color thine own doings, and thou wilt not take the excuses of others.

It were more just that thou shouldst accuse thyself and excuse thy brother.

If thou wilt be borne with bear also with another.

See how far thou art yet from true charity and humility, which knows not how to be angry with anyone, or to have indignation against anyone but one's self.

It is no great thing to be able to converse with them that are good and meek, for this is naturally pleasing to all. And everyone would willingly have peace and love those best that agree with them.

But to live peaceably with those that are harsh and perverse, or disorderly, or such as oppose us, is a great grace, and highly commendable and manly.

3. Some there are who keep themselves in peace and have peace also with others.

And there are some that are neither at peace within themselves, nor suffer others to be in peace; they are troublesome to others, but always more troublesome to themselves.

And some there are who keep themselves in peace and study to restore peace to others.

Yet all our peace in this miserable life is rather to be placed in humble sufferings than in not feeling adversities.

He who knows how to suffer will enjoy much peace.

Such a one is a conqueror of himself and lord of the world, a friend of Christ, and an heir of Heaven.

Practical Reflections

Granting the principle laid down in this chapter, that true peace consists much more in humbly submitting to what is contrary to our inclinations, than in meeting with nothing to thwart them, we must resolve to keep peace in contradictions, and to be calm in the midst of storms, patiently and meekly enduring persecution and all the evil that others may do or say against us. A soul that is truly humble complains only of itself; it endeavors to excuse others, while it blames itself, and is angry with no one but itself. I am resolved therefore, to live in peace with God, by obeying Him in all things; in peace with my neighbor, by not censuring his conduct or interfering with his affairs; and in peace with myself, by combatting and subduing, on all occasions, the emotions and repugnances of my heart.

Prayer

Thou hast said, O Lord, by the mouth of Thy Prophet, seek after peace and pursue it, that is, cease not to seek it until thou hast found it. Only Thou, my Jesus, canst bestow it upon me, for Thou alone didst accomplish my peace and reconciliation with Thy Father upon the Cross. I have long sought to live in peace with Thee, with my neighbor, and with myself; but my infidelities, my selfish feelings, and the sallies of passion are causes of perpetual trouble to my soul, and hinder me from tasting its sweets. O my Saviour, Thou Who didst calm the tempests, Thou Whom the winds and the sea obeyed, calm the agitation of my troubled soul, which can nowhere find true repose but in Thee. Grant that, resigning myself in all things to Thy blessed will, I may find peace and happiness in being, doing, quitting, and suffering whatever Thou shalt appoint. Amen.

Chapter 4

Of a Pure Mind and Simple Intention

WITH two wings a man is lifted up above earthly things: that is, with simplicity and purity.

Simplicity must be in the intention, purity in the affection.

Simplicity aims at God, purity takes hold of Him and tastes Him.

No good action will hinder thee if thou be free from inordinate affections.

If thou intend and seek nothing but the will of God and the profit of thy neighbor, thou shalt enjoy eternal liberty.

If thy heart were right, then every creature would be to thee a mirror of life and a book of holy doctrine.

There is no creature so little and contemptible as not to manifest the goodness of God.

2. If thou wert good and pure within, then wouldst thou discern all things without impediment and understand them rightly.

A pure heart penetrates Heaven and Hell.

According as everyone is interiorly, so he judgeth exteriorly.

If there be joy in the world, certainly the man whose heart is pure enjoys it.

And if there be anywhere tribulation and anguish, an evil conscience feels the most of it. (*Rom.* 2:9).

As iron put into the fire loses the rust and becomes all glowing, so a man that turns himself wholly to God puts off his sluggishness and is changed into a new man.

3. When a man begins to grow lukewarm he is afraid of a little labor and willingly takes external comfort.

But when he begins perfectly to overcome himself and to walk manfully in the way of God, then he makes less account of those things, which before he considered burdensome to him.

Practical Reflections

Purity of heart consists in detachment from everything that can defile it. A voluntary fault, an unguarded glance of the eye, a turning away from God, imprint a blemish upon the soul which defaces its beauty, and disfigures it in the sight of God. Blessed, says Jesus Christ, are the clean of heart, for they shall see God. They shall know Him by a lively and experimental faith in this life, which shall enable them to support the invisible things of God as though they were present to their sight; and in the next life they shall see Him by the light of His glory. We must therefore be determined, as far as we are able, not to commit any known sin, much less to contract a habit of any that can sully the purity of the soul, and make it a slave to self-love, endear it to the pleasures of sense, and render it incapable of elevating itself towards God. We must, moreover, in order to obtain this purity of heart, incessantly ask it of God, saying with the Psalmist: Create a clean heart in me, O God, and renew a right spirit within my bowels, that is, a pure intention, by which I may seek only to please Thee in and before all things. In a word, we must be attached to nothing but God and His holy will; for all attachment to creatures tarnishes the beauty of the soul, and renders it incapable and unworthy of being united with its God.

Prayer

O Jesus, Who hast so strongly recommended us, in the Gospel, to become humble, and simple as little children, if we would enter into the Kingdom of Heaven, grant us that state of holy and spiritual infancy, and that simplicity of mind and purity of heart, which may make us worthy of Thy love. Amen.

Chapter 5

Of the Consideration of One's Self

W E CANNOT trust much to ourselves, because we often want grace and understanding.

There is but little light in us and this we quickly lose through negligence.

Many times also we perceive not that we are so blind interiorly.

We often do ill and do worse in excusing it.

We are sometimes moved with passion, and we mistake it for zeal.

We blame little things in others and pass over great things in ourselves.

We are quick enough at perceiving and weighing what we suffer from others, but we mind not what others suffer from us.

He that would well and duly weigh his own deeds would have no room to judge hardly of others.

2. An internal man prefers the care of himself before all other cares, and he that diligently attends to himself is easily silent with regard to others.

Thou wilt never be internal and devout unless thou pass over in silence other men's concerns and particularly look to thyself.

If thou attend wholly to thyself and to God, thou wilt be little moved with what thou perceivest without thee.

Where art thou when thou art not present to thyself? And when thou hast run over all things, what profit will it be to thee if thou hast neglected thyself? (*Matt.* 16:26).

If thou desirest to have peace and true union thou must set all the rest aside and turn thine eyes upon thyself alone.

3. Thou wilt then make great progress if thou keep thyself free from all temporal care.

But if thou set a value upon anything temporal thou wilt fail exceedingly.

Let nothing be great in thine eyes, nothing high, nothing pleasant, nothing agreeable to thee, except it be purely God or of God.

Look upon all the comfort which thou meetest with from any creature as vain.

A soul that loveth God despiseth all things that are less than God.

None but God, eternal and incomprehensible, who filleth all things, can afford true comfort to the soul and true joy to the heart.

Practical Reflections

Useless reflections upon ourselves and upon exterior things occasion us to lose much time, many graces, and much merit. Did we but endeavor to substitute a respectful remembrance of God, in place of a vain and hurtful attention to ourselves and to creatures, we should be always well employed. To consider God as within us, and ourselves as existing in God: to live under the eye of Jesus Christ by means of recollection, in His hands by resignation, and at His feet by humility and a sincere acknowledgment of our miseries, is to live really as Christians; for we can only be such in proportion as we are devoted to Jesus Christ. Why then are we so much and so frequently attracted by news, curiosities, and vanity, and so little interested with God, our duties, and our salvation? It is because we are indifferent to the things of eternity, and too much attached to those which pass away with time. Let us, therefore, begin to be now what we hope to be forever—occupied only with God, in God, and for God.

Prayer

Correct in me, O Lord, that indolence of mind in which I squander away my time with trifles, and that uselessness of thought which withdraws me from the enjoyment of Thy presence, and distracts my attention in the time of prayer; or if, when I recite my prayers, I cannot always think of Thee, grant that my distractions may not be voluntary, so that whilst they divert my mind, they may never withdraw my heart from Thee. Teach me, O Lord, before prayer, to prepare my soul, that, urged by my many necessities, and by a desire of pleasing Thee, I may fulfill this important duty with a becoming sense of Thine awful presence, and of the subject on which I seek relief from Thy bounty and mercy. Amen.

Chapter 6

Of the Joy of a Good Conscience

THE glory of a good man is the testimony of a good conscience. (*2 Cor.* 1:12).

Keep a good conscience and thou shalt always have joy.

A good conscience can bear very much and is very joyful in the midst of adversity.

A bad conscience is always fearful and uneasy.

Sweetly wilt thou take thy rest if thy heart reprehend thee not. (*Prov.* 3:24).

Never rejoice but when thou hast done well.

The wicked never have true joy, neither do they feel internal peace, because "There is no peace to the wicked, saith the Lord." (*Is.* 48:22).

And if they shall say: We are in peace, evils will not come upon us, and who shall dare to hurt us? Believe them not, for the wrath of God will rise on a sudden, and their deeds shall be brought to nothing, and their projects shall perish.

2. To glory in tribulation is not hard to him that loves, for so to glory is to glory in the Cross of Our Lord. (*Gal.* 6:14).

That glory is short-lived which is given and taken by men.

The glory of this world is always accompanied with sorrow.

The glory of good men is in their own consciences, not in the mouths of men.

The joy of the just is from God and in God, and they rejoice in the truth. (*1 Cor.* 13:6).

He that desires true and everlasting glory values not that which is temporal.

And he that seeks after temporal glory or does not heartily despise it, shows himself to have but little love for that which is heavenly.

That man has great tranquillity of heart who neither cares for praises nor dispraises.

3. He will easily be content and in peace whose conscience is clean.

Thou art not more holy if thou art praised nor anything the worse if thou art dispraised.

What thou art that thou art, nor canst thou be said to be greater than God sees thee to be.

If thou consider well what thou art within thyself thou wilt not care what men say of thee.

Man beholds the face, but God looks upon the heart. Man considers the actions, but God weighs the intentions.

To do always well and to hold one's self in small account is a mark of an humble soul.

To refuse comfort from any created thing is a sign of great purity and interior confidence.

4. He that seeks no outward testimony for himself shows plainly that he has committed himself wholly to God.

"For not he who commendeth himself," saith St. Paul, "is approved, but he whom God commendeth." (*2 Cor.* 10:18).

To walk with God within and not to be held by any affection without, is the state of an internal man.

Practical Reflections

The peace of a good conscience does not always exclude those troubles which are occasioned by temptations and interior trials; but in all the storms which arise, it keeps the heart submissive and faithful to God; submissive in suffering pain, and faithful in not yielding under it, but in resisting, in fighting, and in neglecting nothing on account of it. Thus it is that a suffering and submissive soul is, according to the royal Prophet, an acceptable sacrifice to God, who never rejects a contrite and humble heart, humble from the experience of its own miseries, and contrite for having given cause to God to oblige it to experience them. Let us, therefore, form a strong and constant resolution not to suffer ourselves to be discouraged, either by our falls, or by our trials, or by the experiences of our miseries; but to humble ourselves before God, at the sight of our wretchedness; to crave pardon for the faults we have committed through not resisting, as we ought to have done, the enemy of our salvation; to punish ourselves immediately for them by some act of mortification; and, after that, to remain in peace; for a good conscience is that which is either exempt from sin by fidelity, or cleansed from it by repentance.

Prayer

Thou knowest, O Lord, to how many sinful allurements, interior trials, and dangers we are exposed, both from natural and violent inclinations to evil, our unceasing repugnance to good, and the assaults of temptation. How shall we be able to resist so many and such powerful enemies, bent as they are upon our destruction, if Thou in Thy bounty assist us not? It is to Thee we raise up our hearts and our minds, it is to Thee we look for succor to keep us from yielding to temptation, to deliver us from the greatest of all evils, sin, and to preserve us from perishing everlastingly. Amen.

Chapter 7

Of the Love of Jesus above All Things

BLESSED is he who knows what it is to love Jesus and to despise himself for the sake of Jesus.

We must quit what we love for this Beloved, because Jesus will be loved alone above all things.

The love of things created is deceitful and inconstant.

The love of Jesus is faithful and enduring. He that cleaveth to creatures shall fall with them.

He that embraceth Jesus shall stand firm forever.

Love Him and keep Him for thy friend, who, when all go away, will not leave thee nor suffer thee to perish in the end.

Thou must at last be separated from all things else, whether thou wilt or not.

2. Keep thyself with Jesus both in life and death and commit thyself to His care, who alone can help thee when all others fail.

Thy Beloved is of such a nature that He will admit of no other, but will have thy heart to Himself, and sit there like a king upon his own throne.

If thou couldst but purge thyself well from affection to creatures, Jesus would willingly dwell with thee.

Thou wilt find all that in a manner lost, which thou hast placed in men out of Jesus.

Do not trust or rely upon a frail reed; "for all flesh is grass and all the glory thereof shall fade as the flower of the field." (*Is.* 40:6).

3. Thou wilt soon be deceived if thou only regard the outward show of men.

For if thou seek thy comfort and thy gain in others, thou wilt often meet with loss.

If in all things thou seek Jesus, doubtless thou wilt find Jesus.

But if thou seek thyself thou wilt indeed find thyself, to thine own ruin.

For a man does himself more harm if he seek not Jesus, than the whole world and all his enemies could do him.

Practical Reflections

Apply thy whole mind to know Jesus Christ, thy whole heart to love Him, and all thy care to follow Him, since for this alone thou art a Christian. What difficulty canst thou have in loving a Man God, who assumed humanity only for love of thee and for thy salvation! Be then resolved to study and to contemplate

Him in all His actions, to penetrate into His designs, to enter into His dispositions and the purport of His mysteries; and endeavor to do, to suffer, and to live as He did; for the whole merit of a Christian in this life consists in conformity in all things with Jesus Christ; and, in the next, it will constitute his never-ending happiness. If he endeavor to participate here in the humble and suffering life of his Redeemer, he will hereafter partake of His glorious immortality.

Prayer

As, O Jesus, I can have no pretensions to Heaven but through Thy virtues and merit, I beseech Thee to inspire me with an ardent desire of knowing and following Thee. Grant, O my most amiable Saviour, that I may follow Thy maxims, practice Thy virtues and form myself upon Thine example, that my resemblance to Thee may make me worthy of Thy love, and cause me to find grace in the sight of Thy heavenly Father, who loves us only in proportion as we resemble Thee. Help me then to become imbued with Thy sentiments and conformed to Thine inclinations. Grant that, after Thy example, I may become meek, humble, patient, charitable, and submissive in all things to Thy Father's will. I hope that, presenting myself to Him in and by Thee, I shall not be rejected, and that the attachment which I desire to have for Thee may secure Thy love for me, and my ultimate salvation. Amen.

Chapter 8

Of Familiar Friendship with Jesus

WHEN Jesus is present all things go well, and nothing seems difficult; but when Jesus is absent everything is hard.

When Jesus speaks not within, our comfort is worthless; but if Jesus speak but one word, we feel great consolation.

Did not Mary Magdalen immediately arise from the place where she wept when Martha said to her, "The Master is here, and calleth for thee"? (*John* 11:28).

Happy hour, when Jesus calls from tears to joy of spirit!

How hard and dry art thou without Jesus! How foolish and vain if thou desire anything out of Jesus! Is not this a greater loss than if thou wert to lose the whole world? (*Luke* 9:25).

2. What can the world profit thee without Jesus?

To be without Jesus is a grievous hell and to be with Jesus a sweet paradise.

If Jesus be with thee no enemy can hurt thee. (*Rom.* 8:31).

Whosoever finds Jesus finds a good treasure, yea, good above all goods.

And he that loses Jesus loseth exceeding much, and more than if he lost the whole world.

He is wretchedly poor who lives without Jesus, and he is exceedingly rich who is well with Jesus.

3. It is a great art to know how to converse with Jesus, and to know how to keep Jesus is great wisdom.

Be humble and peaceable, and Jesus will be with thee.

Be devout and quiet, and Jesus will stay with thee.

Thou mayest quickly drive away Jesus and lose His grace if thou dost decline after outward things.

And if thou drive Him away from thee and lose Him, to whom wilt thou fly, and whom then wilt thou seek for thy friend?

Without a friend thou canst not well live, and if Jesus be

not thy friend above all, thou wilt be exceedingly sad and desolate.

Thou actest then foolishly if thou put thy trust or rejoice in any other.

We ought rather choose to have the whole world against us than to offend Jesus.

Of all, therefore, that are dear to thee, let Jesus always be thy special beloved.

4. Let all things be loved for Jesus' sake, but Jesus for His own sake.

Jesus Christ alone is singularly to be loved, who alone is found good and faithful above all friends.

For His sake, and in Him, let both friends and enemies be dear to thee, and for all these thou must pray to Him that all may know and love Him.

Neither desire to be singularly praised nor beloved; for this belongs to God alone, who hath none like to Himself.

Neither desire that anyone's heart should be set on thee; nor do thou let thyself be taken up with the love of anyone, but let Jesus be in thee, and in every good man.

5. Be pure and free interiorly, without being entangled by any creature.

Thou must be naked and carry a pure heart to God, if thou wilt attend at leisure, and see how sweet is the Lord. *(Ps. 33:9)*.

And, indeed, thou wilt never attain to this, unless thou be prevented and drawn by His grace, that so thou mayest all alone be united to Him alone, having cast out and dismissed all others.

For when the grace of God cometh to a man then he is

strong and powerful for all things; and when it departs then he is poor and weak, left as it were only to stripes.

In these he must not be dejected nor despair, but stand with an even mind, resigned to the will of God, and bear, for the glory of Jesus Christ, whatever shall befall him; because after winter comes summer, after the night the day returns, after a storm there follows a great calm.

Practical Reflections

It is difficult to live without someone to whom we can open our hearts and confide our secrets. But to whom can we better disclose them than to Jesus, who, more than all others, is a friend the most faithful, the most constant, and the most worthy of our confidence. Seek, therefore, in Him alone thy consolation and thy peace; lay open thy heart incessantly before Him; have recourse to Him in all thy troubles; and be not discouraged if He seem to hide His countenance, for this is only the effect of His love towards thee, and the trial of thy fidelity towards Him. Pray, entreat, and conjure Him in His bounty to assist thee; and be assured that, sooner or later, thou wilt experience the effects of His goodness. Preserve thy heart free for Him, and detached from every creature; love Him for the sake of His own infinite perfections; and love all things else only as they lead thee to Him and to His love. Let pains, injuries, sorrows, and humiliations become as welcome to thee as they were to Jesus Christ; and let the esteem and the praises of men be to thee objects of dread and contempt, because they were so to Him. In a word, accustom thyself to know Him, to speak to Him, to love Him, and seek to please Him in all things that, living thus in the exercise of His love, the last motion of thy heart may be an act of the love of thy dearest Redeemer.

Prayer

As Thy love for me, O Jesus, is a prevenient love, and as Thou makest me worthy of Thy love, by first loving me, attract and gain my heart, and confirm it in Thy love. Grant that, detached from all things, and uninfluenced by the allurements of self-love, I may breathe only Thy love; that I may be engaged with Thee alone, and attentive only to Thee, and neither seek nor love anything but Thee alone, in all things. Be Thou, my most amiable Saviour, the reigning object and sovereign good of my soul. Grant that, animated by Thy Spirit, formed upon Thine example, faithful to Thy graces, and obedient to Thine orders, I may live for Thee, from Thee, and like Thee, in order to commence that occupation on earth which I hope to continue in Heaven, which is to possess and to love Thee. Amen.

Chapter 9

Of the Want of All Comforts

IT IS not hard to despise all human comfort when we have divine.

But it is much, and very much, to be able to want all comfort, both human and divine; and to be willing to bear this interior banishment for God's honor, and to seek one's self in nothing nor to think of one's own merit.

What great thing is it if thou be cheerful and devout when grace comes! This hour is desirable to all.

He rides at ease that is carried by the grace of God.

And what wonder if he feel no weight who is carried by the Almighty, and led on by the Sovereign Guide?

2. We willingly would have something to comfort us,

and it is with difficulty that a man can put off himself.

The holy martyr Lawrence overcame the world with his Prelate, because he despised whatever seemed delightful in this world, and for the love of Christ he unrepiningly suffered the high priest of God, Sixtus, whom he exceedingly loved, to be taken away from him.

He overcame, therefore, the love of man by the love of the Creator; and instead of the comfort he had in man he made choice rather of God's pleasure.

So do thou also learn to part with a necessary and beloved friend for the love of God.

And take it not to heart when thou art forsaken by a friend; knowing that one time or other we must all part.

3. A man must go through a long and great conflict in himself before he can learn fully to overcome himself, and to draw his whole affection towards God.

When a man stands upon himself he is easily drawn aside after human comforts.

But a true lover of Christ, and a diligent pursuer of virtue, does not hunt after comforts, nor seek such sensible sweetnesses, but is rather willing to bear strong trials and hard labors for Christ.

Therefore, when God gives spiritual comfort, receive it with thanksgiving, but know that it is the bounty of God, not thy merit.

4. Be not puffed up, be not overjoyed, nor vainly presume, but rather be the more humble for this gift and the more cautious and fearful in all thine actions; for this hour will pass away and temptation will follow.

When comfort shall be taken away from thee, do not

presently despair; but wait with humility and patience for the heavenly visit, for God is able to restore thee a greater consolation.

This is no new thing, nor strange to those who have experienced the ways of God: for the great saints and ancient prophets have often felt this kind of variety.

5. Hence one said, at the time when grace was with him: "In my abundance I said I shall never be moved." (*Ps.* 29:7).

But when grace was withdrawn he immediately tells us what he experienced in himself: "Thou turnedst away thy face from me and I became troubled." (*Ps.* 29:8).

Yet in the meantime he despairs not, but more earnestly prays to the Lord, and says: "To thee, O Lord, will I cry, and I will make supplication to my God." (*Ps.* 29:9).

At length he receives the fruit of his prayer, and witnesseth that he was heard, saying, "The Lord hath heard me, and hath had mercy on me: The Lord became my helper." (*Ps.* 29:11).

But in what manner? "Thou hast turned for me," says he, "my mourning into joy, and thou hast compassed me with gladness." (*Ps.* 29:12).

If it has been thus with great saints, we that are weak and poor must not be discouraged if we are sometimes fervent, sometimes cold, because the Spirit comes and goes according to His own good pleasure. Wherefore holy Job says: "Thou visitest him early in the morning, and thou provest him suddenly." (*Job* 7:18).

6. Wherein then can I hope, or in what must I put my trust, but in God's great mercy alone, and in the hope of heavenly grace?

For whether I have with me good men, or devout brethren, or faithful friends, or holy books, or fine treatises, or sweet singing and hymns, all these help little, and give me but little relish, when I am forsaken by grace and left in my own poverty.

At such a time there is no better remedy than patience and self-denial under the will of God.

7. I never found anyone so religious and devout as not to have sometimes a subtraction of grace, or feel a diminution of fervor.

No saint was ever so highly rapt and illuminated as not to be tempted sooner or later.

For he is not worthy of the high contemplation of God who has not, for God's sake, been exercised with some tribulation.

For temptation going before is usually a sign of ensuing consolation.

For heavenly comfort is promised to such as have been proved by temptation. "To him that overcometh," saith Our Lord, "I will give to eat of the tree of life." (*Apoc.* 2:7).

8. Now divine consolation is given that a man may be better able to support adversities.

And temptation follows that he may not be proud of it.

The devil never sleeps, neither is the flesh yet dead: therefore thou must not cease to prepare thyself for battle, for on the right hand, and on the left, are enemies that never rest.

Practical Reflections

As we approach to God by faith, and not by the senses, and as faith of itself is dry and obscure, we must not be surprised if we sometimes experience dryness and desolation, and at other times consolation and joy. All consists in receiving consolation with humility, and in supporting desolation with fortitude and courage. Silver and gold, says the Wise Man, are tried in the fire; and souls, before they can become worthy of being admitted to an intimate friendship with God, are tried in the furnace of the most painful and humiliating tribulations. Humble, then, thy heart, under the all-powerful hand of God, and bear with patience the trials of the Lord, who, by the temptations which we resist, makes us little humble, and dependent upon Him, and would have us, in imitation of the holy martyrs, love Him in suffering, suffer in loving Him, and honor His greatness by our entire destruction of self-love.

Prayer

How happy are we, O Jesus, when we experience no pleasure nor satisfaction but in Thee. But how much more so when, although we receive neither consolation nor delight nor sensible gratification in Thy service, we still, in spite of all disgust, persevere in our spiritual exercises faithful to Thy grace. It is thus, O God, we prove that we love Thee for Thyself; that we seek not human comfort, but to please Thee; and that, dying to self-satisfaction, which is the natural life of the heart, we make it our delight to please Thee and our true satisfaction to sacrifice our own for Thy love. It is just, O Lord, that I should prefer Thy holy will to my own inclinations, and that I should serve Thee more for Thyself than from any selfish motive. This I desire, O Jesus; but do Thou give me courage to accomplish it, and grant that henceforth I may prefer submission to Thy good pleasure before every other consolation. Amen.

Chapter 10

Of Gratitude for the Grace of God

WHY seekest thou rest, since thou art born to labor? Dispose thyself to patience rather than consolation, and to bear the Cross rather than to rejoice.

For who is there among worldly people that would not willingly receive comfort and spiritual joy, if he could always have it?

For spiritual consolation exceeds all the delights of the world and the pleasures of the flesh.

For all worldly delights are either vain or filthy; but spiritual delights alone are pleasant and honorable, springing from virtue, and infused by God into pure minds.

But these divine consolations no man can always enjoy when he will, because the time of temptation is not long absent.

2. But what very much opposes these heavenly visits is a false liberty of mind and a great confidence in one's self.

God doth well in giving the grace of consolation, but man doth ill in not returning it all to God with thanksgiving.

And this is the reason why the gifts of grace cannot flow in us, because we are ungrateful to the Giver, nor do we return all to the Fountainhead.

For grace will always be given to him that duly returns thanks, and what is wont to be given to the humble will be taken away from the proud.

3. I would not have any such consolation as would rob me of compunction, nor do I wish to have any such contemplation as leads to pride.

For all that is high is not holy; nor all that is pleasant good; nor every desire pure; nor is everything that is dear to us pleasing to God.

I willingly accept of that grace which always makes me more humble and fearful, and more ready to forsake myself.

He that has been taught by the gift of grace, and been instructed by the scourge of its withdrawal, will not dare to attribute anything of good to himself, but rather acknowledge himself to be poor and naked.

Give to God what is His (*Matt.* 22:21), and take to thyself what is thine; that is, give thanks to God for His grace; but as to thyself, be sensible that nothing is to be attributed to thee but sin and the punishment due to sin.

4. Put thyself always in the lowest place, and the highest shall be given thee, for the highest stands not without the lowest. (*Luke* 14:10).

The saints that are highest in the sight of God are the least in their own eyes; and the more glorious they are the more humble they are in themselves.

Being full of the truth and heavenly glory they are not desirous of vainglory.

They that are grounded and established in God can by no means be proud.

And they that attribute to God whatsoever good they have received seek not glory from one another, but that glory which is from God alone (*John* 5:44); they desire above all things that God may be praised in themselves, and in all the saints, and to this they always tend.

5. Be grateful then for the least and thou shalt be worthy to receive greater things.

Let the least be to thee as something very great, and the most contemptible as a special favor.

If thou considerest the dignity of the Giver, no gift will seem to thee little which is given by so great a God.

Yea, though He give punishment and stripes, it ought to be acceptable; for whatever He suffers to befall us, He always does it for our salvation. (*Dan.* 3:28).

He that desires to retain the grace of God let him be thankful for grace when it is given, and patient when it is withdrawn: let him pray that it may return; let him be cautious and humble, lest he lose it.

Practical Reflections

Do not exalt thyself on account of the gifts of God, which are often a help to thy weakness, always the effect of His bounty, and ordinarily above thy deserts. When, in the act of offending Him, thou perceivest thy heart touched at the sight of thine ingratitude and infidelity, thou oughtest to humble thyself and be confounded before Him at seeing Him so full of goodness and thyself so replete with wickedness.

Penetrated with a lively sorrow for having offended God, who seeks thee even when thou art fleeing away from Him, and loads thee with His graces, even when thou provest thyself unworthy of them, return to Him by true repentance; ask pardon for thy fault, and think only of avenging Him by punishing thyself.

Prayer

O God, Whose bounty is infinite and Whose mercies are pro-
portioned to our miseries, permit us not to be so ungrateful as
to forget Thy benefits, nor so unfaithful as to become unworthy
of Thy graces. We acknowledge that we deserve only to be aban-
doned by Thee, we merit but Thy hatred and eternal torments;
but we conjure Thee, O Saviour, not to deal with us according
to our deserts, but according to the multitude of Thy tender
mercies, which Thou art ever desirous of imparting to us. Amen.

Chapter 11

Of the Small Number of the Lovers of the Cross of Jesus

JESUS has now many lovers of His heavenly Kingdom
but few that are willing to bear His Cross.

He has many that are desirous of comfort, but few of
tribulation.

He finds many companions of His table, but few of His
abstinence.

All desire to rejoice with Him, few are willing to suffer
with Him.

Many follow Jesus to the breaking of bread, but few to
the drinking of the chalice of His Passion.

Many reverence His miracles, but few follow the igno-
miny of His cross.

Many love Jesus as long as they meet with no adversity.

Many praise Him and bless Him as long as they receive
consolation from Him.

But if Jesus hide Himself, and leave them for a little while, they either fall into complaints or excessive dejection.

2. But they that love Jesus for Jesus' sake and not for any comfort of their own, bless Him no less in tribulation and anguish of heart than in the greatest consolation.

And if He should never give them His comfort, yet would they always praise Him and always give Him thanks.

3. Oh, how much is the pure love of Jesus able to do when it is not mixed with any self-interest or self-love.

Are not all those to be called hirelings who are always seeking consolation?

Are they not proved to be rather lovers of themselves than of Christ who are always thinking of their own profit and gain?

Where shall we find a man that is willing to serve God gratis?

4. Seldom do we find anyone so spiritual as to be stripped of all things.

For who shall be able to find the man that is truly poor in spirit and stripped of all affection to all created things? His price is from afar and from the uttermost coasts. (*Prov.* 31:10).

If a man give his whole substance it is yet nothing. (*1 Cor.* 13:3).

And if he do great penance it is yet little. And if he attain to all knowledge he is far off still.

And if we have great virtue and exceeding fervent devotion there is still much wanting to him, to wit, one thing which is chiefly necessary for him. (*Luke* 10:42).

And what is that? That, having left all things else, he

leave also himself and wholly go out of himself and retain nothing of self-love.

And when he shall have done all things which he knows should be done, let him think that he has done nothing.

5. Let him not make great account of that which may appear much to be esteemed, but let him in truth acknowledge himself to be an unprofitable servant, as Truth itself has said: "When you shall have done all the things that are commanded you, say: We are unprofitable servants." (*Luke* 17:10).

Then may he be truly poor and naked in spirit and may say with the Prophet: "I am alone and poor." (*Ps.* 24:16).

Yet no one is indeed richer than such a man, none more powerful, none more free, who knows how to leave himself and all things and place himself in the very lowest place.

Practical Reflections

How many Christians adore Jesus, poor in the manger, and suffering upon the Cross, who will neither submit to privation, nor endure tribulation for His sake! Yet He was born, and lived, and died in poverty and sufferings, to teach us to renounce all things, and to bear our crosses with patience; to teach us by His preaching and example the virtues necessary for salvation, and to merit for us the grace to practice them. What will it avail thee to adore Jesus Christ, thy Saviour and thy model, if thou dost not imitate Him and place thy whole confidence in Him? Take, then, the generous resolution of renouncing all things by depriving the senses of all dangerous or unprofitable gratifications; by discarding from thy mind all vanity and self-complacency, and all malignity in condemning others; and by stripping thy heart of all attachment to self-satisfaction and self-seeking, on all occasions. Carry this interior poverty and deprivation even so far as to renounce thine own will in all things, to desire only and to accomplish the will of God. It is by thus giving up thy whole self to God that thou wilt constitute Him the sole master and proprietor of thy heart, and by stripping thyself of all things here, make Him thine inheritance forever hereafter.

Prayer

I conceive, O my Saviour, an exalted idea of the bereavement Thou requirest of a Christian heart, since Thou dost oblige it to yield itself up entirely to Thee, and to substitute Thy love in place of the love of itself. But how far am I from practicing it, how incapable of it of myself! Help me, O Lord, to renounce and to die to myself in all things. Suffer not my heart to seek itself, since Thou designest it to be entirely Thine. Grant that whenever it is tempted to live for, or to seek itself in anything, it may immediately renounce and die to itself, to live only in and for Thee. Then may I say with Thine Apostle: Jesus Christ is my life, and it is gain for me to die to all, that I may live only in Him, and by Him, and for Him. Amen.

Chapter 12

Of the Royal Way of The Holy Cross

TO MANY this seems a hard saying: "Deny thyself, take up thy cross, and follow Jesus." (*Matt.* 16:24).

But it will be much harder to hear that last word: "Depart from me, ye cursed, into everlasting fire." (*Matt.* 25:41).

For they that at present willingly hear and follow the

word of the cross shall not then be afraid of eternal condemnation.

This Sign of the Cross will be in Heaven when the Lord shall come to judge.

Then all the servants of the cross, who in their lifetime have conformed themselves to Him that was crucified, shall come to Christ their judge with great confidence.

2. Why then art thou afraid to take up thy cross, which leads to a kingdom?

In the cross is salvation; in the cross is life; in the cross is protection from thine enemies.

In the cross is infusion of heavenly sweetness; in the cross is strength of mind; in the cross is joy of spirit.

In the cross is the height of virtue; in the cross is the perfection of sanctity.

There is no health of the soul nor hope of eternal life but in the cross.

Take up, therefore, thy cross and follow Jesus, and thou shalt go into life everlasting.

He is gone before thee carrying His own Cross; and He died for thee upon the Cross that thou mayest also bear thy cross and love to die on the cross.

Because if thou die with Him thou shalt also live with Him, and if thou art His companion in suffering thou shalt also partake in His glory. (*2 Cor.* 1:7).

3. Behold the cross is all and in dying to thyself all consists, and there is no other way to life and to true internal peace but the holy way of the cross and of daily mortification.

Go where thou wilt, seek what thou wilt, and thou shalt

not find a higher way above, nor a safer way below than the way of the holy cross.

Dispose and order all things according as thou wilt and as seems best to thee, and thou wilt still find something to suffer, either willingly or unwillingly, and so thou shalt still find the cross.

For either thou shalt feel pain in the body, or sustain in thy soul tribulation of spirit.

4. Sometimes thou shalt be left by God, other times thou shalt be afflicted by thy neighbor, and what is more, thou shalt often be a trouble to thyself.

Neither canst thou be delivered or eased by any remedy or comfort, but as long as it shall please God thou must bear it.

For God would have thee learn to suffer tribulation without comfort, and wholly to submit thyself to Him, and to become more humble by tribulation.

No man hath so lively a feeling of the Passion of Christ as he who hath happened to suffer suchlike things.

The cross, therefore, is always ready and everywhere waits for thee.

Thou canst not escape it, whithersoever thou runnest; for whithersoever thou goest thou carriest thyself with thee and shalt always find thyself

Turn thyself upwards, or turn thyself downwards; turn thyself without, or turn thyself within thee, and everywhere thou shalt find the cross.

And everywhere thou must of necessity have patience if thou desirest inward peace and wouldst merit an eternal crown.

5. If thou carry the cross willingly, it will carry thee and bring thee to thy desired end; to wit to that place where there will be an end of suffering, though here there will be no end.

If thou carry it unwillingly thou makest it a burden to thee and loadest thyself the more, and nevertheless thou must bear it.

If thou fling away one cross, without doubt thou shalt find another and perhaps a heavier.

6. Dost thou think to escape that which no mortal ever could avoid? What saint was there ever in the world without his cross and affliction?

Our Lord Jesus Christ Himself was not one hour of His life without suffering: "It behooved Christ to suffer," saith He, "and rise again from the dead, and so enter into his glory." (*Luke* 24:46).

And why dost thou pretend to seek another way than this royal way, which is the way of the holy cross?

7. The whole life of Christ was a cross and a martyrdom, and dost thou seek rest and joy?

Thou errest, thou errest, if thou seekest any other thing than to suffer tribulations; for this whole mortal life is full of miseries and beset on all sides with crosses.

And the higher a person is advanced in spirit the heavier crosses shall he often meet with, because the pain of his banishment increases in proportion to his love.

8. Yet this man, thus many ways afflicted, is not without some allay of comfort, because he is sensible of the great profit which he reaps by bearing the cross.

For whilst he willingly resigns himself to it, all the burden of tribulation is converted into an assured hope of comfort from God.

And the more the flesh is brought down by affliction the more the spirit is strengthened by inward grace.

And it sometimes gains such strength through affection to tribulation and adversity, by loving to be conformable to the Cross of Christ, as not to be willing to be without suffering and affliction; because it is confident that it is so much the more acceptable to God, as it shall be able to bear more and greater things for Him.

This is not man's power, but the grace of Christ, which can and does effect such great things in frail flesh, that what it naturally abhors and flies, even this, through fervor of spirit, it now embraces and loves.

9. To bear the cross, to love the cross, to chastise the body, and bring it under subjection; to fly honors, to be willing to suffer reproaches, to despise one's self and wish to be despised; to bear all adversities and losses, and to desire no prosperity in this world, are not according to man's natural inclination.

If thou look upon thyself, thou canst do nothing of this of thyself.

But if thou confide in the Lord, strength will be given thee from Heaven, and the world and the flesh shall be made subject to thee.

Neither shalt thou fear thine enemy, the devil, if thou be armed with faith and signed with the Cross of Christ.

10. Set thyself then like a good and faithful servant of Christ, to bear manfully the Cross of thy Lord, crucified for the love of thee.

Prepare thyself to suffer many adversities and divers evils in this miserable life; for so it will be with thee wherever thou art, and so indeed wilt thou find it wheresoever thou mayest hide thyself.

It must be so, and there is no remedy against the tribulation of evil and sorrow but to bear them patiently.

Drink of the chalice of thy Lord lovingly if thou desire to be His friend and to have part with Him. (*Matt.* 20:22).

Leave consolations to God, to do with them as best pleaseth Him.

But prepare thou thyself to bear tribulations, and account them the greatest consolations; for the sufferings of this life bear no proportion to the glory to come (*Rom.* 8:18), although thou alone couldst suffer them all.

11. When thou shalt arrive thus far, that tribulation becomes sweet and savory to thee for the love of Christ, then think that it is well with thee, for thou hast found a paradise upon earth.

As long as suffering appear grievous to thee and thou seek to fly from it, so long will it be ill with thee, and the tribulation from which thou fliest will everywhere follow thee.

12. If thou set thyself to what thou oughtst, that is to suffer and die to thyself, it will quickly be better with thee and thou shalt find peace.

Although thou shouldst have been rapt up to the third heaven with St. Paul (*2 Cor.* 12:2), thou art not thereby assured that thou shalt suffer no adversity. "I" said Jesus, "will show him how great things he must suffer for my name." (*Acts* 9:16).

To suffer therefore, is what waits for thee, if thou wilt love Jesus and constantly serve Him.

13. Would to God thou wert worthy to suffer something for the name of Jesus! how great a glory would be laid up for thee, how great joy would it be to all the saints of God and how great edification to thy neighbor.

All recommend patience, but alas! how few there are that desire to suffer.

With good reason oughtst thou willingly to suffer a little for Christ, since many suffer greater things for the world.

14. Know for certain that thou must lead a dying life and the more a man dies to himself the more he begins to live to God.

No man is fit to comprehend heavenly things who has not resigned himself to suffer adversities for Christ.

Nothing is more acceptable to God, nothing more wholesome for thee in this world than to suffer willingly for Christ.

And if thou wert to choose, thou oughtest to wish rather to suffer adversities for Christ than to be delighted with many comforts, because thou wouldst thus be more like unto Christ and more conformable to all the saints.

For our merit and the advancement of our state consist, not in having many sweetnesses and consolations, but rather in bearing great afflictions and tribulations.

15. If, indeed, there had been anything better and more beneficial to man's salvation than suffering, Christ certainly would have showed it by word and example.

For He manfully exhorts both His disciples that followed Him and all that desire to follow Him to bear the cross, saying: "If any one will come after me, let him deny himself and take up his cross and follow me." (*Luke* 9:23).

So that when we have read and searched all let this be the final conclusion, that "Through many tribulations we must enter into the kingdom of God." (*Acts* 14:21).

Practical Reflections

Can we read, believe, and ponder seriously the wonderful advantages of the cross, and the great merits of suffering, as here described, and not love to suffer, to receive crosses from the hands of Jesus Christ, and to submit to endure whatever He pleases, and as much as He pleases, since to suffer much, and in a proper manner, is absolutely requisite for salvation, and is the most tender and efficacious effort of the goodness of God towards us, who will not spare us the pains of time, that He may spare us those of eternity? It is to bear the visible character of the predestinate, which, according to St. Paul, consists in our resemblance to Jesus Christ, an humble, suffering, and persecuted God; it is to render ourselves worthy of His life of glory by participating in His life of suffering; it is to efface the punishment due to our sins by perfect repentance; it is to gain the heart of Jesus Christ, merit His love, avenge Him, and punish ourselves, honor Him by our destruction, and prefer His good pleasure before our own satisfaction. Shall not all this console thee under affliction, and animate thee to bear it with becoming resignation? Say, then, in the time of suffering, in order not to fail: "Hell, which I have deserved, is something more horrible than anything I can now endure; my Saviour has suffered much more for me; and Heaven is worth infinitely more than I can undergo."

Prayer

Penetrate my heart, O Jesus, with these sentiments when Thou sendest me pains, and support me in all my afflictions; for, alas! Thou knowest how naturally I hate and fly from the cross, although I am persuaded that it was by the cross Thou didst save me, and that I cannot gain salvation, nor enter into Heaven, but by the way of Calvary. Inspire me with that patience, that strength, and that courage which Thou didst impart to Thy martyrs: and since I cannot better evince my love and gratitude towards Thee than by suffering for Thee, nor render myself more worthy of Thy grace and glory than by carrying the cross, vouchsafe to support me when sinking under its burden by the desire of pleasing Thee, and the hope of eternal happiness. Amen.

Book III

Of Internal
Consolation

Chapter 1

The Internal Discourse of
Christ to a Faithful Soul

DISCIPLE

I WILL hear what the Lord God will speak in me. (*Ps.* 84:9). Blessed is that soul which heareth the Lord speaking within her (*Prov.* 8:34), and from His mouth receiveth the word of comfort.

Blessed ears which receive the veins of the divine whisper and take no notice of the whisper of the world.

Blessed ears indeed, which hearken to truth itself teaching within and not to the voice which soundeth without.

Blessed eyes which are shut to outward things and attentive to the interior. (*Matt.* 13:16).

Blessed they who penetrate into internal things and endeavor to prepare themselves more and more by daily exercises to the attainment of heavenly secrets.

Blessed they who seek to be wholly intent on God, and who rid themselves of every worldly impediment.

Mind these things, O my soul, and shut the doors of thy sensuality, that thou mayest hear what the Lord thy God speaks within thee.

CHRIST

2. Thus saith thy Beloved, I am thy salvation, thy peace, and thy life. (*Ps.* 34:3).

Abide in Me and thou shalt find peace.

Let alone all transitory things and seek things eternal.

What are all temporal things but deceit? And what will all things created avail thee if thou be forsaken by thy Creator?

Cast off then all earthly things and make thyself agreeable to thy Creator and faithful to Him, that so thou mayest attain to true happiness.

Practical Reflections

The soul disposes itself to hear what the Lord speaks to its interior, when, devoted to retirement, silence, and prayer, loving to be alone with its God, and seeking Him in itself, by a lively and reverential faith, it is attentive and faithful to the motions of His grace, to the interior influence of His presence, and to the attractions of His love. Thus, to maintain a spirit of recollection and of faithful love, ever to keep the mind attentive to the will of God, and the heart resolved to accomplish it, is effectually to dispose ourselves to hear God, and to receive the most intimate communications of His Spirit. God speaks to us incessantly by His inspirations, and the holy views He imparts to us, to engage us to die to ourselves, and to live only to Him. But either we do not hearken to Him, or it is only in a careless manner. When the soul is wholly given to the senses, agitated by the passions, and entirely taken up with exterior things, it is itself incapable and unworthy of the operations of God. We should therefore resolve to think and to speak but little to creatures, and to love silence and retirement, to nourish our minds with God's presence, and our hearts with His love, and to do all for Him and in His sight, if we would become interior men, living in God, and for God, as every Christian should do who would be saved.

Prayer

Wearied with the demands of my senses, the tumult of my passions, and the inefficacy of my desires, I come to Thee, O

Jesus, earnestly to implore Thee to recall my mind and my heart to their center, which is Thy presence and Thy love. I can no longer endure to live without Thee, my God; I can no longer remain a fugitive from Thy presence, nor banish myself from Thy heart. Ah, how frequently do my soul, and the objects which surround me demand: Where is thy God? Everything speaks to me of Thee, yet nothing brings me to Thee. Thou art within me, and I seek Thee in exterior things, which dissipate my mind and remove me at a distance from Thee. O Life of my soul! The Center of my heart! The Supreme and Sovereign object of my mind! When shall I see what I now believe? When shall I possess what I love? Grant that the moment Thy presence strikes my mind, all within my heart may fall prostrate and yield entirely to Thee. Amen.

Chapter 2

The Truth Speaks within Us, Without Noise of Words

DISCIPLE

SPEAK, Lord, for Thy servant heareth. (*1 Kgs.* 3:9).

"I am thy servant, give me understanding that I may know thy testimonies." (*Ps.* 118:125).

Incline my heart to the words of Thy mouth, let Thy speech distill as the dew. (*Ps.* 71:6).

Heretofore the children of Israel said to Moses, "Speak thou to us and we will hear, let not the Lord speak to us lest we die." (*Ex.* 20:19).

Not thus, O Lord, not thus do I pray, but rather with the Prophet Samuel I humbly and longingly entreat Thee,

"Speak, Lord, for Thy servant heareth."

Let not Moses nor any of the Prophets speak to me, but speak Thou rather, O Lord God, Who art the inspirer and enlightener of all the prophets, for Thou alone without them canst perfectly instruct me, but they without Thee will avail me nothing.

2. They may indeed sound forth words, but they give not the spirit.

They speak well, but if Thou be silent they do not set the heart on fire.

They deliver the letter, but Thou disclosest the sense. They publish mysteries, but Thou explainest the meaning of the thing signified.

They declare the Commandments, but Thou enablest us to keep them.

They show the way, but Thou givest strength to walk in it.

They work only outwardly, but Thou instructest and enlightenest the heart.

They water exteriorly, but Thou givest the increase.

They cry out with words, but Thou givest understanding to the hearing.

3. Let not then Moses speak to me but Thou, O Lord my God, the eternal Truth, lest I die and prove fruitless if I be only outwardly admonished and not enkindled within.

Lest the word which I have heard and not fulfilled, which I have known and not loved, which I have believed and not observed, rise up in judgment against me.

Speak then, O Lord, for Thy servant heareth (*1 Kgs.* 3:9), for Thou hast the words of eternal life. (*John* 6:69).

Speak that it may be for me some comfort to my soul

and for the amendment of my whole life and to Thy praise and glory and everlasting honor.

Practical Reflections

God speaks to the understanding by the light of His Spirit, and to the heart by His holy inspirations. All that the Prophets deliver in the Word of God, all the truths which preachers announce to us, cannot enlighten the understanding, nor touch the heart, if God Himself speak not to us by the motions of His grace. We should therefore entreat the Lord to speak to our interior, while we exteriorly attend to or read divine truths, for fear that hearing the word of God and not keeping it, knowing His doctrines and not following them, conscious of His will and not doing it we should become more and more culpable in His sight.

Prayer

Speak to me, O Lord, speak in such a manner to my soul that I may hear and obey Thee. Make known to me Thy designs for my salvation, and enable me to execute them. Teach me and all Christians, O Jesus, what Thou art to us, and what we ought to be to Thee. Instruct us in the sacred maxims of Thy Gospel, and induce us to practice them, for what will it avail us to believe Thy heavenly doctrines, if we endeavor not to follow them, and to live, as well as to believe, as becometh Christians? O eternal Word of the Father, by which He spoke, and all things were made, speak to my soul, say to it, I am thy salvation. Work in me to will and to do, and consummate my salvation. Amen.

Chapter 3

The Words of God Are to be Heard with Humility, and Many Weigh Them Not

CHRIST

M Y SON, hear My words, words most sweet, exceeding all the learning of the philosophers and of the wise men of this world.

My words are spirit and life (*John* 6:69), and not to be estimated by the sense of man. They are not intended to gratify a vain self-complacency, but are to be heard in silence and received with all humility and great affection.

DISCIPLE

2. And I said: "Blessed is the man whom thou shalt instruct, O Lord, and shalt teach him thy law, that thou mayst give him rest from the evil days" *(Ps. 93:12-13)* and that he may not be desolate upon earth.

CHRIST

3. It is I who have taught the prophets from the beginning and even till now I cease not to speak to all, but many are deaf to My voice and hard.

The greater number listen more willingly to the world than to God, and more readily follow the desire of the flesh than the good will of God.

The world promises things temporal and of small value and is served with great eagerness; I promise things most excellent and everlasting and men's hearts are not moved.

Who is there that serves and obeys Me in all things with that great care with which the world and its lords are served? "Be thou ashamed, O Sidon," saith the sea. (*Is.* 23:4). And if thou ask why, hear the reason.

For a small living men run a great way, for eternal life many will scarce move a single foot from the ground.

An inconsiderable gain is sought after; for one penny sometimes men shamefully quarrel, they are not afraid to toil day and night for a trifle or some slight promise.

4. But, alas, for an unchangeable good, for an inestimable reward, for the highest honor and never-ending glory they are unwilling to take the least pains.

Be ashamed then thou slothful servant who art so apt to complain, seeing that they are more ready to labor for death than thou for life.

They rejoice more in running after vanity than thou in the pursuit of truth.

And indeed they are sometimes frustrated of their hopes, but My promise deceives no man nor sends away empty him that trusts in Me.

What I have promised I will give, what I have said I will make good, provided a man continue to the end faithful in My love.

I am the rewarder of all the good and the strong trier of all the devout.

5. Write My words in thy heart and think diligently on them, for they will be very necessary in the time of temptation.

What thou understandest not when thou readest thou shalt know in the day of visitation.

I am accustomed to visit My elect in two ways, that is by trial and by comfort.

And I read them daily two lessons, one to rebuke their vices, the other to exhort them to the increase of virtues.

He that hath My words and slighteth them, hath that which shall condemn him at the last day. (*John* 12:48).

A Prayer to Impose the Grace of Devotion

6. O Lord, my God, Thou art all my good, and who am I that I should dare speak to Thee?

I am Thy most poor servant and a wretched little worm, much more poor and contemptible than I can conceive or dare express.

Yet remember, O Lord, I am nothing, I have nothing can do nothing. (*2 Cor.* 12:11).

Thou alone art good, just and holy; Thou canst do all things; Thou givest all things; Thou fillest all things, leaving only the sinner empty.

Remember Thy tender mercies and fill my heart with Thy grace, Thou Who wilt not have Thy works to be empty.

7. How can I support myself in this wretched life, unless Thy mercy and grace strengthen me?

Turn not Thy face from me; delay not Thy visitation; withdraw not Thy comfort, lest my soul become as earth without water unto Thee. (*Ps.* 142:6).

O Lord, teach me to do Thy will (*Ps.* 142:10), teach me to converse worthily and humbly in Thy sight, for Thou art my Wisdom, Who knowest me in truth and didst know me before the world was made and before I was born in the world. (*Ps.* 138:16).

Practical Reflections

It is astonishing to witness how much men undertake, urged on by vain and deceitful hope, to obtain temporal and perishable goods, and how very little they do to obtain spiritual and eternal rewards, though encouraged by a solid and certain hope founded upon the word of God, which never fails. The prospect of interest, or the uncertain hope of riches, animates every heart, enhances every pleasure, dries up every tear, lightens every labor; and we think ourselves well repaid for our trouble when we have acquired the honor, the pleasure, or the advantage we had in view. The hope of Heaven alone, the prospect of eternal happiness, which may be obtained by patience and good works, animates us not, it neither supports nor consoles us: we are as much cast down and discouraged at the thought of gaining Heaven by patient suffering as though we esteemed it of no value. Whence comes this? It is because we are too much attached to things present and too indifferent about the things to come. Our hope is faint because our faith is weak.

Prayer

What confusion for me, O Lord, that I should give myself so much trouble to please the world and to gratify my passions, and take so little pains to satisfy Thy justice by works of penance, or Thy goodness by punctuality in the discharge of my duties! Alas! why do I not undergo as much for Thee as for myself? Why is not my ardor to please Thee as fervent as my eagerness to gratify myself? Change, O Lord, change the object and inclinations of my heart. Take Thou the place of self within me, and grant that my love for Thee may be as ardent to please Thee as my own self-love is to satisfy myself. Give me such a love for Thee as may be called a love of reparation, that is, such as

may, by its ardor and constancy, make amends for the languor
and inconstancy of mine. Amen.

Chapter 4

We Ought to Walk in Truth and Humility in God's Presence

CHRIST

SON, walk before Me in truth and always seek Me in the
simplicity of thy heart.

He that walks before Me in truth shall be secured from
evil occurrences and truth shall deliver him from deceivers
and from the detractions of the wicked.

If truth be on thy side thou wilt be free from all anxiety
(*John* 8:32) and unconcerned at all that vain man can say
against thee.

DISCIPLE

2. Lord, this is true; as Thou sayst so I beseech Thee, let
it be done with me. Let Thy truth teach me, let Thy truth
guard me and keep me till I come to a happy end. (*Ps.* 24:3).

Let the same deliver me from all evil affections and all
inordinate love and I shall walk with Thee in perfect freedom of heart.

CHRIST

3. I who am Truth will teach thee those things which are
right and pleasing in My sight.

Think on thy sins with great compunction and sorrow

and never esteem thyself to be anything for thy good works.

Thou art indeed a sinner, subject to and entangled with many passions.

Of thyself thou always tendest to nothing, thou quickly fallest, thou art quickly overcome, easily disturbed and dissolved.

Thou has not anything in which thou canst glory, but many things for which thou oughtst to humble thyself, for thou art much weaker than thou art able to comprehend.

4. Let nothing then seem much to thee of all thou dost.

Let nothing appear great; nothing valuable or admirable; nothing worthy of esteem, nothing high, nothing truly praiseworthy or desirable, but what is eternal.

Let the eternal truth please thee above all things and thine own excessive vileness ever displease thee.

Fear nothing so much, blame and abhor nothing so much as thy vices and sins, which ought to displease thee more than any losses whatsoever.

Some persons walk not sincerely before Me; but being led with a certain curiosity and pride, desire to know the hidden things of My providence and to understand the high things of God, neglecting themselves and their own salvation.

These often fall into great temptations and sins through their pride and curiosity, because I stand against them.

5. Fear the judgments of God; dread the anger of the Almighty; but presume not to examine the works of the Most High, but search into thine own iniquities, how many ways thou hast offended and how much good thou hast neglected.

Some only carry their devotions in their books, some in pictures and some in outward signs and figures.

Some have Me in their mouths, but little in their hearts.

There are others, who, being enlightened in their understanding and purified in their affection, always breathe after things eternal, are unwilling to hear of earthly things and grieve to be subject to the necessities of nature, and such as these perceive what the spirit of truth speaks in them.

For it teaches them to despise the things of the earth and to love heavenly things; to disregard the world and all day and night to aspire after Heaven.

Practical Reflections

Nothing can more effectually teach thee what thou art, than the consideration of thy many miseries. As thou becomest convinced of thine evil inclinations, so wilt thou not elevate thyself by thoughts of vanity or self-complacency. Happy then the soul that knows itself, that knows and bewails its own miseries, weakness, and evil inclinations. It is this which subjects it to God, and obliges it to have frequent recourse to Him, and to humble itself under His all-powerful hand. The continual danger it apprehends of yielding to temptation keeps it in a state of perpetual dependence upon Him, and of sincere and constant deprivation for His sake. Be determined, then, willingly to receive from the hand of God whatever trials He is pleased to send thee, to enter into His designs, and to submit to His good pleasure.

Prayer

As I am sensible, O God, that nothing is more pleasing to Thee than the disposition of a soul which depends upon Thee in all things, and which applies itself to know and to do Thy will, so the grace which I now ask of Thee is that I may be docile to Thine inspirations, and faithful in following them. I well know that Thou requirest of me a sincere and constant adherence to Thy service, an exact fidelity to my duties, and an absolute conformity to Thy blessed will. I know that Thou requirest me to direct all my actions by an interior spirit, and a real desire of pleasing Thee. This, above all things, I ask of Thee, my God, to be employed only on Thee and for Thee, to esteem nothing but what is eternal, and to reckon as nothing all that passes away with time. When, O God, shall an interior life, a life of death to all things, a life hidden with Jesus Christ in Thee, become my portion, as it is now my desire? Unite my soul intimately to Thyself, captivate and confirm my heart in Thy love both for time and eternity. Amen.

Chapter 5

The Wonderful Effects of Divine Love

DISCIPLE

I BLESS Thee, O heavenly Father, Father of my Lord Jesus Christ; because Thou hast vouchsafed to be mindful of so poor a wretch as I am.

O Father of mercies and God of all comfort (*2 Cor.* 1:3), I give thanks to Thee, who sometimes art pleased to cherish with Thy consolation, me who am unworthy of any comfort.

I bless Thee and glorify Thee forevermore, together with Thine only-begotten Son and the Holy Ghost, the Comforter to all eternity.

O Lord God, my holy Lover, when Thou shalt come into my heart all that is within me will be filled with joy. (*Prov.* 23:5).

Thou art my Glory and the Joy of my heart.

Thou art my Hope and my Refuge in the day of my trouble. *(Ps.* 58:17).

2. But because I am as yet weak in love and imperfect in virtue, therefore do I stand in need of being strengthened and comforted by Thee. For this reason visit me often and instruct me in Thy holy discipline.

Free me from evil passions and heal my heart of all disorderly affections, that being healed and well purified in my interior, I may become fit to love, courageous to suffer and constant to persevere.

3. Love is an excellent thing, a great good indeed, which alone maketh light all that is burdensome and equally bears all that is unequal.

For it carries a burden without being burdened and makes all that which is bitter sweet and savory.

The love of Jesus is noble and generous; it spurs us on to do great things and excites us to desire always that which is most perfect.

Love will tend upwards and is not to be detained by things beneath.

Love will be at liberty and free from all worldly affections, lest its interior sight be hindered, lest it suffer itself to be entangled with any temporal interest or cast down by losses.

Nothing is sweeter than love; nothing stronger, nothing higher, nothing more generous, nothing more pleasant, nothing fuller or better in Heaven or on earth; for love proceeds from God and cannot rest but in God above all things created.

4. The lover flies, runs and rejoices, he is free and not held.

He gives all for all and has all in all, because he rests in one sovereign good above all, from whom all good flows and proceeds.

He looks not at the gifts, but turns himself to the giver above all goods.

Love often knows no measure, but is inflamed above all measure.

Love feels no burden, values no labors, would willingly do more than it can; complains not of impossibility, because it conceives that it may and can do all things.

It is able therefore to do anything and it performs and effects many things where he that loves not faints and lies down.

5. Love watches, and sleeping, slumbers not.

When weary is not tired; when straitened is not constrained; when frighted is not disturbed, but like a lively flame and a torch all on fire it mounts upwards and securely passes through all opposition.

Whosoever loveth knoweth the cry of this voice.

A loud cry in the ears of God is the ardent affection of the soul, which saith, O my God, my love, Thou art all mine and I am all Thine. (*Cant.* 2:16).

6. Give increase to my love, that I may learn to taste with the interior mouth of the heart how sweet it is to love and to swim and to be dissolved in love. (*Ps.* 33:9).

Let me be possessed by love, going above myself through excess of fervor and ecstasy.

Let me sing the canticle of love, let me follow Thee my Beloved on high, let my soul lose herself in Thy praises, rejoicing exceedingly in Thy love.

Let me love Thee more than myself and myself only for Thee, and all others in Thee, who truly love Thee as the law of love commands, which shines forth from Thee.

7. Love is swift, sincere, pious, pleasant, and delightful; strong, patient, faithful, prudent, long-suffering, courageous, and never seeking itself.

For where a man seeks himself there he falls from love.

Love is circumspect, humble, and upright, not soft, not light, not intent upon vain things; is sober, chaste, stable, quiet, and keeps a guard over all the senses.

Love is submissive and obedient to superiors, in its own eyes mean and contemptible, devout and thankful to God; always trusting and hoping in Him, even when it tastes not the relish of God's sweetness, for there is no living in love without some pain or sorrow.

8. Whosoever is not ready to suffer all things and to stand resigned to the will of his Beloved, is not worthy to be called a lover.

He that loveth must willingly embrace all that is hard and bitter, for the sake of his Beloved, and never suffer himself to be turned away from Him by any contrary occurrences whatsoever.

Practical Reflections

Who shall ever conceive or explain the wonderful effects of the love of God in a soul that is faithful to its impressions, and firm in the time of trial? It is much better to feel them than to speak of them; and it is more perfect to practice them than to feel them. What does not the love of God effect when it is active, solid, and constant, in a soul that is captivated with the beauty and goodness of its God, and inflamed with the ardor of His holy charity! It often thinks of Him, for we cannot forget what we love; it does all to please Him; it suffers all for His sake; it carefully avoids the slightest faults; for how can we love God and be willing to offend Him? It desires for God all the good which He is and possesses; it would that all the hearts of men were but one, and this the heart of a seraph; it rejoices in all the glory that is given to Him in Heaven and on earth; it invites all creatures to love and praise Him; it would procure for Him, at the expense of its very life and being, if it were possible, any addition of happiness and delight; it cannot be consoled for His absence; it sighs incessantly for the happiness of seeing Him; it considers this life an exile, which the will of God alone makes supportable; it looks upon death with joy, as being the only means of coming to the possession of Him, and of no more offending Him; it burns with a secret fire, which with lively ardor consumes it before God, in God, and for God; it lives no longer for itself, but for Him whom it loves more than itself; it seeks, it finds, it beholds, everywhere its God. Its joy and its felicity in this world is to suffer, to renounce, and to annihilate itself; and to die to all sensible objects in order to gain the love of Jesus. It believes, it hopes, it loves with a sovereign love, through the respect, esteem, and attachment which it has for the Author of its faith, hope, and charity. God exists, it says, and that is enough for my happiness, my consolation, and my joy. God deserves to be served; He wills that I should do or suffer this for Him; Jesus Christ was most willing to do and to suffer all for me. It is not satisfied with submitting itself in everything to the orders of its God; it seeks but to know His inclinations, and His good pleasure is its law. In a word a soul that loves its God no longer lives by its own life, but it is God who lives within it.

Prayer

Is it possible, O Lord, that Thou Who art infinitely amiable, and Who lovest us with an infinite love, shouldst find in us so little love for Thee? Revive in our hearts that fire of divine charity which Thou, my Saviour, didst bring from Heaven upon the earth, and which Thou desirest should glow within us. Grant that, becoming insensible and indifferent to all creatures, we may feel neither ardor nor attachment but for Thee alone; and that, being ever disposed to suffer all, and to lose all, rather than Thy love, but for one moment, we may love Thee in preference to all things else, and esteem our whole self of infinitely less consideration than Thee. Preserve us in that habitual love of Thee which is Sanctifying Grace; inspire us with an active love to animate us in all our actions. Give us that perpetual love which, causing us to do all for and by Thee, may procure for us the happiness of dying in the exercise of Thy love, to continue it throughout a blessed eternity. Amen.

Chapter 6

The Proof of a True Lover

CHRIST

MY SON, thou art not as yet a valiant and prudent lover.

DISCIPLE

Why, O Lord?

CHRIST

Because thou fallest off from what thou hast begun, upon meeting with a little adversity and too greedily seekest after consolation.

A valiant lover stands his ground in temptations and yields not to the crafty persuasions of the enemy.

As he is pleased with Me in prosperity so I displease him not when I send adversity.

2. A prudent lover considers not so much the gift of the lover as the love of the giver.

He looks more at the good will than the value, and prizes his Beloved above all His gifts.

A generous lover rests not in the gift, but in Me above every gift.

All is not lost if sometimes thou hast not that sense of devotion towards Me or My saints which thou wouldst have.

That good and delightful affection, which thou sometimes perceivest, is the effect of present grace and a certain foretaste of thy heavenly country, but thou must not rely too much upon it, because it goes and comes.

But to fight against the evil motions of the mind which arise, and to despise the suggestions of the devil is a sign of virtue and of great merit.

3. Let not, therefore, strange fancies trouble thee, of what kind soever they be that are suggested to thee.

Keep thy resolution firm and thine intention upright towards God.

Neither is it an illusion that sometimes thou art rapt into an ecstasy and presently returnest to the accustomed weakness of thy heart.

For these thou rather sufferest against thy will than pro-curest, and as long as thou art displeased with them and dost resist them it is merit and not loss.

4. Know that the old enemy strives by all means to hin-der thy desire after good and to divert thee from every devout exercise, namely from the veneration of the saints, from the pious meditation of My Passion, from the prof-itable remembrance of thy sins, from keeping a guard upon thine own heart and from a firm purpose of advanc-ing in virtue.

He suggests to thee many evil thoughts that he may weary thee out, and frighten thee that he may withdraw thee from prayer and the reading of devout books.

He is displeased with humble confession, and if he could he would cause thee to omit Communion.

Give no credit to him, value him not, although he often lays his deceitful snares in thy way.

Charge him with it when he suggests wicked and unclean things and say to him:

Begone, unclean spirit; be ashamed, miserable wretch; thou art very filthy indeed to suggest such things as these to Me.

Depart from me, thou wicked imposter, thou shalt have no share in me, but my Jesus will be with me as a valiant warrior and thou shalt be confounded.

I would rather die and undergo any torment whatsoever than yield to thy suggestions.

Be silent, I will hear no more of thee, although thou so often strivest to be troublesome to me. "The Lord is my light and my salvation, whom shall I fear? The Lord is the protector of my life, of whom shall I be afraid?" *(Ps.* 26:1).

"If armies in camp should stand together against me, my heart shall not fear. The Lord is my helper and my Redeemer." *(Ps.* 69:6).

5. Fight like a good soldier, and if sometimes thou fallest through frailty rise up again with greater strength than before, confiding in My more abundant grace, but take great care thou yield not to any vain complacency and pride.

Through this many are led into error and sometimes fall into incurable blindness.

Let this fall of the proud, who foolishly rely on their own strength, serve thee for a warning and keep thee always humble.

Practical Reflections

I know that the true love of God may consist more in suffering, for His sake, dryness, disgust, and the most grievous temptations, without yielding to them, than in the enjoyment of interior delights, sweetnesses, and consolations; for in the one instance we receive much from God, in the other we give much to Him. In the one we love the gifts of God, in the other we love Himself and His holy will preferably to all His gifts; and the love by which we love God for what He is, is much more perfect than that by which we love Him for what He bestows upon us. Ah, how pleasing to Almighty God to behold a soul ever watchful over itself to keep its heart free from the least faults, ever attentive to its duties, in obedience to His orders, and in resignation to His holy will, and ever willing generously to resist the demands of nature and the temptations of the devil! A soul which neither allows nor pardons itself anything, but endeavors to correspond with the holy designs of God in its regard, to destroy in itself everything human, and to overthrow self-love, takes for the rule of its conduct that rule of true love: All to please God, and nothing to gratify myself. But what most pleases God is to see that this soul, really clothed with the strength and grace of His spirit in all its contests with itself and its passions, can endure nothing contrary to His good pleasure; to see that it neither asks, nor seeks, nor finds any consolation or sensible support, its delight being the delight which God takes in seeing it suffer, even without being sensibly assured that He takes pleasure in it. Its submission and its self-renunciation are its consolation and support, happy in becoming a victim of immolation to the love of God.

Prayer

Abandon me not, O Lord, to the sensitiveness of self-love, which will suffer nothing; nor to the inefficacy of my desires, by which I ever will what I never perform. Penetrate my heart with a conviction of the happiness and obligation of suffering all for Thee, and as Thou didst suffer. Grant that, having no other interest but Thine, and willing only what Thou willest, I may receive pains of mind as cheerfully as consolations of spirit; and hoping that, punishing me here, Thou wilt spare me hereafter, I may often say to Thee, in the time of suffering, may Thy justice be satisfied whatever I may have to endure in this life. The less I enjoy Thee, the more will I love Thee; the more will I resist the irregular desires of my heart, that I may ultimately deserve the more to possess Thee. O my God! My Saviour! I am willing to be deprived of all consolation here below, provided I never offend Thee. What a happiness to become a victim of Calvary, a martyr to Thy crucified Heart, and entirely devoted to Thy good pleasure! Amen.

Chapter 7

Grace Is to Be Hid under the Guardianship of Humility

M Y SON, it is more profitable and more safe for thee to hide the grace of devotion and not to be elevated with it, not to speak much of it, not to consider it much, but rather to despise thyself the more and to be afraid of it, as given to one unworthy.

Thou must not depend too much on this affection which may be quickly changed into the contrary.

When thou hast grace think with thyself how miserable and poor thou art wont to be when thou art without it.

Nor does the progress of a spiritual life consist so much in having the grace of consolation, as in bearing the want of it with humility, resignation, and patience, so as not to grow remiss in thine exercise of prayer at that time, nor to suffer thyself to omit any of thine accustomed good works.

But that thou willingly do what lies in thee, according to the best of thy ability and understanding, and take care not wholly to neglect thyself through the dryness or anxiety of mind which thou feelest.

2. For there are many who when things succeed not well with them presently grow impatient or slothful.

Now the way of man is not always in his own power (*Jer.* 10:23), but it belongs to God to give and to comfort when He will, and as much as He will, and to whom He will, and as it shall please Him and no more.

Some, wanting discretion, have ruined themselves upon occasion of the grace of devotion, because they were desirous of doing more than they could, not weighing well the measure of their own weakness, but following rather the inclinations of the heart than the dictates of reason.

And because they presumptuously undertook greater things than were pleasing to God, therefore they quickly lost His grace.

They became needy and were left in a wretched condition, who had built themselves a nest in Heaven to the end, that being thus humbled and impoverished they might learn not to trust to their own wings, but to hide themselves under Mine. (*Ps.* 90:4).

Those who are yet but novices and unexperienced in the way of the Lord, if they will not govern themselves by the counsel of discreet persons, will be easily deceived and overthrown.

3. And if they will rather follow their own judgment than believe others who have more experience, their future is full of danger if they continue to refuse to lay down their own conceits.

They that are wise in their own eyes seldom humbly suffer themselves to be ruled by others. (*Prov.* 3:7; *Rom.* 11:25).

It is better to have little knowledge with humility and a weak understanding, than greater treasures of learning with self-conceit.

It is better for thee to have less than much, which may puff thee up with pride.

He is not so discreet as he ought to be who gives himself up wholly to joy, forgetting his former poverty and the chaste fear of God, which apprehends the loss of that grace which is offered.

Neither is he so virtuously wise who, in the time of adversity or any tribulation whatsoever, carries himself in a desponding way and conceives and reposes less confidence in Me than he ought.

4. He who is too secure in time of peace will often be found too much dejected and fearful in time of war.

If thou couldst but always continue humble and little in thine own eyes and keep thy spirit in due order and subjection, thou wouldst not fall so easily into dangers and offenses.

It is a good counsel that when thou hast conceived the spirit of fervor, thou shouldst meditate how it will be with thee when that light shall leave thee.

Which, when it shall happen, remember that the light may return again, which, for thine instruction and My glory I have withdrawn from thee for a time.

5. Such a trial is oftentimes more profitable than if thou wert always to have prosperity according to thy will.

For a man's merits are not to be estimated by his having many visions or consolations, nor by his knowledge in scriptures, nor by his being placed in a more elevated station.

But by his being grounded in true humility and replenished with divine charity; by his seeking always purely and entirely the honor of God; by his esteeming himself as nothing and sincerely despising himself, and being better pleased to be despised and humbled by others than to be the object of their esteem.

Practical Reflections

Man in the state of innocence would have perfect love, because all within him would have submitted without difficulty to His orders; but in the state of sin in which we now are we cannot serve Him without continually fighting against ourselves; nor can we love Him without hating ourselves; we can do but little for Him but what we do against ourselves. Hence we should humbly submit to the dryness, disgust, and irksomeness which we frequently experience in our exercises of piety; we should enter into the designs of Almighty God, make a merit of seeking to please Him without gratifying ourselves; and willingly consent to become victims of His love, and to sacrifice all for His honor. Did the truly Christian soul know how far a state of suffering may be made a holy and sanctifying state, a state of proved and purified love for God, in a word, a state in which we neither seek nor find ourselves in anything but purely God, how would that soul esteem it! What care would it not take to profit by it, that is, to suffer patiently, to support the Lord with courage, and to neglect nothing, whatever uneasiness might arise. Were we thoroughly persuaded of, and deeply impressed with a conviction of the continual merit of a life of dryness when supported without dejection, we should without doubt endeavor to correspond with the designs of God, who would thus oblige us not to seek ourselves in anything, but to endeavor only to please Him, and to make a real merit of His good pleasure. We should esteem ourselves happy in sacrificing to God the gratifications of our hearts, in yielding ourselves up to Him, and in doing our duty, even without the satisfaction of knowing that we please Him!

Prayer

Purify my heart, O Lord, from the pursuits of self-love, which is never satisfied with what is done for Thee unless it also be gratified by it. Grant that, in all my exercises of piety, I may seek rather to please Thee than to gratify myself: that dying daily to the natural life of my soul, in which consists true satisfaction, I may seek no other pleasure than fidelity in Thy service and exactness in following Thy holy will in all things; that so, approaching to Thee, my God, more by faith than by sense, I may do and suffer all for Thy love, notwithstanding my natural aversion and the deprivation of all the sweetness and sensible charms of piety, persuaded of the truth of what Thou didst once say to St. Gertrude, that Thou reservest until death the consolation of all we perform without consolation during life. Grant, therefore, that my whole employment and all my happiness may be to serve and to love Thee much more for Thyself than for my own gratification. Amen.

Chapter 8

Of Acknowledging Our Unworthiness in the Sight of God

DISCIPLE

I WILL speak to my Lord, I who am but dust and ashes. (*Gen.* 18:27). If I think anything better of myself, behold Thou standest against me and my sins bear witness to the truth, and I cannot contradict it.

But if I humble myself and acknowledge my own nothingness, and cast away all manner of esteem of myself and (as I really am) account myself to be mere dust, Thy grace will be favorable to me and Thy light will draw nigh to my heart; and all self-esteem, how small soever, will be sunk in the depth of my own nothingness and there lose itself forever.

It is there Thou showest me to myself, what I am, what I have been and what I am to come to; for I am nothing and I knew it not. (*Ps.* 72:22).

If I am left to myself, behold I am nothing and all weakness; but if Thou shouldst graciously look upon me, I presently become strong and am filled with a new joy.

And it is very wonderful that I am so quickly raised up and so graciously embraced by Thee; I, who by my own weight, am always sinking to the bottom.

2. It is Thy love that effects this, freely preventing me and assisting me in so many necessities, reserving me also from grievous dangers, and as I may truly say, delivering me from innumerable evils.

For by an evil loving of myself, I lost myself, and by seeking Thee alone and purely loving Thee, I found both myself and Thee, and by this love have more profoundly annihilated myself.

Because Thou, O most sweet Lord, art bountiful to me above all desert and above all I dare hope or ask for.

3. Blessed be Thou, O my God, for though I am unworthy of all good, yet Thy generosity and infinite goodness never ceaseth to do good, even to those who are ungrateful and that are turned away from Thee.

Oh, convert us unto Thee, that we may be thankful, humble, and devout; for Thou art our salvation, our power, and our strength. (*Ps.* 61:8).

Practical Reflections

When we perceive within ourselves any feelings of vanity or self-complacency, we need but consider, for one moment, the unfathomable depth of our corruption, and descend into the abyss of our miseries, to stifle them in their very birth. For how can we represent to ourselves that universal incapacity which we experience for supernatural good, our inclination for evil, how violently we are carried towards wickedness, the blindness of our understandings, the malice of our hearts and the fury of our passions, which are always revolting against reason; in a word, how can we consider what we really are, and not despise and humble ourselves beneath all creatures? And if we consider ourselves with reference to God; if we reflect what He is and what we are in His sight, a mere nothing, sinners, but sinners loaded with the numberless crimes we have committed, not knowing whether they have ever been pardoned; creatures so weak and feeble, so inconstant in good, and so constant in evil; alas! perhaps in the sight of God, living and dying in the state of sin, and worthy only of His eternal hatred; how, in the midst of such reflections, can we possibly consent to the least thought of vanity? How true it is that to esteem ourselves is not to know, but to forget what we are.

Prayer

Suffer not pride, O Lord, to deprive us of the sight and conviction of our manifold miseries. Oblige us to do justice to ourselves and to Thee, by referring the glory of all things to Thee, to Whom alone it belongs: and by giving to ourselves nothing but contempt, which is truly our desert and appropriate portion. How does a Christian who knows that he is all Thine, my Saviour, and that he carries within himself an inexhaustible source of malice and corruption, give Thee alone the honor of all the good he may do by the help of Thy grace, and attribute nothing to himself but the evil which he commits, since without Thee he is incapable of doing anything but sin! Fill my heart with this true humility, without which it is impossible ever to become worthy of Thy love. Amen.

Chapter 9

All Things are to be Referred to God as to our Last End

CHRIST

M Y SON, I must be thy chief and last end if thou desirest to be truly happy.

By this intention shall thine affection be purified, which too often is irregularly bent upon thyself and things created.

For if in anything thou seek thy self thou presently faintest away within thyself and growest dry.

Refer, therefore, all things principally to Me, for it is I that have given thee all.

Consider everything as flowing from the Sovereign Good, and therefore they must all be returned to Me as to their origin.

2. Out of Me, both little and great, rich and poor, as out of a living fountain, draw living water. (*Is.* 12:3).

And they who freely and willingly serve Me shall receive grace for grace. (*John* 10:6).

But he that would glory in anything else besides me, or delight in any good as his own (not referred to Me), shall not be established in true joy, nor enlarged in his heart, but in many kinds shall meet with perplexities and anguish.

Therefore thou must not ascribe anything of good to thyself, nor attribute virtue to any man, but give all to God, without whom man is nothing. (*Ps.* 113:1).

I have given all, I will have all returned to Me again and

I very strictly require thanks for all that I give. (*Matt.* 25:28).

3. This is that truth by which all vainglory is put to flight.

And if heavenly grace and true charity come in there shall be no envy or narrowness of heart, nor shall self-love keep its hold.

For divine charity overcomes all and dilates all the powers of the soul.

If thou art truly wise thou wilt rejoice in Me alone; thou wilt hope in Me alone, for none is good but God alone, who is to be praised above all and to be blessed in all. (*Dan.* 3:56).

Practical Reflections

Let an upright and pure intention of pleasing God direct all thine actions, and endeavor to give Him the whole glory of all the good thou performest, for He is the plenitude and source of all good. Glory only in thine infirmities, and turn them to thine advantage by frequently offering them to the God of all mercy, who is ever well pleased in a soul that is penetrated with a sense of its own nothingness. Dwell not upon thoughts of vanity and self-complacency, and do not desire to be praised and esteemed by men; for God confounds and despises those who seek to please men and to obtain their praises. The only means by which thou canst please God and gain His love is to despise and hate thyself.

Prayer

Permit me not, O Lord, to attribute the least good to myself, but to refer all to Thee, Who alone art the Author of every good work. Glory is Thy portion, and I will give it wholly and entirely to Thee; confusion is mine, and I will accept it from Thy hand, happy if, by joyfully resigning myself to contempt, I become worthy of Thy favors, and if, by living an humble and concealed life, I die to myself and to the world, and live only to Thee. Amen.

Chapter 10

It Is Sweet to Serve God, Despising this World

DISCIPLE

NOW will I speak, O Lord, and will not be silent; I will say in the hearing of my God, my Lord and my King that is on high.

Oh, how great is the multitude of Thy sweetness, O Lord, which Thou hast hidden for them that fear Thee. (*Ps.* 30:20). But what art Thou to those that love Thee? What to those that serve Thee with their whole heart?

Unspeakable indeed in the sweetness of Thy contemplation, which Thou bestowest on those that love Thee.

In this most of all hast Thou shown me the sweetness of Thy love, that when I had no being Thou hast made me, and when I strayed far from Thee Thou hast brought me back again, that I might serve Thee, and Thou hast commanded me to love Thee.

2. O Fountain of everlasting love, what shall I say of Thee?

How can I ever forget Thee who hast vouchsafed to remember me, even after I was corrupted and lost.

Thou hast, beyond all hope, showed mercy to Thy servant, and beyond all my desert bestowed Thy grace and friendship upon me.

What returns shall I make to Thee for this favor? for it is a favor not granted to all to forsake all things and renounce the world and choose a monastic life.

Can it be much to serve Thee whom the whole creation is bound to serve?

It ought not to seem much to serve Thee, but this seems rather great and wonderful to me, that Thou vouchsafest to receive one so wretched and unworthy into Thy service and to associate him to Thy beloved servants.

3. Behold all things are Thine which I have and with which I serve Thee.

Although, on the contrary, Thou dost rather serve me than I Thee.

Lo! Heaven and earth, which Thou hast created for the service of man, are ready at Thy beck and daily do whatever Thou hast commanded them.

And this is yet but little, for Thou hast also appointed the angels for the service of man. (*Heb.* 1:14).

But what is above all this is that Thou Thyself hast vouchsafed to serve man and hast promised that Thou wilt give him Thyself.

4. What shall I give Thee for so many thousands of favors? Oh, that I could serve Thee all the days of my life!

Oh, that I were able, if it were but for one day, to serve Thee worthily!

Indeed Thou art worthy of all service, of all honor, and of eternal praise!

Thou art truly my Lord and I am Thy poor servant, who am bound with all my strength to serve Thee and ought never to grow weary of praising Thee.

This is my will, this is my desire, and whatever is wanting to me do Thou vouchsafe to supply.

5. It is a great honor, a great glory to serve Thee and to despise all things for Thee.

For they who willingly subject themselves to Thy most holy service shall have great grace.

They shall find the most sweet consolations of the Holy Ghost who, for the love of Thee, have cast away all carnal delights.

They shall gain great freedom of mind who, for Thy name, enter upon the narrow way and neglect all worldly care.

6. O pleasant and delightful service of God, which makes a man truly free and holy!

O sacred state of religious bondage, which makes men equal to angels, pleasing to God, terrible to the devils and commendable to all the faithful.

O service worthy to be embraced and always wished for, which leads to the supreme good and procures a joy that will never end.

Practical Reflections

To judge ourselves unworthy of every grace; to correspond with those we receive; to refer to God all the glory of our fidelity in His service; often to thank Him for His goodness in seeking us when we go astray, and receiving us again after we have sinned; to hope all things from His mercy, and to place ourselves entirely in His hands, is what should be done by every Christian soul who knows what Jesus Christ is to him, and what he ought to be to Jesus Christ.

How fortunate are we in not being able to find in ourselves any real cause for feelings of vanity or self-complacency, for this obliges us to forsake ourselves, and abide only in God! Ah, how does the sense of our miseries establish us in the heart of the God of mercy! And how does the experience of our inability to do good, and our inclination for evil, oblige us to adhere to God, and to have continual recourse to Him.

Prayer

How can I forget Thee, O Lord, Who hast so often preserved me from Hell, into which I might have precipitated myself by my irregular or useless life? Cure me of that vain complacency and swelling pride which would persuade me that there is something of good in me. It is in Thee, O Lord, it is all from Thee: for without Thee I can do nothing but offend Thee. Suffer me not to exalt myself before Thee by voluntary pride, lest I draw upon myself the same chastisement with which Thou didst visit the first angels. I would rather be despised by men and loved by Thee, then be esteemed by them and reproved by Thee. Grant that I may do Thee justice by referring all that is good to Thee, and to myself naught but the evil I have committed, that I may thus obtain Thy merciful pardon. Amen.

Chapter 11

The Desires of Our Hearts Are to be Examined and Moderated

CHRIST

SON, thou hast many things still to learn which thou hast not yet well learned.

DISCIPLE

2. What are these things, O Lord?

CHRIST

3. That thou conform in all things thy desires to My good pleasure, and that thou be not a lover of thyself, but earnestly zealous that My will be done.

Desires often inflame thee and violently hurry thee on, but consider whether it is for My honor or thine own interest that thou art most moved.

If thou hast no other view but Me thou wilt be well contented with whatever I shall ordain, but if there lurk in thee anything of self-seeking, behold, this it is that hinders thee and troubles thee.

4. Take care then not to rely too much upon any desire which thou hast conceived before thou hast consulted Me, lest afterwards thou repent or be displeased with that which before pleased thee and which thou zealously desirest as the best.

For every inclination which appears good is not presently to be followed nor every contrary affection at first sight to be rejected.

Even in good desires and inclinations it is expedient sometimes to use some restraint, lest by too much eagerness, thou incur distraction of mind; lest thou create scandal to others, by not keeping within discipline or even lest by the opposition which thou mayest meet with from others, thou be suddenly disturbed and fall.

5. In some cases thou must use violence and manfully

resist the sensual appetite and not regard what the flesh has a mind for, or what it would fly from, but rather labor that, whether it will or not, it may become subject to the spirit.

And it must be chastised and kept under servitude, until it readily obeys in all things and learns to be content with a little and to be pleased with what is plain and ordinary, and not to murmur at any inconvenience.

Practical Reflections

Our desires should be regulated by the will of God, moderated by the influence of His Grace, and referred to His glory. True mortification of the heart consists in repressing the ardor of our desires, in turning their earnestness against self, and in directing them all to their proper object, which is God. The holy practice of self-renunciation, which is absolutely necessary for salvation, and which is included in the spirit of the Gospel and the engagements of our Baptism, consists entirely in repressing our irregular desires, in raising our indifferent or natural inclinations to a supernatural end, and in grounding our hopes of salvation, through the merits of Christ, on the fulfillment of our good resolutions.

Prayer

When, O Lord, shall I become so wearied with my irregular and fruitless desires as to be induced to regulate them by Thy holy will, and to practice the good which I desire to perform. Shall I be satisfied with continually saying I desire earnestly to be all Thine, and to serve Thee faithfully, without doing it with constancy, or desiring it effectually? Alas! my God, I know that Hell is filled with good desires and resolutions, yet it is Hell.

Can I be converted and gain salvation by only desiring it, as so many condemned Christians have desired and do still desire it? Root out, O Lord, this inefficacy of my desires, which may lead me to perdition; and grant that I may ever unite to the desire the use of those means Thou affordest me of pleasing Thee and of saving my soul. Amen.

Chapter 12

Of Learning Patience and of Fighting against Concupiscence

DISCIPLE

O LORD God, patience, as I perceive, is very necessary for me; for this life is exposed to many adversities.

For, notwithstanding all I can do to live in peace, my life cannot be without war and sorrow.

CHRIST

2. So it is, son; but I would not have thee seek for such a peace as to be without temptations or meet with no adversities.

But even then to think that thou has found peace, when thou shalt be exercised with divers tribulations and tried in many adversities.

If thou shalt say thou art not able to suffer so much, how then wilt thou endure the fire of Purgatory?

Of two evils one ought always to choose the less.

That thou mayest, therefore, escape the everlasting punishments to come labor to endure present evils with patience for God's sake.

Dost thou think the men of this world suffer little or nothing? Thou shalt not find it so, though thou seek out the most delicate.

3. But thou wilt say they have many delights and follow their own wills and, therefore, make small account of their tribulations.

4. Suppose it to be so, that they have all they desire, but how long dost thou think this will last?

Behold, like smoke they shall vanish away (*Ps.* 36:20), who abound in this world and there shall be no more remembrance of their past joys.

Nay, even whilst they are living they enjoy them not without a mixture of bitterness, irksomeness and fear.

For the very same thing in which they conceive a delight doth often bring upon them a punishment of sorrow.

It is but just it should be so with them that, since they inordinately seek and follow pleasures, they should not enjoy them without confusion and bitterness.

Oh, how short, how deceitful, how inordinate and filthy are all these pleasures!

Yet, through sottishness and blindness, men understand this not, but like brute beasts, for a small pleasure in this mortal life, they incur the eternal death of their souls.

But thou, my son, go not after thy lusts, but turn away from thine own will. (*Ecclus.* 18:30).

Delight in the Lord and He will give thee the requests of thy heart. (*Ps.* 36:4).

5. For if thou wilt be delighted in truth and receive

more abundant consolation from Me, behold in the contempt of all worldly things and the renouncing of all those mean pleasures, thou shalt be blessed and an exceeding great comfort be derived to thy soul.

And the more thou withdrawest thyself from all comfort in things created, the more sweet and the more powerful consolations wilt thou find in Me.

But thou shalt not at first attain to these without some sorrow and labor in the conflict.

The old custom will stand in thy way but by a better custom it shall be overcome.

The flesh will complain, but by the fervor of the spirit it shall be kept under.

The old serpent will tempt thee and give thee trouble, but by prayer he shall be put to flight; moreover, by keeping thyself always employed in useful labor his access to thee shall be in a great measure impeded.

Practical Reflections

True peace of soul consists in an humble and constant submission to the will of God under the severest pains and the most violent temptations. When thou findest within thyself nothing but repugnance, trouble, and despondency, it is then that by renouncing thyself, and giving thyself entirely into the hands of God, thou wilt obtain true peace of soul. To separate thyself from everything pleasing, to accept everything that is disagreeable as coming from the hand of God, to conquer on all occasions thy repugnance, is the surest way to arrive at true peace.

Prayer

Thou alone, O Jesus, canst impart to us this interior peace, this peace of God, this ineffable peace, and this humble submission. We ask it of Thee, and we hope it from Thee. Give us this precious gift, we beseech Thee, which may keep our minds and our hearts in Thy faith and love. Amen.

Chapter 13

The Obedience of an Humble Subject, After the Example of Jesus Christ

CHRIST

SON, he who strives to withdraw himself from obedience withdraws himself from grace, and he that seeks to have things for his own particular use loses such as are common.

If a man doth not freely and willingly submit himself to his superior, it is a sign that his flesh is not, as yet, perfectly obedient to him, but oftentimes rebels and murmurs.

Learn then to submit thyself readily to thy superior if thou desire to subdue thine own flesh.

For the outward enemy is sooner overcome if the inward man be not laid waste.

There is no more troublesome or worse enemy to the soul than thou art thyself, when not agreeing well with the Spirit.

Thou must, in good earnest, conceive a true contempt of thyself if thou wilt prevail over flesh and blood.

Because thou hast yet too inordinate a love for thyself,

therefore art thou afraid to resign thyself wholly to the will of others.

2. But what great matter is it if thou, who art but dust and a mere nothing, submit thyself for God's sake to man, when I, the Almighty and the Most High, who created all things out of nothing, have for thy sake humbly subjected Myself to man?

I became the most humble and most abject of all, that thou mightest learn to overcome thy pride by My humility.

Learn, O dust, to obey; learn to humble thyself, thou that art but dirt and mire, and to cast thyself down under the feet of all men.

Learn to break thine own will and to yield thyself up to all subjection.

3. Conceive an indignation against thyself; suffer not the swelling of pride to live in thee, but make thyself so submissive and little, that all may trample on thee and tread thee underfoot as the dirt of the streets.

What hast thou, vain man, to complain of?

What answer canst thou make, O wretched sinner, to those that reproach thee, thou that hast so often offended God and many times deserved Hell?

But Mine eye hath spared thee (*1 Kgs.* 24:11), because thy soul was precious in My sight, that thou mightest know My love and mightest be always thankful for My favor and that thou mightest give thyself continually to true subjection and humility, and bear with patience to be despised by all.

Practical Reflections

We must not be satisfied with exteriorly submitting to obedience and in things that are easy, but we must obey with our whole heart, and in things the most difficult. For the greater the difficulty, the greater also is the merit of obedience. Can we refuse to submit to man for God's sake, when God, for love of us, submits to man, even to His very executioners?

Jesus Christ was willingly obedient during His whole life, and even unto the death of the Cross; and am I unwilling to spend my life in the exercise of obedience, and to make it my cross and my merit? Independence belongs to God, who has made man dependent upon others, that his subordination may be to him the means of his sanctification. I will therefore form myself upon the model of my submissive, dependent, and obedient Saviour, and dispose of nothing in myself, not even of my own will.

Prayer

O my Saviour, Who, in obedience to Thy Father, wast conceived in the womb of Mary, Who didst go down to Nazareth, and wast subject to Thy parents for thirty years, Who wouldst be born and live, and die in obedience, induce us to follow Thine example, to obey Thee in all things in the persons of our superiors, who hold Thy place in our regard. Grant that, doing willingly what is ordained us, and endeavoring to believe it best, we may spend our whole lives in continual obedience, and thus secure for ourselves Thy grace in time, and Thy glory for all eternity. Amen.

Chapter 14

On the Consideration of God's Secret Judgments, Lest We be Puffed Up With Our Own Good Works

DISCIPLE

THOU thunderest forth over my head Thy judgments, O Lord, and Thou shakest all my bones with fear and trembling and my soul is terrified exceedingly. (*Job* 4:14).

I stand astonished and consider that the heavens are not pure in Thy sight. (*Job* 15:15).

If in the angels Thou hast found sin and hast not spared them, what will become of me?

Stars have fallen from Heaven and I that am but dust, how can I presume? (*Apoc.* 6:13).

They whose works seemed praiseworthy have fallen to the very lowest, and such as before fed upon the bread of angels I have seen delighted with the husks of swine. (*Luke* 15:16).

2. There is then no sanctity, if Thou, O Lord, withdraw Thy hand.

No wisdom avails if Thou cease to govern us.

No strength is of any help if Thou support us not.

No chastity is secure without Thy protection.

No guard that we can keep upon ourselves will profit us, if Thy holy providence watch not over us. (*Ps.* 126:1).

For if we are left to ourselves we sink and we perish; but if Thou visit us we are raised up and we live.

For we are unsettled, but by Thee we are strengthened; we are tepid, but by Thee we are inflamed.

3. Oh, how humble and lowly ought I to think of myself; how little ought I to esteem whatever good I may seem to have!

Oh, how low ought I to cast myself down under the bottomless depths of Thy judgments, O Lord, where I find myself to be nothing else but nothing, nothing!

O immense weight! O sea, that cannot be passed over, where I find nothing of myself but altogether nothing!

Where then can there be any reason for glorying in myself? Where any confidence in any conceit of my own virtue?

All vainglory is swallowed up in the depth of Thy judgments over me.

4. What is all flesh in Thy sight? Shall the clay glory against Him that formed it? (*Is.* 45:9).

How can he be puffed up with the vain talk of men whose heart in truth is subjected to God?

The whole world will not move him whom truth hath established in humility. Neither will he be moved with the tongues of all that praise him who hath settled his whole hope in God.

For behold, they also that speak are all nothing, for they shall pass away with the sound of their words, but the truth of the Lord remaineth forever.

Practical Reflections

The contemplation of the holiness and purity of God, in whose sight the heavens are not clean, and the conviction of our own sinfulness and corruption, should stifle in us every rising sentiment of pride. An angel sins, and God cannot endure him; He rejects him, and casts him off forever. Man sins, and He bears with him; He offers him His mercy, and opens to him the gates of Heaven. In the fallen angels we behold the horrid nature of sin, and the awful character of God's justice; in the redeeming love of Jesus we are invited to confide entirely in His tender mercy: from both we derive motives of a speedy conversion from sin, to awaken our gratitude, and to animate us to a life of holiness.

Prayer

O God of sanctity, Who canst not endure iniquity, how canst Thou endure me, an unworthy sinner, who am committing iniquity without ceasing, and am continually displeasing Thee? O God of purity, before Whom the heavens are not clean, and Who didst discover corruption even in the angels, why dost Thou not reject me, who am naught but defilement and sin? Lord, if Thou wilt, Thou canst make me clean. I cast myself upon Thy mercy, and conjure Thee to enable me to correct and to punish all my sins and to destroy within me everything that is contrary to Thine infinite sanctity. Amen.

Chapter 15

How We are to be Disposed, and What We are to Say when We Desire Anything

CHRIST

MY SON, say thus on every occasion: Lord, if it be pleasing to Thee let this be done in this manner.
Lord, if it be to Thine honor let this be done in Thy name.
Lord, if Thou see that this is expedient and approve it as

profitable unto me, then grant that I may use it to Thine honor.

But if Thou know that it will be hurtful to me and not expedient for the salvation of my soul, take away from me such a desire.

For every desire is not from the Holy Ghost, though it seems to a man right and good.

And it is oftentimes hard to judge truly, whether it be a good or bad spirit that urges thee on to desire this or that; or whether thou art moved to it by thine own spirit.

Many in the end have been deceived, who at first seemed to be led by a good spirit.

2. Whatsoever, therefore, presents itself to thy mind as worthy to be desired, see that it be always with the fear of God and humility of heart that thou dost desire or ask for it, and above all, thou oughtest, with a resignation of thyself, to commit all to Me and to say:

Thou knowest, O Lord, what is best, let this or that be done as Thou wilt.

Give what Thou wilt, how much Thou wilt, and at what time Thou wilt.

Do with me as Thou knowest and best pleaseth Thee, and is most for Thine honor.

Put me where Thou wilt and do with me in all things according to Thy will.

I am in Thy hand, turn me round which way Thou wilt.

Lo, I am Thy servant (*Ps.* 118:125), ready to obey Thee in all things; for I do not desire to live for myself but for Thee; Oh, that I could do so, after a faithful and perfect manner!

Prayer for the Fulfilling of the Will of God

DISCIPLE

3. Grant me Thy grace most merciful Jesus, that it may be with me and may labor with me and continue with me to the end. *(Wis.* 9:10).

Grant me always to will and desire that which is most acceptable to Thee and which pleaseth Thee best.

Let Thy will be mine and let my will always follow Thine and agree perfectly with it.

Let me always will or not will the same with Thee, and let me not be able to will or not will any otherwise than as Thou willest or willest not.

4. Grant that I may die to all things that are in the world, and for Thy sake love to be despised and not to be known in this world.

Grant that I may rest in Thee above all things desired and that my heart may be at peace in Thee.

Thou art the true peace of the heart, Thou art its only rest; out of Thee all things are hard and uneasy. In this peace, in the selfsame, that is in Thee, the one sovereign eternal good, I will sleep and I will rest. *(Ps.* 4:9). Amen.

Practical Reflections

As it is God who wills all that happens to us, and wills it for our good, for our salvation, so we ought in all things to resign ourselves to His holy appointments, that is, we should, first, will only what God wills, and when He wills it; secondly, we should never separate our will from His by any voluntary transgression, and never say or do anything contrary to it; thirdly, we should never knowingly sin, or resist God in what He requires from us.

A firm and constant resolution to do, to renounce, and to suffer whatever He at present requires, or may in future demand of our fidelity, is all that is necessary to make us victims of His love and good pleasure, and to commence here upon earth what we hope to continue in Heaven. Wherefore let us often pray that the will of God may be accomplished in us in time as it will be in eternity.

Prayer

O my God, Whose holy will is the rule and principle of all good, mayest Thou be the soul of all my actions, and the object of all the motions of my heart. Grant that in my whole conduct, and in all trials, I may seek only to do and to suffer whatever Thou willest, because it is Thy will, and as Thou pleasest; that I may renounce my own will in everything; that I may make Thee the sole master and proprietor of my heart, that in all things it may be submissive to Thy will, and never depart from it. Amen.

Chapter 16

True Comfort Is to Be Sought in God Alone

DISCIPLE

WHATSOEVER I can desire or imagine for my comfort, I look not for it in this life, but hereafter.

For if I alone should have all the comforts of this world, and might enjoy all its delights, it is certain they could not last long.

Wherefore, thou canst not, O my soul, be fully comforted, nor perfectly delighted but in God, the comforter of the poor and the support of the humble.

Expect a little while, my soul, wait for the divine promise, and thou wilt have plenty of all that is good in Heaven.

If thou desirest too inordinately these present things, thou wilt lose those that are heavenly and everlasting.

Let temporal things serve thine use, but the eternal be the object of thy desire.

Thou canst not be fully satisfied with any temporal good, because thou wast not created for the enjoyment of such things.

2. Although thou shouldst have all created goods, yet this could not make thee happy and blessed; but in God, who created all things, thy beatitude and happiness consist.

Not such a happiness as is seen or extolled by the foolish admirers of this world, but such as good Christians look for, and of which they have sometimes a foretaste who are spiritual and clean of heart, whose conversation is in Heaven. (*Phil.* 3:20).

All human comfort is vain and short.

Blessed and true is that comfort which is inwardly received from truth.

A devout man always carries about him Jesus, his comforter, and saith to Him: Be with me, O Lord Jesus, in all places and at all times.

Let this be my consolation, to be willing to want all human comfort.

And if Thy comfort also be withdrawn, let Thy will and just appointment for my trial be to me as the greatest of comforts.

"For thou wilt not be angry always, nor wilt thou threaten forever." (*Ps.* 102:9).

Practical Reflections

God is the center of our hearts, says St. Augustine, and we cannot rest till we rest in God; that is, so long as we are attached to ourselves and to creatures, we seek happiness where it is not to be found, out of God. We should therefore withdraw our hearts from all that is not God, and die to all things else, if we would enjoy true happiness, which can only result from an entire dedication of our souls to God. Wherefore let us not say, with those of the world: Happy they who possess abundance of all things they desire, and want none of the goods and pleasures of the earth! Rather let us say: Blessed is the heart for which God sufficeth! happy the Christian who loves that only now which he shall love forever.

Prayer

When, O God, shall I become so detached from created objects as to sigh only for the happiness of pleasing and loving Thee? When wilt Thou become more to me than all things else, all in all, even as Thou art to the blessed in Heaven? Grant that I may deny myself every gratification, and delight only in pleasing Thee. Pains, crosses, and afflictions shall be from henceforth the joy of my soul, or at least the subjects of my patience, because they have been consecrated by Thee, my Jesus! and it is Thy blessed will I should endure them. And if, as I deserve, Thou deprivest me of consolation, grant that humble submission may support me, whilst Thou hidest the light of Thy countenance. Amen.

Chapter 17

We Ought to Cast All Our Care upon God

CHRIST

SON, suffer Me to do with thee what I will; I know what is best for thee.

Thou thinkest as man; thou judgest in many things as human affection suggests.

DISCIPLE

2. Lord, what Thou sayest is true; Thy care over me is greater than all the care I can take of myself.

For he stands at too great a hazard that does not cast his whole care on Thee. (*1 Ptr.* 5:7).

Lord, provided that my will remain but right and firm towards Thee, do with me whatsoever it shall please Thee.

For it cannot but be good whatever Thou shalt do by me.

If Thou wilt have me to be in darkness, be Thou blessed, and if Thou wilt have me to be in light, be Thou again blessed; if Thou vouchsafe to comfort me, be Thou blessed, and if it be Thy will I should be afflicted, be Thou always equally blessed.

CHRIST

3. Son, it is in this manner thou must stand affected if thou desire to walk with Me.

Thou must be as ready to suffer as to rejoice. Thou must be willing to be poor and needy as to be full and rich.

DISCIPLE

4. Lord, I will suffer willingly for Thee whatsoever Thou art pleased should befall me.

I will receive with indifference from Thy hand good and evil, sweet and bitter, joy and sorrow, and will give Thee thanks for all that happens to me. (*Job* 2:10).

Keep me only from all sin and I will fear neither death nor Hell.

Cast me not off forever, nor blot me out of the Book of Life, and what tribulation soever befalleth me shall not hurt me. (*Apoc.* 3:5).

Practical Reflections

To preserve peace in time of trouble our will must remain firm in God, and be ever directed towards Him, that is, we should be disposed to receive all things from the hand of God, from His justice, and from His bounty, with humble submission to His blessed will. Good and evil, health and sickness, prosperity and adversity, consolation and dryness, temptation and tranquillity, interior sweetness, trials, and chastisements, all should be received by the soul with humility, patience, and resignation, as coming to us by the appointment of God. This is the only means of finding peace in the midst of great troubles and adversities.

Prayer

Grant, O God, that I may rely entirely on Thy power and goodness. Thou canst and wilt assist me; this shall be my support and confidence in the midst of the most grievous afflictions. Keep me from sin, and I am content to suffer all things else. When assailed by violent temptations, and, as it were, in the midst of the shadow of death, I will place my trust in Thee, and fear no evil, because Thou wilt be with me. All I ask, O God, is that my trials may be as pleasing to Thee as they are painful to me, that by patient endurance they may become to me the way of penance, and conduct me to salvation. Amen.

Chapter 18

Temporal Miseries Are to Be Borne with Patience, after the Example of Jesus Christ

CHRIST

SON, I came down from Heaven for thy salvation. I took upon Me thy miseries, not of necessity, but moved thereto by charity, that thou mightest learn patience and mightest bear without repining the miseries of this life.

For from the hour of My Incarnation till My expiring on the Cross, I was never without suffering.

I underwent a great want of temporal things; I frequently heard many complaints against Me; I meekly bore with confusions and reproaches; for My benefits I received ingratitude; for My miracles, blasphemies; and for My heavenly doctrine, reproaches.

DISCIPLE

2. Lord, because Thou wast patient in Thy lifetime, in thus chiefly fulfilling the commandment of Thy Father, it is fitting that I, a wretched sinner, should, according to Thy

will, take all with patience and, as long as pleaseth Thee, support the burden of this corruptible life, in order to my salvation. (*2 Mach.* 6:25).

For though this present life be burdensome, yet it is now become, through Thy grace, very meritorious and, by the help of Thine example and the footsteps of Thy saints, more supportable to the weak and more lightsome.

It is also much more consoling than it was formerly under the Old Law, when the gate of Heaven remained shut and the way to it seemed more obscure, when so few concerned themselves to seek the Kingdom of Heaven.

Neither could they, who were then just and to be saved, enter into Thy heavenly Kingdom, before Thy Passion and the payment of our debt by Thy sacred death.

Oh, what great thanks am I obliged to return to Thee for having vouchsafed to show to me and to all the faithful a right and good way to an everlasting Kingdom.

For Thy life is our way, and by holy patience we walk on to Thee, Who art our crown. (*John* 14:6).

If Thou hadst not gone before and instructed us who would have cared to follow?

Alas, how many would have stayed afar off and a great way behind, if they had not before their eyes Thine excellent example?

Behold we are still tepid, notwithstanding all Thy miracles and the instructions we have heard: what then would it have been if we had not this great light to follow Thee.

Practical Reflections

To animate ourselves to suffer in a proper manner we should often think of the Passion of Jesus Christ, who suffered the punishment due to our sins. The afflictions which God sends us are intended either to prove our fidelity or to punish us for our offenses. We should therefore receive them with humble submission, and in a truly penitential spirit; happy in being allowed to satisfy the justice of God in time, that we may contemplate His bounty for eternity. Our greatest trials are from ourselves. The rebellions of our passions, the bitterness of our hearts, our constitutional fretfulness, the wandering of our imagination, and the whole man so opposite to God, would be insupportable did we not frequently think of the patience with which God waits for us, and endeavor to imitate Him who bears with our infirmities. Let us, then, be patient under sufferings, that so, at the last hour, we may enjoy the consolation of having sanctified the evils of this life by a spirit of patience, and thus rendered them most available to salvation.

Prayer

Can we behold Thee, O Jesus, suffer so much for us and yet be unwilling to suffer anything for Thee? Can we believe that we must suffer with Thee on earth, if we would reign with Thee in Heaven, and yet resist Thy chastisements or bear them with impatience? Dearest Saviour, give us strength to suffer, and grant that the patience which Thou impartest to us may make us worthy of those eternal rewards which Thou hast promised us in the Kingdom of Heaven. Amen.

Chapter 19

On Supporting Injuries, and Who Is Proved to Be Truly Patient

CHRIST

WHAT is it thou sayest, My son? Cease to complain, considering My Passion and the sufferings of the saints. Thou hast not yet resisted unto blood. (*Heb.* 12:4).

What thou sufferest is but little in comparison to them who have suffered so much; who have been so strongly tempted, so grievously afflicted, so many ways tried and exercised. (*Heb.* 11:33, 37).

Thou must then call to mind the heavy sufferings of others, that thou may the more easily bear the little things thou sufferest.

And if to thee they seem not little, take heed lest this also proceed from thine impatience.

But whether they be little or great strive to bear them with patience.

2. The better thou disposest thyself for suffering, the more wisely dost thou act, and the more dost thou merit: and thou wilt bear it more easily, thy mind being well prepared for it and accustomed to it.

Say not: I cannot take these things from such a man, and things of this kind are not to be suffered by me for he has done me a great injury, and he upbraids me with things I never thought of; but I will suffer willingly from another, and as far as I shall judge fitting for me to suffer.

Such a thought is foolish, which considers not the virtue

of patience, nor by whom it shall be crowned, but rather weighs the persons and the offense committed.

3. He is not truly a patient man who will suffer no more than he thinks good and from whom it pleases him.

The truly patient man minds not by whom it is he is exercised, whether by his superior, or by one of his equals, or by an inferior: whether by a good and holy man, or by one that is perverse and unworthy.

But how much soever and how often soever any adversity happens to him from anything created, he takes it all with equality of mind, as from the hand of God, with thanksgiving and esteems it a great gain.

For nothing, how little soever, that is suffered for God's sake, can pass without merit in the sight of God.

4. Be thou therefore, ready prepared to fight if thou desirest to gain the victory.

Without fighting thou canst not obtain the crown of patience.

If thou wilt not suffer, thou refusest to be crowned; but if thou desirest to be crowned, fight manfully and endure patiently. (*2 Tim.* 2:5).

Without labor there is no coming to rest, nor without fighting can the victory be obtained.

DISCIPLE

5. May Thy grace, O Lord, make that possible to me which seems impossible to me by nature. *(Luke* 18:27).

Thou knowest that I can bear but little and that I am quickly cast down by a small adversity.

Let all exercises of tribulation become amiable and agreeable to me, for Thy name's sake; for to suffer and to be afflicted for Thee is very healthful to my soul.

Practical Reflections

The practice of patience consists, first, in receiving all misfortunes as coming from the hand of God; secondly, in bearing all things with resignation; thirdly, in never murmuring under contradictions; fourthly, in believing that, having deserved Hell, no one can do us wrong or injustice; fifthly, in complaining only of ourselves; sixthly, in not speaking when the heart is full; seventhly, in thanking God for evil as well as for good; in a word, in frequently saying with holy Job: The Lord gave, and the Lord hath taken away; blessed be His holy name. Such is the practice of patience, which is so necessary for salvation, and yet so rare among Christians: for although there is no one but who suffers much, yet very few suffer as they ought.

Long and constant patience in our trials and difficulties is a penitential and powerful means of effacing sin, which when God punishes in this life, we may hope He will not punish in the next.

Prayer

Grant, O my Saviour, that Thy patience in bearing with me and suffering for me may be the model and principle of my patience in suffering for Thee; and that, entering into Thy designs for my salvation, which Thou wouldst secure for me by the good use I make of afflictions, I may receive all things with humble submission to Thy holy will. Amen.

Chapter 20

The Confession of Our Own Infirmity
And the Miseries of This Life

DISCIPLE

I WILL confess against myself my injustice. *(Ps.* 21:5). I will confess to Thee, O Lord, my infirmity.

It is oftentimes a small thing which casts me down and troubles me.

I make a resolution to behave myself valiantly; but when a small temptation comes I am brought into great straits.

It is sometimes a very trifling thing from which proceeds a grievous temptation.

And when I think myself somewhat safe, I find myself sometimes, when I least apprehend it, almost overcome with a small blast.

2. Behold, then, O Lord, my abjection and frailty (*Ps.* 24:18), every way known to Thee.

Have pity on me and draw me out of the mire (*Ps.* 118:15), that I stick not fast therein, that I may not be utterly cast down forever.

This it is which often drives me back and confounds me in Thy sight, to find that I am so subject to fall and have so little strength to resist my passions.

And although I do not altogether consent, yet their assaults are troublesome and grievous to me, and it is exceedingly irksome to live thus always in a conflict.

Hence my infirmity is made known to me, because wicked thoughts do always much more easily rush in upon me than they can be cast out again.

3. Oh, that Thou, the most mighty God of Israel, the zealous lover of faithful souls, wouldst behold the labor and sorrow of Thy servant, and stand by me in all my undertakings.

Strengthen me with heavenly fortitude, lest the old man, the miserable flesh, not fully subject to the spirit, prevail and get the upper hand, against which we must fight as long as we breathe in this most wretched life.

Alas! what kind of life is this, where afflictions and miseries are never wanting; where all things are full of snares and enemies.

For when one tribulation or temptation is gone another cometh: yea, and whilst the first still lasts, many others come on and these unexpected.

4. How can a life be loved that hath such great bitterness, that is subject to so many calamities and miseries.

How can it be called life since it begets so many deaths and plagues?

And yet it is loved and many seek their delight in it.

Many blame the world that it is deceitful and vain, yet they are not willing to quit it, because the concupiscence of the flesh overmuch prevails.

But there are some things that draw them to love the world—others to despise it.

The concupiscence of the flesh, the concupiscence of the eyes, and the pride of life (*John* 2:16), draw to the love of the world; but the pains and miseries, which justly follow these things, breed a hatred and loathing of the world.

5. But alas! the pleasure of sin prevails over the worldly

soul and under these briers she imagines there are delights (*Job* 30:7); because she has neither seen nor tasted the sweetness of God, nor the internal pleasures of virtue.

But they that perfectly despise the world and study to live to God under holy discipline, experience the divine sweetness that is promised for those who forsake all; and such clearly see how grievously the world is mistaken and how many ways it is imposed upon.

Practical Reflections

It is not sufficient to know and to feel our weaknesses and miseries, and our continual danger of perishing eternally by yielding to our passions; we should also at the sight of them humble ourselves before God, and place our whole confidence in Him. We should incessantly bewail our exile, and cast and support ourselves upon the bounty of God. We should never remain in the state of sin, tepidity, or infidelity in which our weakness too often engages us, but immediately arise after we have fallen and speedily return to our heavenly Father when we find we have gone astray.

This life is so replete with temptations, pains, and miseries, that it becomes insupportable to a soul that loves God, and is afraid of offending Him. How shall I live, does it exclaim, and not sin? Yet how shall I sin and still live? to be ever falling, and then rising again; ever resisting my passions, and fighting against the irregular desires of my heart, is this life? It is continual death. But let us not grow weary of repressing, of fighting, and conquering our predominant passions, for in this consists the merit of a supernatural life, of a life conducting to eternal happiness.

Prayer

I acknowledge, O God, that life would be unsatisfactory had I no trial of suffering for Thy sake. Grant, therefore, that, when weary of myself, and fatigued with the miseries of this life, I may commit them all to Thy most merciful providence. Support me by Thy bounty, and give me patience and fidelity to endure myself, and to suffer whatever Thou shalt appoint. Amen.

Chapter 21

We Are to Rest in God Above All Goods and Gifts

DISCIPLE

ABOVE all things, and in all things, do thou, my soul, rest always in the Lord, for He is the eternal rest of the saints.

Give me, O most sweet and loving Jesus, to repose in Thee above all things created; above all health and beauty, above all glory and honor, above all power and dignity, above all knowledge and subtlety, above all riches and arts, above all joy and gladness, above all fame and praise, above all sweetness and consolation, above all hope and promise, above all merit and desire.

Above all the gifts and presents that Thou canst give and infuse, above all the joy and jubilation that the mind can contain and experience.

In fine, above angels and archangels, and all the hosts of Heaven, above all things visible and invisible, and above all that which is less than Thee, my God!

2. For Thou, O Lord, my God! art the best above all things. Thou alone most high; Thou alone most powerful; Thou alone most sufficient and most full; Thou alone most sweet and most comfortable.

Thou alone most beautiful and most loving; Thou alone most noble and most glorious above all things; in whom all things are found together in all their perfection, and always have been and always will be.

And, therefore, whatever Thou bestowest upon me, that is not Thyself, or whatever Thou revealest to me concerning Thyself, or promisest, as long as I see Thee not, nor fully enjoy Thee, is too little and insufficient.

Because, indeed, my heart cannot truly rest, nor be entirely contented, till it rest in Thee, and rise above all Thy gifts and all things created.

3. O my most beloved spouse, Christ Jesus, most pure lover, Lord of the whole creation, who will give me the wings of true liberty, to fly and repose in Thee? (*Ps.* 54:7).

Oh, when shall it be fully granted me to attend at leisure, and see how sweet Thou art, O Lord, my God? (*Ps.* 33:9).

When shall I fully recollect myself in Thee, that through the love of Thee I may not feel myself, but Thee alone, above all feeling and measure, in a manner not known to all?

But now I often sigh and bear my misfortune with grief.

Because I meet with many evils in this vale of miseries, which frequently disturb me, afflict me; and cast a cloud over me; often hinder and distract me, allure and entangle me, so that I cannot have free access to Thee, nor enjoy Thy sweet embraces, which are ever enjoyed by blessed spirits.

Let my sighs move Thee, and this manifold desolation under which I labor upon earth.

4. O Jesus! the brightness of eternal glory, the comfort of a soul in its pilgrimage, my tongue cannot express the sentiments of my heart, but my silence itself speaks to Thee.

How long doth my Lord delay to come?

Let Him come to me, His poor servant, and make me joyful; let Him stretch forth His hand, and deliver me, a wretch, from all anguish. (*Ps.* 137:7).

Oh, come, oh, come (*Apoc.* 22:20), for without Thee, I can never have one joyful day, nor hour, for Thou art my joy, and without Thee my table is empty.

I am miserable, and in a manner imprisoned, and loaded with fetters, till Thou comfort me with the light of Thy presence, and restore me to liberty and show me a favorable countenance.

5. Let others seek instead of Thee, whatever else pleases them; nothing else doth please me or shall please me, but Thou my God, my hope, my eternal salvation.

I will not hold my peace, nor cease to pray, till Thy grace returns and Thou speak to me interiorly.

CHRIST

6. Behold here I am, behold I come to thee, because thou hast called upon Me. Thy tears and the desire of thy soul, thy humiliation and contrition of heart have inclined and brought Me to thee. (*Is.* 38:5).

DISCIPLE

7. And I said, O Lord, I have called upon Thee and have desired to enjoy Thee, and am ready to renounce all things for Thee.

For Thou didst first stir me up that I might seek Thee.

Be Thou, therefore, blessed, O Lord; Who hast showed this goodness to Thy servant, according to the multitude of Thy mercies.

What hath Thy servant more to say in Thy presence, but to humble himself exceedingly before Thee; always remembering his own iniquity and vileness.

For there is none like to Thee amongst all things that are wonderful in Heaven or on earth. (*Ps.* 85:8).

Thy works are exceedingly good, Thy judgments are true and by Thy providence all things are ruled.

Praise, therefore, and glory be to Thee, O Wisdom of the Father! let my tongue, my soul and all things created, join in praising and blessing Thee.

Practical Reflections

We should prefer God before all things; that is, we should labor to forsake and renounce ourselves in all things, die to all self-satisfaction and deny ourselves many lawful pleasures, to punish ourselves for having indulged in those which are criminal. We should submit, give up, and immolate ourselves to God, rise superior to all created things, direct our hearts towards Him, and lose ourselves in His perfections; keep ourselves in a state of sovereign and interior adoration, to which all should yield; and by our actions, by the sacrifice of everything that is dear to us, establish Him the absolute Master and God of our hearts. To love God, so as to delight only in Him, is indeed a Heaven upon earth, and as it were, a foretaste of a happy eternity; but to arrive at this, we must disengage ourselves from those amusements of the mind which dissipate and withdraw it from God, and from those attachments of the heart which bind it to creatures; that so the soul, being free from itself and from the servitude of the passions, may take the wings of the dove, fly away towards God, and repose in Him alone.

Prayer

My God, my Sovereign Good, and only consolation, how dare I raise myself towards Thee, draw Thee to myself, and firmly unite myself to Thee, I who am filled, penetrated, and loaded with so many miseries, irregular inclinations towards evil, and continual repugnance to good; I who am every moment falling from Thee to myself, and from myself into sin, in a word, I who meet with so many obstacles within myself, which, like a wall of separation, would hinder me from being united to Thee? But what, O Lord, is impossible to me is easy to Thee; in Thy power and bounty I place all my hopes. Thou knowest my condition, and if Thou wilt Thou canst assist me. I groan incessantly under the load of my infirmities. I address myself to Thee, to be delivered from them by Thy mercy. I find no rest nor content nor happiness but in and by Thee. Come, then, O God, give consolation and support to my soul, which desires only Thee, to live only by and for its God. I languish and am on fire with the desire of possessing Thee without the fear of ever losing Thee. Reject me not, O infinitely amiable God! for I can no longer live separated and removed at a distance from Thee. Amen.

Chapter 22

Of the Remembrance
of the Manifold Benefits of God

OPEN, O Lord, my heart in Thy law and teach me to walk in Thy Commandments. (*2 Mach.* 1:4).

Give me grace to understand Thy will, and to commemorate with great reverence and diligent consideration all Thy benefits, as well in general as in particular, that so I may be able worthily to give Thee thanks for them.

But I know and confess that I am not able to return Thee due thanks, not even for the least point.

I am less than any of Thy benefits bestowed upon me (*Gen.* 32:10); and when I consider Thine excellency, my spirit loses itself in the greatness of Thy majesty.

2. All that we have in soul and body, all that we possess outwardly, or inwardly, by nature or grace, are Thy benefits and commend Thy bounty, mercy, and goodness from whom we have received all good.

And though one has received more, another less, yet all is Thine, and without Thee even the least cannot be had.

He that has received greater things cannot glory in his own merit, nor extol himself above others, nor exult over the lesser; because he is indeed greater and better who attributes less to himself and is more humble and devout in returning thanks.

And he who esteems himself the vilest of men and judges himself the most unworthy, is fittest to receive the greatest blessings.

3. But he that has received fewer, must not be troubled,

nor take it ill, nor envy him that is more enriched; but attend rather to Thee, and very much praise Thy goodness, that Thou bestowest Thy gifts so plentifully, so freely and willingly, without respect to persons. (*Rom.* 2:11).

All things are from Thee and therefore Thou art to be praised in all.

Thou knowest what is fit to be given to everyone; and why this person hath less and the other more, is not our business to decide, but Thine, who keepest an exact account of the merits of each one.

4. Wherefore, O Lord God, I take it for a great benefit not to have much, which outwardly and according to men might appear praiseworthy and glorious, so that a person considering his own poverty and meanness ought not, upon that account, to be weighed down or to be grieved and dejected, but rather to receive comfort and great pleasure.

Because Thou, O God, hast chosen the poor and humble, and those that are despised by this world, for Thy familiar friends and domestics. (*1 Cor.* 1:27).

Witness Thine Apostles themselves whom Thou didst appoint rulers over all the earth. (*Ps.* 44:17).

And yet they conversed in this world without complaint, so humble and simple, without any malice or guile, that they were even glad when they suffered affronts and reproaches for Thy name (*Acts* 5:41); and what the world flies from they embraced with great affection.

5. Nothing, therefore, ought to give such great joy to him that loves Thee and knows Thy benefits, as the accomplishment of Thy will in himself and the pleasure of Thine eternal appointment.

With which he ought to be so far contented and comforted as to be as willing to be the least as anyone would wish to be the greatest and to enjoy as much peace and content in the lowest place *(Luke* 14:10) as in the highest, and to be as willing to be despicable and mean and of no name and repute in the world as to be preferred in honor and greater than others.

For Thy will and the love of Thine honor ought to be regarded above all, and to comfort and please him more than any benefits whatsoever, which he hath received or can receive.

Practical Reflections

Happy the soul that is little in its own eyes, and is as content to be below all men, as others are desirous to be above them; that makes its merit and delight consist in being unknown, abject, and despised, and longs as ardently to become the reproach and the outcast of the world as others do to be esteemed and honored by it. Such a soul is after God's own heart; it is great in the eyes of His majesty, and by its humility renders itself worthy of His greatest graces. To arrive at this degree of perfection we must love an abject and hidden life, do nothing for the sake of esteem or praise, cheerfully receive contempt and adversity as our due; accept with humble submission blame, contradiction, and calumny, and nourish ourselves with reproaches in imitation of Jesus Christ, esteeming it our greatest honor thus to resemble Him.

Prayer

When, O my Saviour, shall the esteem of men, and the honor of the world become, as they ought to be, the disdain and the dread of my soul; humiliation and contempt, its joy and delight? Grant that the love which Thou hadst for contempt, Thou Who art the adoration of the angels, may be the motive and the rule of my patience in bearing with it, who have deserved to become the eternal object of Thy hatred and malediction. Amen.

Chapter 23

Four Things which Bring Much Peace

CHRIST

SON, I will teach thee now the way of peace and true liberty.

DISCIPLE

2. Do, Lord, as Thou sayest, for this is delightful for me to hear.

CHRIST

3. Endeavor, My son, rather to do the will of another than thine own.

Ever choose rather to have less than more.

Always seek the lowest place and to be inferior to everyone.

Always wish and pray that the will of God may be entirely fulfilled in thee.

Behold such a man as this enters upon the coasts of peace and rest.

DISCIPLE

4. Lord, this Thy short speech contains much perfection. It is short in words, but full in sense and plentiful in its fruit. For if I could faithfully observe it I should not be so easily troubled.

For as often as I find myself disquieted and disturbed I am sensible it is because I have strayed from this doctrine.

But Thou, O Lord, who canst do all things, and always lovest the progress of the soul, increase in me Thy grace that I may accomplish these Thy words and perfect my salvation.

A Prayer against Evil Thoughts

5. O Lord my God, depart not far from me; O my God, have regard to help me (*Ps.* 70:12), for divers evil thoughts have risen up against me, and great fears afflict my soul.

How shall I pass without hurt? How shall I break through them?

CHRIST

6. I will go before thee, says He, and will humble the great ones of the earth. (*Is.* 45:2). I will open the gates of the prison and reveal to thee hidden secrets.

DISCIPLE

7. Do, Lord, as Thou sayst, and let all these wicked thoughts flee from before Thy face.

This is my hope and my only comfort: to fly to Thee in all tribulations, to confide in Thee, to call on Thee from my heart, and patiently to look for Thy consolations.

A Prayer for Enlightening the Mind

8. Enlighten me, O good Jesus, with the brightness of eternal light, and cast out all darkness from the dwelling of my heart.

Restrain my many wandering thoughts and suppress the temptations that violently assault me.

Fight strongly for me and overcome these wicked beasts (*Lev.* 26:6), I mean these alluring concupiscences, that peace may be made in Thy power (*Ps.* 121:7), and the abundance of Thy praise may resound in Thy holy court, which is a clean conscience.

Command the winds and storms; say to the sea, be thou still, and to the north wind, blow thou not, and a great calm shall ensue. (*Matt.* 8:26).

9. Send forth Thy light and Thy truth (*Ps.* 42:3), that they may shine upon the earth; for I am as earth that is empty and void (*Gen. 1:2),* till Thou enlighten me.

Pour forth Thy grace from above, water my heart with the dew of Heaven; send down the waters of devotion to wash the face of this earth, to bring forth good and perfect fruit.

Lift up my mind, oppressed with the load of sins, and raise my whole desires towards heavenly things, that, having tasted the sweetness of the happiness above, I may have no pleasure in thinking of the things of the earth.

10. Draw me away and deliver me from all unstable comfort of creatures; for no created thing can fully quiet and satisfy my desires.

Join me to Thyself by an inseparable bond of love; for

Thou alone canst satisfy the lover, and without Thee all other things are frivolous.

Practical Reflections

As no one can escape the sight or the justice of God, so we should, in the first place, keep a continual watch over ourselves; secondly, we should never allow ourselves anything that may displease God; thirdly, we should walk always in His presence, and do all things with an intention of pleasing Him, follow on all occasions the motions of His grace, never resist His holy will, nor defer its accomplishment for one moment; so that there may be no interval between our knowing, willing, and performing what He requires of us. Nothing is so agreeable to God as to confide in Him, to trust in all things to Him, to abandon ourselves entirely to Him, and to depend completely upon Him. Happy the soul which, receiving all from His hands, resigns itself in all things to His holy will, wills only what He wills, and wills all that happens to it, because He so ordains it.

Prayer

Each day do I ask of Thee, O Lord, that Thy will may be done on earth as it is in Heaven. Hearken to my prayer, I beseech Thee, and grant that I may perform all my actions in compliance with Thy holy will, and ever make it the sole rule of my conduct. Deliver my soul from the slavery of its passions. Grant that they may all yield to Thine empire, and that to please and love Thee may ever be the predominant desire of my soul. Amen.

Chapter 24

We Should Refrain from Curious Inquiry into the Lives of Others

CHRIST

SON, be not curious and give not way to useless cares. (*1 Tim.* 1:4).

What is this or that to thee? Do thou follow Me. (*John* 21:22).

For what is it to thee whether this man be such or such; or that man do or say this or the other.

Thou art not to answer for others, but must give an account for thyself; why, therefore, dost thou meddle with them?

Behold, I know every one and see all things that are done under the sun (*Eccles.* 1:14); and I know how it is with every one, what he thinks, what he would have and at what his intention aims.

All things, therefore, are to be committed to Me; but as for thy part, keep thyself in good peace and let the busybody be as busy as he will.

Whatsoever he shall do or say will come upon himself, because he cannot deceive Me.

2. Be not solicitous for the shadow of a great name; neither seek to be familiarly acquainted with many, nor to be particularly loved by men.

For these things beget distractions and great darkness in the heart.

I would willingly speak My words to thee and reveal My secrets to thee, if thou wouldst diligently observe My coming and open to Me the door of thy heart.

Be careful and watch in prayer and humble thyself in all things. (*1 Ptr.* 4:7).

Practical Reflections

In order to enjoy true peace, we must, in the first place, avoid all curiosity as to what regards our neighbor; secondly, we must receive with patience all the afflictions which arise either from the justice of God, or the injustice of man; thirdly, we must suffer and accustom ourselves to the privation of all joy and consolation; sacrifice to God all the pleasures of our mind, heart, and senses; and thank Him for not permitting us to find any real satisfaction but in Him.

Prayer

I acknowledge, O God, that my only desire and the only curiosity of my mind is to know whether I am at present in the state of grace, and whether I shall so continue until death; whether Thou hast pardoned me my sins, and whether Thou wilt grant me that greatest of all Thy mercies, final perseverance. But I will resign this desire to Thee, I will sacrifice this security, and will hope from Thy pure bounty this greatest of all graces. Amen.

Chapter 25

In What Things Firm Peace of Heart And True Progress Consist

CHRIST

SON, I have said, Peace I leave with you, My peace I give unto you; not as the world giveth do I give unto you. (*John* 14:27).

Peace is what all desire; but all care not for those things which appertain to true peace.

My peace is with the humble and meek of heart. Thy peace shall be in much patience.

If thou wilt hear Me and follow My voice thou shalt enjoy much peace.

DISCIPLE

2. What then shall I do, Lord?

CHRIST

3. In everything attend to thyself, what thou art doing and what thou art saying; and direct thy whole intention to this, that thou mayest please Me alone, and neither desire nor seek anything out of Me.

And as for the sayings or doings of others, judge of nothing rashly, neither busy thyself with things not committed to thy care, and thus may it be brought about that thou shalt be little or seldom disturbed.

But never to feel any trouble, nor to suffer any grief of heart or pain of body, is not the state of this present life, but of everlasting rest.

Think not, therefore, that thou hast found true peace if thou feel no burden; nor that then all is well if thou hast no adversary, nor that thou hast attained to perfection if all things be done according to thine inclination.

Neither do thou then conceive a great opinion of thyself, nor imagine thyself to be especially beloved, if thou experience great devotion and sweetness; for it is not in such things as these that a true lover of virtue is known, nor doth the progress and perfection of a man consist in these things.

DISCIPLE

4. In what then, O Lord?

CHRIST

5. In offering thyself with thy whole heart to the will of God, not seeking the things that are thine, either in little or great, either in time or eternity.

So that with the same equal countenance thou mayest continue giving thanks, both in prosperity and adversity, weighing all things with an equal balance.

If thou come to be so valiant and long-suffering in hope, that when interior comfort is withdrawn thou canst prepare thy heart to suffer still more, and dost not justify thyself, as if thou oughtest not to suffer such great things.

But acknowledgest My justice in all thine appointments and praisest My holy name, then it is that thou walkest in the true and right way of peace and mayest hope, without any doubt, to see My face again with great joy. (*Job* 33:26).

And if thou arrive to an entire contempt of thyself, know then that thou shalt enjoy an abundance of peace, as much as is possible in this state of banishment.

Practical Reflections

We should sacrifice ourselves entirely to the will of God, and meet with equanimity whatever He decrees for us; that is, we should, first, desire nothing which is not the will of God; secondly, we should not refuse any of the adversities He sends us;

thirdly, we should bring ourselves to a state of perfect self-contempt, so as to receive humiliations and contradictions as our due; fourthly, we should remain firm, constant, and faithful to what God desires of us, although we experience neither consolation nor delight nor security; fifthly, we should, in a word, make our delight the delight of God's own heart, that is, we should accomplish His holy will.

Prayer

Yes, O Jesus, in all things I resign myself entirely to Thy dominion, I will confide in Thee, and abandon myself wholly to Thee, persuaded that my salvation can never be more secure than when entrusted to Thee, my Saviour.

Grant, therefore, that I may live under Thine eyes and in Thy hands, in a reverential and continual remembrance of Thy presence, and an exact dependence upon Thy holy will, being assured that Thou wilt promote my salvation in proportion as I endeavor to please and love Thee, and to mortify and hate myself. Amen.

Chapter 26

The Eminence of a Free Mind, which Humble Prayer Produces Better than Reading

DISCIPLE

LORD, this is the work of a perfect man, never to let one's mind slacken from attending to heavenly things and to pass through many cares, as it were without care, not like one torpid, but by a certain prerogative of a free mind, which does not cleave by an inordinate affection to anything created.

2. Preserve me, I beseech Thee, O my most merciful God, from the cares of this life (*Luke* 21:34), that I be not too much entangled by them; from the many necessities of the body, that I may not be ensnared by pleasure, and from all hindrances of the soul, lest being overcome by troubles I be cast down.

I do not say from those things which worldly vanity covets with so much eagerness, but from those miseries, which, by the general curse of our mortality, as punishments weigh down and keep back the soul of Thy servant from being able, when it will, to enter into liberty of spirit.

3. O my God, who art unspeakable sweetness, turn unto bitterness for me all carnal comfort which withdraws me from the love of things eternal, and wickedly allures me to itself, by setting before me a certain present delightful good.

O my God, let not flesh and blood prevail over me (*1 Cor.* 15:50), let it not overcome me; let not the world and its transitory glory deceive me (*1 John* 2:17); let not the devil overreach me by his devices. (*2 Cor.* 2:11).

Give me fortitude that I may stand my ground; patience, that I may endure, and constancy, that I may persevere.

Give me, in lieu of all the comforts of this world, the most delightful unction of Thy spirit, and instead of carnal love, infuse into me the love of Thy name.

4. Behold! eating, drinking, clothing, and other necessaries appertaining to the support of the body, are burdensome to a fervent spirit. (*Wis.* 9:15).

Grant that I may use such things with moderation, and not be entangled with an inordinate affection to them.

It is not lawful to cast them all away, for nature must be supported; but to require superfluities and such things as are most delightful Thy holy law forbids; for otherwise the flesh would grow insolent against the spirit. (*Gal.* 5:17).

In all this I beseech Thee let Thy hand govern and direct me, that I may no way exceed.

Practical Reflections

The mortification of the senses, and the victory over our own humors, are so essential for salvation, that, in truth, the soul which gives itself to exterior objects, and is often more engaged upon itself than upon God, is totally unworthy of Him; because, when it gives itself to its passions, it can have no desire to please God. Ah! how will it change its ideas and sentiments at the hour of death! when alone with God it shall hear from Him this reproach: I have not been thine in time, I will not be thine for eternity! Thou hast preferred the pleasures of sense to the happiness of pleasing Me; it is just thou shouldst now be consigned to all the horrors of a miserable eternity! Thou didst receive good things in thy lifetime, was it said to the rich man when he complained in Hell of the rigor of his torments; and so will it one day be said to those sensual souls who will not now restrain nor mortify themselves in anything, unless they endeavor to prefer the happiness of eternity to the pleasures of time, and to merit Heaven by self-control.

Prayer

Grant me, O God, strength and courage to restrain the desires of my heart, that I may be free to possess Thee; grant that, renouncing all sensual gratifications, I may become pleasing and acceptable to Thee; happy in sacrificing all that can give me pleasure, for the sake of pleasing Thee, and in spending my life in repairing Thy past displeasure by penance, and in preventing it in the future by fidelity. O penance, what charms hast thou for a soul that is penetrated with the love of God, and is resolved to avenge Him, and to punish itself. Amen.

Chapter 27

Self-Love Chiefly Keeps a Person Back from the Sovereign Good

CHRIST

MY SON, thou must give all for all, and be nothing of thine own.

Know that the love of thyself is more hurtful to thee than anything in the world.

Everything, according to the love and inclination which thou hast to it, cleaveth to thee more or less.

If thy love be pure, simple, and well ordered, thou shalt not be a captive to anything. *(Matt.* 6:22).

Covet not that which thou mayest not have.

Seek not to have that which may curb or rob thee of thine inward liberty.

It is wonderful that thou wilt not from the very bottom of thy heart commit thyself wholly to Me with all things that thou canst desire or have.

2. Why dost thou pine away with vain grief? Why dost thou suffer thyself to be overwhelmed with useless cares?

Be resigned to My good pleasure and thou shalt suffer no loss.

If thou seek this or that, or would be here or there, for the sake of thine own interest, or of thine own will, thou shalt never be at rest, nor free from solicitude, for in everything thou wilt find some defect, and in every place there will be someone that will cross thee.

3. It is not, therefore, the obtaining or multiplying things exteriorly that avails thee, but rather the despising of them and cutting them up by the root out of thy heart.

This I would not have thee to understand only with regard to money and riches, but also with regard to the ambition of honor and the desire of empty praise, all which things pass away with the world. (*John* 2:17).

The place avails little if the spirit of fervor be wanting; neither shall that peace stand long which is sought from abroad, if the state of thy heart want the true foundation; that is, if thou stand not in Me, thou mayest change, but not better thyself.

For when occasion happens, thou shalt find that which thou didst fly from and even more.

A Prayer to Cleanse the Heart and Obtain Heavenly Wisdom

DISCIPLE

4. Confirm me, O God, by the grace of Thy Holy Spirit. Give me power to be strengthened in the inward man and to cast out of my heart all unprofitable care and trouble; let me not be drawn away with various desires of anything whatsoever, whether it be of little or great value; but teach me to look upon all things as passing away and

myself as passing along with them.

For nothing is lasting under the sun, where all is vanity and affliction of spirit. *(Eccles.* 2:11). Oh, how wise is he who considers things in this manner!

5. Give me, O Lord, heavenly wisdom that I may learn above all things to seek Thee and to find Thee *(Wis.* 9:10); above all things to relish Thee, and to love Thee, and to understand all other things as they are, according to the order of Thy wisdom.

Grant that I may prudently decline him that flatters me and patiently bear with him that contradicts me.

For it is great wisdom not to be moved with every wind of words, nor to give ear to the wicked, flattering siren; for thus shall we go on securely in the way we have begun.

Practical Reflections

If we would give ourselves unreservedly to God, we must, first, seek ourselves in nothing we present to Him; secondly, we must yield ourselves to Him on all occasions, and prefer His will to the suggestions of self-love; thirdly, we must not allow nor forgive ourselves anything we know to be displeasing to Him; fourthly, we must make Him the absolute master and proprietor of our whole hearts, so that He may dispose of all that we have and are according to His holy will; fifthly, we must live in a state of dependence and constant docility to the motions of His grace.

To give ourselves thus to God without reserve is the true means of possessing Him and living in peace. But, alas! how few give themselves thus to Him! and how many are His only by halves, divide their hearts between Him and creatures, and love themselves while they pretend to love Him, although they are well aware that all division is injurious to Him, and hinders Him from reigning absolutely in their hearts, of which He cannot be the master if He be not the sole possessor; nor reign as God within them, if He reign not alone and be preferred before all things else.

Prayer

Suffer not my heart, O Lord, which was made only for Thee, which is entirely the work of Thy hands, and the price of Thy Blood, to belong to any other but Thee, or to love anything equally or in preference to Thee. Thy delight is to be with the children of men, and why is not Thy presence my felicity? Why art Thou not more to me than all things else, Thou Who art my only and sovereign good? I am resolved henceforth absolutely to love Thee alone. I will be all Thine, seek to please Thee in all things, and breathe only Thy love. Amen.

Chapter 28

Against the Tongues of Detractors

CHRIST

SON, take it not to heart if some people think ill of thee, and say of thee what thou art not willing to hear.

Thou oughtest to think worse of thyself and to believe that no one is weaker than thyself.

If thou walk interiorly thou wilt make small account of flying words.

It is no small prudence to be silent in the evil time, and to turn within to Me, and not to be disturbed with the judgment of men.

2. Let not thy peace be in the tongues of men, for whether they put a good or bad construction on what thou

dost, thou art not for all that other than thou art. Where is true peace and true glory? Is it not in Me?

And he who covets not to please men, nor fears their displeasure, shall enjoy much peace. (*Col.* 3:22).

All disquiet of heart and distraction of the senses arise from inordinate love and vain fear.

Practical Reflections

Nothing is so apt to give us uneasiness and trouble as the judgments and observations of others concerning us. We consider it a happiness to please men, and a misfortune to meet with their contempt: and yet what is the esteem or the frown of the world but a shadow, a smoke, a vapor which passes away, and adds nothing to what we really are or ought to be? Whatever we are in the eyes of God, so much are we and no more, and therefore we should make no account of the favorable or mean opinions of others.

O human respect! when wilt thou give place to the reverence which we owe to God? Alas! how do human considerations destroy in us all that is pleasing to Him! Instead of inquiring what will be most pleasing to Jesus Christ, we think only of what others will say of us. But is it not better to obey God rather than men, to please Him rather than to please the world? Why then do we not endeavor to do so?

Prayer

Suffer not, O Lord, human respect ever to take place of the reverence which I owe to Thee; but grant that a respectful and predominant sense of Thy presence and of Thy will may induce me to perform all my actions, to quit and to suffer all things, for Thy love. O my Saviour and my Judge, unite my heart to Thyself by a dread of displeasing Thee, and a desire of being always agreeable in Thy sight. Grant that, dying incessantly to myself, I may live only to Thee, and by often renewing my intention of pleasing Thee, succeed in gaining Thy love. Grant that I may so accustom myself to love Thee during life that the last motion of my heart may be a fervent act of my love for Thee. Amen.

Chapter 29

How God is to be Invoked and Blessed in the Time of Tribulation

DISCIPLE

B LESSED, O Lord, be Thy name forever, who hast been pleased that this trial and tribulation should come upon me. (*Dan.* 3:26).

I cannot fly from it, but must of necessity fly to Thee that Thou mayest help me, and turn it to my good.

Lord, I am now in tribulation, and my heart is not at ease; but I am much afflicted with my present suffering.

And now, dear Father, what shall I say? I am taken, O Lord, in these straits: O save me from this hour. (*John* 12:27).

But for this reason I came unto this hour, that Thou mightest be glorified when I shall be exceedingly humbled and delivered by Thee.

May it please Thee, O Lord, to deliver me; for, poor wretch that I am, what can I do and whither shall I go without Thee? (*Ps.* 108:21).

Give me patience, O Lord, at this time also.

Help me, O my God, and I will not fear how much soever I may be oppressed.

2. And now, in the midst of these things, what shall I say? Lord, Thy will be done (*Matt.* 6:10), I have well deserved to be afflicted and troubled.

I must needs bear it, and would to God it may be with patience, till the storm pass over and it be better.

But Thine almighty hand is able to take away from me this temptation also, and to moderate its violence, lest I quite sink under it, as Thou hast often done heretofore for me, O my God, my mercy! (*Ps.* 58:18).

And the more difficult this is to me, the easier to Thee is this change of the right hand of the Most High. (*Ps.* 76:11).

Practical Reflections

Temptations must ever be resisted with firmness and constancy; and, that we may be able to overcome them, we must go with confidence to the throne of God. He often permits us to be so hard pressed, and so weighed down by the load of our miseries, as to leave us no other means of making resistance and maintaining our ground, but that of keeping ourselves closely united to Him, and relying upon Him for the assistance of His grace. The fewer resources we find within ourselves, the more should we be induced to seek for them in God, and when temptation has nearly overcome us, and we are in danger of yielding, cry out with the Apostles: Lord, save us, or we perish; our eyes are raised up to Thee, Who art our Father and our God, able and willing to assist us, our Saviour and Redeemer, engaged to rescue and to save us. The more I experience my own weakness and inability, the more do I hope for strength from Thee. It is Thy glory and Thy delight to defend me, for my soul is the work of Thy hands, and the price of Thy Precious Blood.

Prayer

We are sensible, O Lord, that without Thee, of ourselves, in the time of temptation we should lose courage, yield to sin, and be vanquished; but we know also that Thou canst do all things, and art willing to assist and to save us. Penetrated with a sense of our own miseries, yet full of confidence in Thy mercy, we place ourselves in Thy hands, repose all our hopes in Thee, trust in Thy bounty, renounce whatever is displeasing to Thee, and desire only the accomplishment of Thy will. Grant us the grace of living and dying in those holy dispositions; and may they ever induce Thee to show us Thy mercy. Amen.

Chapter 30

Of Asking the Divine Assistance, and of Confidence of Recovering Grace

CHRIST

SON, I am the Lord, who give strength in the day of trouble. (*Nahum* 1:7).

Come to Me when it is not well with thee.

This is that which most of all hinders heavenly comfort, that thou art slow in turning thyself to prayer.

For before thou earnestly prayest to Me thou seekest in the meantime many comforts and delightest thyself in outward things.

And hence it comes to pass that all things avail thee little till thou take notice that I am He that delivers those that trust in Me. Nor is there out of Me any powerful help, or profitable counsel, or lasting remedy.

But now having recovered spirit after the storm, grow thou strong again in the light of My tender mercies; for I am at hand to repair all, not only to the full, but even with abundance and above measure.

2. Is anything difficult to Me? or shall I be like one that promises and does not perform? (*Jer.* 32:27; *Num.* 23:19).

Where is thy faith? Stand firmly and with perseverance.

Have patience and be of good courage, comfort will come to thee in its proper season.

Wait for Me, wait, I will come and cure thee.

It is a temptation that troubles thee, and a vain fear that frightens thee.

What does that solicitude about future accidents bring thee but only sorrow upon sorrow? "Sufficient for the day is the evil thereof." (*Matt.* 6:34).

It is a vain and unprofitable thing to conceive either grief or joy for future things, which perhaps will never happen.

3. But it is incident to man to be deluded with such imaginations; and a sign of a soul that is yet weak and to be easily drawn away by the suggestions of the enemy.

For he cares not whether it be with things true or false that he abuses and deceives thee, whether he overthrow thee with the love of things present or the fear of things to come.

"Let not, therefore, thy heart be troubled and let it not be afraid." (*John* 14:27).

Believe in Me and trust in My mercy. When thou thinkest I am far from thee, I am often nearest to thee.

When thou judgest that almost all is lost, then oftentimes

it is that thou art in the way of gaining the greatest merit.

All is not lost when anything falls out otherwise than thou wouldst have it.

Thou must not judge according to thy present feeling, nor give thyself up in such manner to any trouble, from whence soever it comes, nor take it so as if all hope were gone of being delivered out of it.

4. Think not thyself wholly forsaken, although for a time I have sent thee some tribulation, or withdrawn from thee the comfort which thou desirest; for this is the way to the Kingdom of Heaven.

And without doubt it is more expedient for thee, and for the rest of My servants, that thou be exercised by adversities than that thou shouldst have all things according to thine inclination.

I know thy secret thoughts; I know that it is very expedient for thy soul that thou shouldst sometimes be left without consolation, lest thou shouldst be puffed up with much success and shouldst take a complacence in thyself, imagining thyself to be what thou art not.

What I have given I can justly take away, and restore it again when I please.

5. When I give it, it is still Mine; when I take it away again I take not anything that is thine; for every good gift and every perfect gift is Mine. (*James* 1:17).

If I send thee affliction or any adversity, repine not, neither let thy heart be cast down.

I can quickly raise thee up again and turn all thy burden into joy.

Nevertheless, I am just and greatly to be praised when

I deal thus with thee.

6. If thou think rightly and consider things in truth thou oughtst never to be so much dejected and troubled for any adversity, but rather to rejoice and give thanks.

Yea, even to account this as a special subject of joy, that afflicting thee with sorrows I spare thee not. (*Job* 6:10).

"As my Father hath loved me I also have loved you," said I to My beloved disciples (*John* 15:9), whom certainly I did not send to temporal joys, but to great conflicts; not to honors, but to contempt; not to idleness, but to labors; not to rest, but to "bring forth much fruit in patience." (*Luke* 8:13). Remember these words, O My son.

Practical Reflections

I am the Lord, saith the Almighty, by the mouth of one of His prophets, who give strength to souls in the day of trouble, and deliver those from danger who put their trust in Me. How consoling, how encouraging and supporting, are these words to a soul that, in the time of temptation and adversity, is faithful and constant to what God requires of it! This is what the Scripture calls to wait for and to support the Lord.

Believe in Me, says our blessed Saviour, and thy heart shall not be troubled nor fear. Wherefore, upon occasion of interior or exterior affliction, we should, in the first place, have recourse to God with confidence; secondly, we should resign ourselves to His blessed will; thirdly, we should not neglect any of our spiritual exercises; fourthly, we should subdue ourselves, restrain and renounce ourselves in all things, that we may act in concert with God; fifthly, we should consider it our welfare and our merit to be afflicted, tormented, and, as it were, annihilated for the honor of God's majesty; sixthly, we should be content to carry a crucified heart, a heart suffering and penetrated with bitterness and sorrow, in imitation of our crucified Jesus.

Prayer

No, Lord, I will not give up all as lost when Thou seemest to withdraw Thyself from me; but, on the contrary, I will believe all gained when my soul, though sinking under fatigue, and withered with bitterness, shall resign itself to Thy holy will, and live only in Thee, saying with the Prophet, I commit to Thee all my strength, for my soul is in Thy hands, and Thy mercy supports and encourages my heart to profit by the sense of my miseries. Abandon me not, O God, to the disorder of my passions, but be Thou their master by Thy grace, and keep me always in the possession of Thy love. Amen.

Chapter 31

Of Disregarding All Things Created, That We May Find the Creator

Disciple

L ORD, I stand much in need of a grace yet greater, if I must arrive so far, that it may not be in the power of any man, nor anything created, to hinder me.

For as long as anything holds me I cannot freely fly to Thee.

He was desirous to fly freely to Thee who said: "Who will give me wings like a dove, and I will fly and be at rest." (*Ps.* 54:7).

What can be more at rest than a simple eye that aims at nothing but God? And what can be more free than he who desires nothing upon earth?

A man ought, therefore, to pass and ascend above everything created, and perfectly to forsake himself, and in ecstasy of mind to stand and see that Thou, the Creator of all, infinitely transcendest all creatures.

And unless a man be at liberty from all things created, he cannot freely attend to things divine.

And this is the reason why there are found so few contemplative persons, because there are few that wholly wean themselves from transitory and created things.

2. For this a great grace is required, which may elevate the soul and carry her up above herself.

And unless a man be elevated in spirit, and set at liberty from all creatures, and wholly united to God, whatever he knows, and whatever he has, is of no great weight.

Long shall he be little and lie grovelling beneath, who esteems anything great but only the one immense, eternal good.

And whatsoever is not God is nothing, and ought to be accounted as nothing.

There is a great difference between the wisdom of an illuminated and devout man and the knowledge of a learned and studious scholar.

Far more noble is that learning which flows from above, from the divine influence, than that which with labor is acquired by the industry of man.

3. Many are found to desire contemplation, but they care not to practice those things which are required thereunto.

It is a great impediment that we so much regard signs and sensible things, and have but little of perfect mortification.

I know not what it is, by what spirit we are led, or what we pretend to, who seem to be called spiritual persons, that we take so much pains, and have a greater solicitude for transitory and mean things, and scarce ever have our senses fully recollected to think of our own interior.

4. Alas! after a slight recollection we presently wander out of ourselves again, neither do we weigh well our works by a strict examination.

We take no notice where our affections lie, nor do we lament the great want of purity in all we do.

For all flesh had corrupted its way *(Gen.* 6:12), and therefore the great flood ensued.

As, therefore, our interior affection is much corrupted it must needs be that the action which follows should also be corrupted, which is the testimony of the want of inward vigor.

From a pure heart proceeds the fruit of a good life. (*1 Tim.* 1:3).

5. We are apt to inquire how much a man has done, but with how much virtue he has done it is not so diligently considered.

We ask whether he be strong, rich, beautiful, talented, a good writer, a good singer, or a good workman; but how poor he is in spirit, how patient and meek, how devout and internal, is what few speak of.

Nature looks upon the outward things of a man, but grace turns herself to the interior.

Nature is often deceived, but grace hath her trust in God that she may not be deceived.

Practical Reflections

Nothing is worthy of a Christian's affections but what is eternal; he should never love anything but what he may love forever. Wherefore let us endeavor, in the first place, to prefer the will of God to all other satisfactions; secondly, to seek in all things to please Him; thirdly, to receive, as coming from His hands, with humble submission, whatever He is pleased to send us; fourthly, to recollect ourselves frequently in His presence, and depend upon Him in all things.

Why should we be busied about trifles, with vain reflections about ourselves, and disquieted about others, while God is residing within us, and expecting from us the homage of our hearts, and the dedication of our whole selves to Him? We know how dangerous it is to neglect the grace of God, and yet we make small account of the losses we sustain by yielding to a spirit of dissipation, paying but little attention to what God requires of us.

Prayer

O my God and my All! O amiable and most loving God! how little attention do I pay to Thy presence, how unfaithful am I to Thy grace, and how little courage do I evince for the sacrifice of all satisfaction to Thee! And yet Thou art the God of my heart, and, as I hope, my portion forever. To become worthy of this happiness I desire to keep my mind constantly fixed on Thee, to sacrifice to Thy love everything which may divert me from Thee, and neither to say nor to do anything but in order to gain Heaven.

Grant, O Lord, that I may avoid whatever is offensive to Thee, and love and practice that only which is well pleasing in Thy sight; and that, frequently recollecting myself in Thee, I may apply my whole self to Thy presence, and do Thy holy will in all things. Amen.

Chapter 32

Denying Ourselves and Renouncing All Cupidity

CHRIST

SON, thou canst not possess perfect liberty unless thou wholly deny thyself. (*Matt.* 16:24).

All self-seekers and self-lovers are bound in fetters full of desires, full of cares, unsettled, and seeking always their own ease, and not the things of Jesus Christ (*Phil.* 3:21), but oftentimes devising and framing that which will not stand.

For all shall come to nothing that proceeds not from God.

Take this short and perfect word: Forsake all and thou shalt find all, leave thy desires and thou shalt find rest. (*Matt.* 11:29).

Consider this well, and when thou shalt put it in practice thou shalt understand all things.

DISCIPLE

2. Lord, this is no one day's work, no child's play; yea, in this short sentence is included the whole perfection of a religious man.

CHRIST

3. Son, thou must not be turned back, nor presently cast down, when thou hearest what the way of the perfect is: but rather be incited thereby to undertake great things,

or at least to sigh after them with an earnest desire.

I would it were so with thee, and that thou wert come so far that thou wert no longer a lover of thyself, but didst stand wholly at My beck, and at his whom I have appointed father over thee; then wouldst thou exceedingly please Me, and all thy life would pass in joy and peace.

Thou hast yet many things to forsake, which, unless thou give up to Me without reserve, thou wilt not attain to that which thou demandest.

I counsel thee to buy of Me gold firetried, that thou mayest be made rich (*Apoc.* 3:18); that is, heavenly wisdom, which treads underfoot all things below.

Set aside the wisdom of the earth, that is, all seeking to please the world and thyself.

4. I have said that thou shouldst give the things that are high and of great esteem with men to purchase those which are esteemed contemptible.

For true heavenly wisdom seems very mean and contemptible, and is scarcely thought of by men; that wisdom, which teaches to think meanly of one's self, and not to seek to become great upon earth; which many praise in words, but in their life are far from it; yet this same is that precious pearl (*Matt.* 13:46), which is hidden from many.

Practical Reflections

What is it to quit all things? It is, first, to renounce and to die to ourselves; secondly, to mortify the senses, the mind, and the heart; thirdly, to detach ourselves from everything that affords us pleasure, and to receive with willingness and submission whatever gives us pain; fourthly, to love our friends in God, our enemies for God, and to hate only ourselves; fifthly, to attach ourselves only to God, to our duties, and to our salvation; sixthly, to direct all the energies of our hearts towards God and against ourselves; seventhly, to desire nothing but to please Him, and to fear nothing but to offend Him; eighthly, to make it our happiness and our merit to gain the light of His countenance, and to become worthy of His love.

How easy to say, I desire to quit all and to belong entirely to God! But how difficult to perform, unless we withdraw ourselves with fixed determination from everything which does not lead us to Him! A small degree of divine love makes this dedication and sacrifice of ourselves to God possible and easy. We should constantly desire it, ask for it, and practice it.

Prayer

Suffer not my heart, O Lord, which was created to love and to possess Thee, to be attached to creatures or to itself, preferably to Thee. Thou alone canst satisfy it and make it happy; to Thee, therefore, should it solely and constantly adhere. O my God, I can indeed sin without Thee, but I cannot rise again without Thee, nor withdraw myself from anything that would seduce my mind and corrupt my unsteady heart. Succor, support, and strengthen me in the combats which I am obliged to sustain with myself in my endeavors to renounce all, that in all I may seek and find Thee. How it distresses me to behold myself the slave of my passions, and the victim of my wayward humors! Break asunder my chains, O Lord, and grant that, detaching myself from all things else, I may adhere only to Thee. Amen.

Chapter 33

The Inconstancy of Our Hearts, and of Directing Our Final Intentions to God

CHRIST

SON, trust not to thy present affection, it will quickly be changed into another.

As long as thou livest thou art subject to change, even against thy will; so as to be sometimes joyful, at other times sad; now easy, again troubled; at one time devout, at another dry; sometimes fervent, at other times sluggish; one day heavy, another lighter.

But he that is wise and well instructed in spirit, stands above all these changes; not minding what he feels in himself, nor on what side the wind of mutability blows; but that the whole bent of his soul may advance towards his due and wished-for end.

For so he may continue one and the selfsame, without being shaken, by directing without ceasing, through all this variety of events, the single eye of his intention towards Me. (*Matt.* 6:22).

2. And by how much purer the eye of the intention is, with so much greater constancy mayest thou pass through these divers storms.

But in many the eye of pure intention is dark, for men quickly look towards something delightful which comes in their way.

And it is rare to find one wholly free from all blemish of self-seeking.

So the Jews heretofore came into Bethania, to Martha and Mary, not for Jesus only, but that they might see Lazarus also. (*John* 12:9).

The eye of the intention therefore must be purified that it may be single and right, and must be directed unto Me, beyond all the various objects that interpose themselves.

Practical Reflections

In order to fix the instability of our hearts in what regards the service of God, and the care of our salvation, we should, first, mistrust ourselves and confide in God; secondly, we should have recourse to Him and implore His assistance on all occasions; thirdly, we should often renew our intention of pleasing Him, without wishing to please ourselves; fourthly, we should fight without ceasing against our natural repugnances; fifthly, we should desire only what God wills, and endeavor to execute it; sixthly, we should habituate our hearts to love God, and, as it were, contract those holy bonds by which He desires to be united with us forever; and, seventhly, we should punctually attend to the inspirations and motions of His grace.

Prayer

When shall Thy grace, O God, inspire me with some degree of that firmness and faithful adherence to Thee which Thy glory imparts to the blessed? Suffer not my heart to be overcome by that inconstancy which is so natural to it, nor my life to be a perpetual succession of good desires and evil practices, of promises, and infidelities. Not to love Thee at all times is to love Thee not as God; Thy reign over our hearts, to be worthy of Thee, should be constant and invariable.

Grant then, O God, that my soul may be all Thine, at all times, and forever; and that, by my perpetual fidelity, I may merit eternal happiness. Amen.

Chapter 34

He Who Loves God Relishes Him Above All Things, and in All Things

DISCIPLE

BEHOLD, "my God, and my all!" What would I have more and what can I desire more happy.

O sweet and savory word! but to him that loves the word, not the world, nor the things that are in the world. (*1 John* 2:15).

My God and my All! Enough is said to him that understands; and it is delightful to him that loves to repeat it often.

For when Thou art present all things yield delight; but when Thou art absent all things are loathsome.

Thou givest tranquillity to the heart, and great peace and pleasant joy.

Thou makest us to think well of all and praise Thee in all things; nor can anything without Thee afford any lasting pleasure; but to make it agreeable and relishing, Thy grace must be present, and it must be seasoned with the seasoning of Thy wisdom.

2. What can be distasteful to him who has no satisfaction but in Thee? and what can yield any true delight to him who relishes not Thee?

But the wise of this world and the admirers of the flesh

are mistaken in their wisdom; because in the world is much vanity, and following the flesh leads to death. (*Rom.* 8:6).

But they that follow Thee by despising the things of this world, and mortifying the flesh, are found to be wise indeed, for they are translated from vanity to truth, from the flesh to the spirit.

Such as these have a relish of God, and what good soever is found in creatures they refer to the praise of their Maker.

But great, yea very great, is the difference between the relish of the Creator and the creature, of eternity and of time, of light uncreated and of light enlightened.

3. O Light eternal! transcending all created lights, dart forth Thy light from above, which may penetrate the most inward parts of my heart.

Cleanse, gladden, enlighten, and quicken my spirit with its powers, that I may be absorbed in Thee with ecstasies of joy.

Oh, when will this blessed and desirable hour come when Thou shalt fill me with Thy presence and become to me all in all. (*1 Cor.* 15:28).

As long as this is not granted to me my joy will not be full.

Alas! the old man is still living in me; he is not wholly crucified; he is not perfectly dead. (*Rom.* 6:6).

He still lusts strongly against the spirit; he wages war within me, and suffers not the kingdom of my soul to be quiet. (*Gal.* 5:17).

4. But, O Lord, who "rulest the power of the sea and appeasest the motion of the waves thereof" (*Ps.* 88:10), "arise and help me." (*Ps.* 43:26).

"Scatter thou the nations that delight in wars." (*Ps.* 67:31).

Crush them by Thy power.

Show forth, I beseech Thee, Thy wonderful works (*Ecclus.* 17:7), and let Thy right hand be glorified (*Ps.* 88:14); for there is no hope nor refuge for me but in Thee, O Lord, my God.

Practical Reflections

To love God alone, to love Him above all things, is to delight only in Him, to seek only Him, and to renounce everything which by nature is pleasing to us, according to that of the royal Prophet: My soul refused to be comforted: I remembered God, and was delighted, and was exercised, and my spirit swooned away. (*Ps.* 67).

Wherefore, if we would love only God, let us mortify the senses, captivate the mind, restrain the heart, subdue the flesh, and refuse ourselves numberless gratifications, in order to please God. Happy the soul that is willing to live a crucified life with Jesus upon the Cross, that so it may be able to say with the Apostle, Jesus Christ is my life, and it is my gain to die to all, that I may live for Him alone.

Prayer

How sweet, O Lord, to breathe only Thy love, and to say to Thee with my whole heart, "My God and my All! my Lord and my God!" Grant that these words may enter into my soul; do Thou impress them upon my mind and in my heart; grant me to understand and to practice them. O great God, Thou art, and this doth satisfy me, because I love Thee more for Thyself than for my own sake.

But, O God! Thou art my Saviour: all that Thou art in this respect, Thou art for me, and this redoubles my confidence and love for Thee. O my God! how can I live without Thee?

How can I not live for Thee? O my Lord! reign absolutely over me. O my God! may my whole self be Thine, and may I live only for Thee! My Lord and my God! mayest Thou be so in time, that Thou mayest be my portion for all eternity. Amen.

Chapter 35

There Is No Security from Temptation in This Life

CHRIST

SON, thou art never secure in this life; but as long as thou livest thou hast always need of spiritual arms.

Thou art in the midst of enemies, and art assaulted on the right hand and on the left.

If then thou dost not make use of the buckler of patience on all sides thou wilt not be long without a wound.

Moreover, if thou dost not fix thy heart on Me with a sincere will of suffering all things for My sake thou canst not support the heat of this warfare, nor attain to the victory of the saints.

It behooveth thee, therefore, to go through all manfully, and to use a strong hand against all things that oppose thee.

For to him that overcometh is given manna *(Apoc.* 2:17), and to the sluggard is left much misery.

2. If thou seek rest in this life how then wilt thou come to rest everlasting?

Set not thyself to seek for much rest, but for much patience.

Seek true peace, not upon earth, but in Heaven; not

in men, nor in other things created, but in God alone. (*John* 14:27).

Thou must be willing, for the love of God, to suffer all things, to wit: labors and sorrows, temptations and vexations, anxieties, necessities, sickness, injuries, detractions, reprehensions, humiliations, confusions, corrections, and contempts. (*James* 1:2).

These things help to obtain virtue; these try a novice of Christ; these procure a heavenly crown.

I will give an everlasting reward for this short labor, and glory without end for transitory confusion.

Dost thou think to have always spiritual consolations when thou pleasest?

My saints had not these always; but met with many troubles, and various temptations and great desolations.

But they bore all with patience, and confided more in God than in themselves; knowing that the sufferings of this life bear no proportion to the greatness of the glory to come. (*Rom.* 8:18).

Wouldst thou have that immediately which others after many tears and great labors have hardly obtained.

"Expect the Lord, do manfully and let thy heart take courage" (*Ps.* 26:14); do not despond, do not fall off, but constantly offer both soul and body for the glory of God.

I will reward thee most abundantly, and will be with thee in all thy tribulation. (*Ps.* 91:15).

Practical Reflections

Prepare thy soul for temptation, says the Wise Man; that is, first, let not thy happiness consist in being free from sufferings, but in bearing them patiently; secondly, expose not thyself voluntarily to temptation, nor to the occasions of sin; but if thou shouldst be attacked by the one or engaged in the other, resist, fight, fly, and have recourse to God with all confidence; thirdly, watch, pray, humble thyself before God, and be penetrated with a reverential fear in His presence, a holy diffidence in thyself, and a firm confidence in Him who will support thee against all the attacks of thy spiritual enemies.

A truly Christian soul should dwell upon Calvary, in the wounds of Jesus, and there suffer with patience, fortitude, and fidelity, whatever He is pleased to appoint. For to be true Christians, and to fulfill the duties of our state, we must be ever resolved to suffer and to die for God; since, as St. Cyprian remarks, Christians are the heirs of a crucified Jesus.

Prayer

Thou knowest, O God, that nothing is so contrary to our natural inclinations as to suffer and to die; but, to accomplish this, Thou canst and wilt assist us. Give us, therefore, courage to conquer our unwillingness to suffer ills and contradictions, and our repugnance to the discharge of our duties; and grant that neither the delight of pleasure, nor the fear of pain, may ever induce us to become wanting in fidelity or submission to Thee. Amen.

Chapter 36

Against the Vain Judgments of Men

CHRIST

SON, cast thy heart firmly on the Lord, and fear not the judgment of man when thy conscience gives testimony of thy piety and innocence.

It is good and happy to suffer in this manner, neither will this be grievous to an humble heart, nor to him that trusts in God more than in himself.

Many say many things, and therefore little credit is to be given to them.

Neither is it possible to satisfy all.

Though Paul endeavored to please all in the Lord and made himself all unto all (*1 Cor.* 9:22), yet he made little account of his being judged by the judgment of men. (*1 Cor.* 4:3).

2. He labored for the edification and salvation of others as much as he could and as lay in him, but he could not prevent his being sometimes judged or despised by others.

Therefore he committed all to God, who knows all, and defended himself, by patience and humility, against the tongues of those that spoke evil, or that thought and gave out at pleasure vain and faulty things of him.

However, he answered them sometimes, lest his silence might give occasion of scandal to the weak.

3. "Who art thou, that thou shouldst be afraid of a mortal man?" (*Is.* 51:12). Today he is, and tomorrow he appears no more. (*1 Mach.* 2:63).

Fear God, and thou shalt have no need of being afraid of man.

What can anyone do against thee by his words or injuries? He rather hurts himself than thee, nor can he escape the judgment of God whoever he be. (*2 Mach.* 7:35).

See thou have God before thine eyes and do not contend with complaining words. (*2 Tim.* 2:14).

And if at present thou seem to be overcome, and to suffer a confusion which thou hast not deserved, do not repine at this and do not lessen thy crown by impatience.

Rather look up to Me in Heaven, who am able to deliver thee from all confusion and wrong, and to repay everyone according to his works. (*Matt.* 16:27).

Practical Reflections

A Christian, when assailed by the shafts of calumny, should, in reality, regard these trials in a favorable point of view, because they subject him to the happy necessity of flying to God, and of appealing to Him as the secret witness of his conscience. Although we are fully convinced that, in reality, the esteem or contempt of men, their good or bad opinion respecting us, can neither make us more happy nor more miserable, yet do we strive to obtain their approbation. Why do we not rather endeavor to establish ourselves in the favor of God, who will decide our eternal doom?

Prayer

O Lord, Who didst sacrifice Thy life by a cruel and disgraceful death, and didst give Thy heart to perpetual sorrow and bitterness for my sake, can I refuse to sacrifice to Thee the sensibilities of my heart, when troubled on account of the remarks and disadvantageous judgments of others concerning me? Grant, O divine Jesus, that at the sight of the outrages Thou didst endure for me, my heart may reproach itself for suffering so little, and that so unwillingly, for Thee. And, since the wounds which are inflicted upon the reputation of our neighbor fall always, either in this life or in the next, upon him who does the injury, for Thy glory, and not for mine, deliver my enemies from their blindness, forgive their malice, and inflame them with the fire of Thy charity. Amen.

Chapter 37

Of a Pure and Full Resignation of Ourselves for Obtaining Freedom of Heart

CHRIST

SON, leave thyself and thou shalt find Me. Stand without choice or any self-seeking, and thou shalt always gain.

For greater grace shall always be added to thee, when thou hast perfectly given up thyself, without resuming thyself again.

DISCIPLE

2. Lord, how often shall I resign myself and in what things shall I leave myself?

CHRIST

3. Always and at all times, as in little, so also in great: I make no exception, but will have thee to be found in all things divested of thyself.

Otherwise how canst thou be Mine and I thine, unless thou be both within and without freed from all self-will?

The sooner thou effectest this the better will it be for thee; and the more fully and sincerely thou dost it the more wilt thou please Me and the more shalt thou gain.

4. Some there are that resign themselves, but it is with some exception, for they do not trust wholly to God, and, therefore, are busy to provide for themselves.

Some also, at the first, offer all; but afterward, being assaulted by temptation, return again to what they left, and, therefore, they make no progress in virtue.

These shall not attain to the true liberty of a pure heart, nor to the grace of a delightful familiarity with Me, unless they first entirely resign themselves and offer themselves a daily sacrifice to Me; for without this, divine union neither is nor will be obtained.

5. I have often said to thee and I repeat it again, forsake thyself, resign thyself, and thou shalt enjoy a great inward peace. (*Matt.* 16:24).

Give all for all; seek nothing, call for nothing back; stand purely and with a full confidence in Me, and thou shalt possess Me.

Thou shalt be at liberty within thine own heart, and darkness shall not overwhelm thee.

Aim only at this, pray for this, desire this, that thou mayest be divested of all self-seeking; and, thus naked, follow thy naked Jesus; that thou mayest die to thyself and live eternally to Me.

Then shall vanish all vain imaginations, all evil disturbances and superfluous cares.

Then also immoderate fear shall leave thee and inordinate love shall die.

Practical Reflections

What is it to quit, to renounce, to abandon ourselves entirely to God, without any reserve? It is, first, to act only from the influence of His grace, and an actual desire to please Him, a desire which should be kept up and oftentimes renewed; secondly, it is to yield to Him on all occasions, and to prefer His pleasure to our own; thirdly, it is to renounce our own will in all things and to follow only the will of God; fourthly, it is to make our pleasure consist in pleasing Him, and to have no other interest than His glory; fifthly, to be docile to the inspirations of the Holy Spirit, and the impressions of His love. But alas! who is there that lives after this manner? Who is there that thus renounces himself and abandons himself unreservedly to God? We renounce ourselves on some occasions, and on others we adhere to self-love; we quit ourselves for a time, and then again we seek ourselves. The Spirit of the Lord, says the royal Prophet, only passes by certain souls, but does not stay; and when He returns He knoweth His place no more; He finds them given more to themselves than to their God.

Prayer

How am I wearied, O Lord, with being so much given to myself, and so little devoted to Thee; with seeking myself so often and Thee so seldom! Alas! it is because I am vehemently alive to self, and but very little sensible to Thee. O my God! take Thou place of self within me, and make Thy love reign in place of my self-love. When shall I become free and disengaged from myself, and seek only to love and to please Thee? Give me, in this respect, what Thou commandest, and command what Thou pleasest. I desire that from this moment Thou mayest be the God of my heart, that Thou mayest be my portion forever. Amen.

Chapter 38

The Good Government of Ourselves In Outward Things, and of Having Recourse to God in Dangers

CHRIST

SON, thou must diligently make it thine aim, that in every place and in every action, or outward employment, thou be inwardly free and master of thyself, and that all things be under thee and not thou under them.

That thou mayest be lord and ruler of thine actions, not a slave or bondsman.

But rather a freeman and a true Hebrew, transferred to the lot and to the liberty of the children of God. (*Rom.* 8:21).

Who stand above the things present and contemplate those that are eternal.

Who look upon transitory things with the left eye, and with the right the things of Heaven.

Who suffer not themselves to be drawn away by temporal things to cleave to them, but rather draw these things to that end for which they were ordained by God and appointed by that sovereign artist, who has left nothing in all His works but what is regular and orderly.

2. If likewise, in all events, thou rule not thyself by the outward appearance, nor look on what thou seest or hearest

with a carnal eye, but presently, on every occasion, dost enter, like Moses, into the tabernacle, to consult the Lord, thou shalt sometimes hear the divine answer and come out instructed in many things, present and to come.

For Moses always had recourse to the tabernacle, for the deciding of all doubts and questions, and fled to the help of prayer against the dangers and wickedness of men.

So must thou in like manner fly to the closet of thy heart, and there most earnestly implore the divine assistance. (*Matt.* 6:6).

For Josue, and the children of Israel, as we read, were therefore deceived by the Gabaonites because they did not first consult the Lord, but too easily giving credit to fair words were deluded with counterfeit piety. (*Jos.* 9:15).

Practical Reflections

Exterior occupations oftentimes withdraw the soul from within, and hinder it from being recollected, and from keeping itself in the presence of God, particularly when we give ourselves wholly to them, and reserve not for God the freedom of our hearts. But when we only lend ourselves to exterior employments, and give ourselves, while performing them, to the accomplishment of the will of God, who requires them of us, then we do not become dissipated, but in the diversity of our employments we do the one thing, which is to seek to please God. The desire to please God should include every other desire, and constitute our peace and happiness. No exterior actions can distract that soul which reduces all to unity, that is, which seeks only to please God and finds it all in Him.

Prayer

I am well aware, my God, that the peace of the soul in this life is not what it will be in the next; for in eternity we shall enjoy the certainty of pleasing Thee, and of possessing Thy love; but in time, we can be certain of neither. Ah! how hard and painful is this uncertainty to a soul that loves Thee, O God, and loves but Thee alone! If Thou wilt not assure me that I love Thee, grant at least that I may live as though I were sure I did love Thee, that thus Thou mayest have all the satisfaction of my love, and I all the merit of it. Amen.

Chapter 39

A Man Must Not Be Over-Eager in His Affairs

CHRIST

SON, always commit thy cause to Me; I will dispose well of it in due season.

Wait for My disposal and thou shalt find it will be for thine advantage.

DISCIPLE

2. Lord, I willingly commit all things to Thee; for my care can profit little.

Would that I were not too much set upon future events, but offered myself with all readiness to Thy divine pleasure.

CHRIST

3. My son, oftentimes a man eagerly sets about a thing which he desires; but when he has obtained it he begins to be of another mind. For men's inclinations are not wont to continue long upon the same thing, but rather pass from one thing to another.

It is therefore a thing of no little importance to forsake thyself even in the least things.

4. A man's true progress consists in denying himself, and the man who has renounced himself is much at liberty and very safe.

But the old enemy, who opposes all that is good, fails not to tempt; but day and night lays his dangerous plots to draw the unwary into his deceitful snares.

"Watch and pray," says the Lord, "that ye enter not into temptation." (*Matt.* 26:41).

Practical Reflections

It is vain to trouble ourselves about the future, and to be discouraged at the sight of our infirmities; all consists in relying entirely upon God; in leaving ourselves in His hands, and in sparing no pains to please Him.

It often happens that God wills or permits our anxiety concerning salvation to bring us into a state bordering on despair, in order to oblige us to place our whole confidence in Him. For the less we are supported by creatures, the more we are upheld by God, whose will and pleasure it is to assist us when all others abandon us. Let us therefore endeavor to cast all our care upon Jesus, who will be mindful of us, and let us faithfully correspond with His holy designs.

Prayer

O my God! Who art able and willing to assist me, what grounds have I not to place my whole confidence in Thee, to throw myself into the arms of Thy providence, and wait the effects of Thy bounty? Thou hast care of all: I will therefore give myself up entirely to Thee, live always in Thy presence, and ever guide myself by Thy fear and love. It is this grace I now ask of Thee, the God of my heart, and my portion forever. Grant me to weigh well, and to follow Thine admonition: "Be not solicitous; for your heavenly Father knoweth that you have need of all these things." Amen.

Chapter 40

Man Hath No Good of Himself, and Cannot Glory in Anything

DISCIPLE

LORD, what is man that Thou art mindful of him; or the son of man that Thou visitest him? (*Ps.* 8:3).

What hath man deserved that Thou shouldst give him Thy grace?

Lord, what cause have I to complain if Thou forsake me? or what can I justly allege if Thou refuse to grant my petition?

This, indeed, I may truly think and say, Lord, I am nothing, I can do nothing, I have nothing of myself that is good; but I fail and am defective in all things, and ever tend to nothing.

And unless I am supported and interiorly instructed by

Thee, I become quite tepid and dissolute.

2. But Thou, O Lord, art always the same and endurest forever; always good, just, and holy; doing all things well, justly, and holily; and disposing them in wisdom. (*Wis.* 12:13).

But I, who am more inclined to go back than to advance, continue not always in one state; for seven different seasons are changed over me. (*Dan.* 4:15).

Yet it quickly becomes better when it pleaseth Thee, and Thou stretchest out Thy helping hand; for Thou alone without man's aid can assist me, and so strengthen me that my countenance shall be no more changed in various ways, but my heart shall be converted and take its rest in Thee alone.

3. Wherefore, if I did but well know how to cast away from me all human comfort, either for the sake of devotion, or through the necessity of seeking Thee, because there is no man that can comfort me, then might I justly depend on Thy grace, and rejoice in the gift of new consolation.

4. Thanks be to Thee, from whom all proceeds, as often as it goes well with me.

But, for my part, I am but mere vanity, and nothing in Thy sight; an inconstant and weak man.

What have I then to glory in? or why do I desire to be esteemed?

Is it not for nothing? and this is most vain.

Truly vainglory is an evil plague, a very great vanity, because it draws us away from true glory, and robs us of heavenly grace.

For whilst a man takes complacency in himself, he displeaseth Thee; whilst he seeks after the praises of men, he is deprived of true virtues.

5. But true glory and holy joy is to glory in Thee and not in one's self; to rejoice in Thy name, and not to be delighted in one's own virtue, nor in any creature, save only for Thy sake.

Let Thy name be praised, not mine; let Thy work be extolled, not mine; let Thy holy name be blessed, but to me let nothing be attributed of the praises of men.

Thou art my glory, Thou art the joy of my heart.

In Thee will I glory and rejoice all the day; but for myself I will glory in nothing but in my infirmities. (*2 Cor.* 12:5).

6. Let the Jews seek the glory which one man receives from another; I will seek that which is from God alone. (*John* 5:44).

All human glory, all temporal honor, all worldly grandeur, compared to Thine eternal glory is but vanity and foolishness.

O my truth and my mercy, O my God, O blessed Trinity! to Thee alone be all praise, honor, power, and glory, for endless ages of ages. (*Deut.* 26:19).

Practical Reflections

I am sensible of my natural corruption, which renders me incapable of all supernatural good and prone to all evil: but I cast myself on the mercies of a God who can bring much out of little, as He produced all things out of nothing; since it is not sufficient for me to know my own nothingness, and that I ought to glory in nothing, save only in my infirmities; I should also (for this is most important) be guided by an humble diffidence in myself, and a firm confidence in God, to whom nothing is impossible. When I find no consolation in man, then it is I feel indeed the happy necessity of having recourse to God, and of depending upon Him: happy that, all being wanting to me without Thee, O Lord, I should find my all in Thee! Well might holy Job thus express himself: Thine eyes are upon me, and I shall be no more. For when I think of Thee, my God! I feel within me an ardent desire of pleasing Thee; and everything disappears from before me, when Thou dost present Thyself to my soul.

Prayer

Do Thou, O God, reign absolutely over my soul, and may all that it contains yield and be immolated to Thee? Grant that, by corresponding with Thy holy grace, I may be enabled to suffer the loss of all human and natural satisfaction, to seek in Thee alone my consolation, and to sacrifice my whole self to Thee.

O great God! Who knowest my condition, Who art able and willing to assist me, have compassion on the excess of my miseries! withdraw me from myself, raise me above all visible things, grant that, quitting and renouncing myself, I may desire and seek only Thee. Amen.

Chapter 41

The Contempt of All Temporal Honor

CHRIST

MY SON, take it not to heart if thou see others honored and advanced and thyself despised and debased.

Lift up thy heart to Me in Heaven and thou wilt not be concerned at thy being condemned by men upon earth.

DISCIPLE

2. Lord, we are in blindness, and are quickly seduced by vanity.

If I look well into myself, never was any injury done me by any creature, and therefore I cannot justly complain of Thee.

For, because I have often and grievously sinned against Thee, all creatures have reason to take up arms against me.

To me, therefore, confusion and contempt is justly due; but to Thee praise, honor, and glory. (*Dan.* 9:7; *Bar.* 1:15).

And unless I put myself in this disposition: to be willing to be despised and forsaken of all creatures, and to be esteemed nothing at all, I cannot arrive at inward peace and strength, nor be spiritually enlightened, nor fully united to Thee.

Practical Reflections

The eye of God, being always upon us, should impress us with a profound respect for Him, and the sight of Him in our souls should inspire us with a perfect confidence in Him. God beholds me: when I think of this, how can I offend Him? I behold God: how then can I be discouraged? God exists: that suffices to console the true Christian in all his disappointments; because he loves God more for His infinite perfections than for the favors he receives from Him. But God is my Father, what more can I have to allay all my uneasiness? And is it not sufficient to reflect that He is Goodness itself, to induce me to confide with certainty in Him, and to feel secure of His care and protection? He knows, conducts, and disposes all for my salvation; and where can I be so secure as under the wings of my beloved Saviour?

Prayer

In Thy loving embraces, O Jesus, I desire to live, in them I wish to die; into the abyss of Thy mercies I cast all my miseries, there to obtain forgiveness for my sins, though enormous, by sincerely renouncing them. Yes, for Thy name's sake, O Lord, my Saviour and Father, Thou wilt pardon me my sins because they are great, and because the more enormous they are, the more wilt Thou display the magnitude of Thy mercy in their forgiveness. Be propitious, therefore, to me a miserable sinner, who desires to no longer remain so; and grant that I may love Thee the more as my fears yield to the reflection that though Thou hast power to destroy me, Thou desirest to save me. Amen.

Chapter 42

Our Peace Is Not to be Placed in Men

CHRIST

SON, if thou place thy peace in any person, for the sake of thy contentment in his company, thou shalt be unsettled and entangled.

But if thou have recourse to the everlasting and subsisting truth, thou shalt not be grieved when a friend departs or dies.

In Me the love of thy friend must stand, and for Me he is to be loved whoever he be that appears to thee good, and is very dear to thee in this life.

Without Me no friendship is of any strength, nor will be durable; nor is that love true and pure of which I am not the bond.

Thou oughtest to be so far mortified to such affections of persons beloved, as to wish for, as much as appertains to thee, to be without any company of man.

A man draws nigher to God the farther he withdraws himself from all earthly comfort.

He ascends the higher into God, the lower he descends into himself, and the meaner he esteems himself.

2. But he that attributes anything of good to himself stops the grace of God from coming into him; for the grace of the Holy Ghost ever seeks an humble heart. (*1 Ptr.* 5:5).

If thou couldst perfectly annihilate thyself, and cast out from thyself all created love, then would abundance of grace flow into thee.

When thou lookest towards creatures the sight of the Creator is withdrawn from thee.

Learn, for the Creator's sake to, overcome thyself in all things, and then thou shalt be able to attain to the knowledge of God.

How little soever it be, if a thing be inordinately loved and regarded, it keeps thee back from the sovereign good and corrupts the soul.

Practical Reflections

The more we descend into the abyss of our own nothingness, the more do we become exalted before God. We should therefore, in the first place, be little and humble, dependent upon the Almighty, and abide only in Him; secondly, the more we experience our own weakness and misery, the more earnestly should we apply to the mercy of God; thirdly, the less we find of good in ourselves, the more should we debase ourselves before

Him, hoping all things from His bounty; fourthly, we should never suffer our hearts to become attached to anything but God, our duties and salvation, love only that which we shall love forever, and thus commence in time what we may hope to continue throughout eternity. All friendship which is not in God and for God is faulty, because we should love God alone, with our whole heart. The heart, therefore, should be kept free and disengaged from all things, that it may belong only to Him who is the center of our hearts, and who alone can satisfy our desires.

Prayer

Grant, O God, that my heart, which was made for Thee alone, may be ever wholly Thine; that free from all undue affection to creatures, it may refer all to Thee, and seek Thee alone in all things. Yes, my God, I know with St. Augustine, that Thou art the center of our hearts, because Thou art their last end and sovereign good, and that they cannot rest until they rest in Thee. Grant me therefore what I now ask, a faithful, sovereign, and constant adherence to Thee. Amen.

Chapter 43

Against Vain and Worldly Learning

CHRIST

SON, be not moved with the fine and subtle sayings of men, for the Kingdom of God is not in speech, but in power. (*1 Cor.* 4:20).

Attend to My words which inflame the heart and enlighten the mind, which excite to compunction and afford manifold consolations.

Never read anything that thou mayest appear more learned or more wise.

Study rather to mortify thy vices, for this will avail thee more than the being able to answer many hard questions.

2. When thou shalt have read, and shalt know many things, thou must always return to one beginning.

I am He that teach men knowledge, and I give a more clear understanding to little ones than can be taught by man. (*Ps.* 93:10).

He to whom I speak will quickly be wise, and will make great progress in spirit.

Woe to them that inquire of men after many curious things, and are little curious of the way to serve Me.

The time will come when Christ, the Master of masters, the Lord of angels, shall appear to hear the lessons of all men, that is, to examine the consciences of everyone.

And then He will search Jerusalem with candles (*Soph.* 1:12), and the hidden things of darkness shall be brought to light (*1 Cor.* 4:5), and the arguments of tongues shall be silent.

3. I am He that in an instant elevates an humble mind to comprehend more reasons of the eternal truth than could be acquired by ten years' study in the schools.

I teach without noise of words, without confusion of opinions, without ambition of honor, without contention of arguments.

I teach to despise earthly things, to loathe things present, to seek and relish things eternal, to fly honors, to endure scandals, to repose all hope in Me, to desire nothing out of Me, and above all things, ardently to love Me.

4. For a certain person, by loving Me entirely, learned divine things and spoke wonders.

He profited more by forsaking all things than by studying subtleties.

But to some I speak things common, to others things more particular; to some I sweetly appear in signs and figures, to others in great light I reveal mysteries.

The voice of the books is the same, but it teacheth not all men alike; because I within am the teacher of truth, the searcher of hearts, the understander of thoughts, the promoter of actions; distributing to everyone as I judge fitting. (*1 Cor.* 12:1).

Practical Reflections

God scarcely communicates Himself at all to proud and presumptuous souls who entertain a vain complacency in themselves, because they rob Him of that glory which belongs to Himself alone. But to the humble He communicates His most enlivening and efficacious graces, because they confide not in themselves, but, from a sense of their own misery and sinfulness, depend solely upon Him who alone can make them worthy of His love.

What will it avail a Christian to know the duties of religion unless he practice them? What will it avail him to dispute upon the efficacy and the operations of grace if he be not faithful in corresponding with it, and in punctually following the inspirations of the Holy Spirit? Not everyone, says Jesus Christ, that saith to Me, Lord, Lord, shall enter into the Kingdom of Heaven: but he that doth the will of My Father, who is in Heaven, he shall enter into the Kingdom of Heaven. We hear this declaration, and why does it not influence our conduct?

Prayer

Come, O Holy Spirit! enlighten the minds of all with Thy sacred light, and inflame their hearts with the fire of Thy love. Teach us what we are to believe, and engage us to practice it. For, alas! what will it avail us to know what is required of us, in order to be saved, if we do not endeavor to reduce it to practice?

Suffer not our faith to condemn us at the last day, by bearing witness to what we ought to have done to gain Heaven, and to our having neglected to perform it; but grant that both our minds and our hearts by belief and practice may equally conspire to prepare us for eternal bliss. Amen.

Chapter 44

Of Not Drawing to Ourselves Exterior Things

CHRIST

SON, in many things it behooveth thee to be ignorant, and to esteem thyself as one dead upon earth; as one to whom the whole world is crucified.

Many things also must thou pass by with a deaf ear, and think rather of those things that appertain to thy peace.

It is more profitable to turn away thine eyes from such things as displease thee, and to leave to everyone his own way of thinking, than to give way to contentious discourses.

If thou stand well with God, and look at His judgment, thou wilt more easily bear to see thyself overcome.

DISCIPLE

2. O Lord, to what are we come? Behold a temporal loss is greatly bewailed; for a small gain men labor and toil, but the loss of the soul is little thought of, and hardly returns to mind.

That which is of little or no profit takes up our thoughts; and that which is above all things necessary, is negligently passed over; for the whole man sinks down into outward things, and unless he quickly recovers himself, he willingly continues immersed in them.

Practical Reflections

To regard one's self as crucified and dead to the world, is, first, to entertain no attachment for anything but God, one's duty, and salvation; secondly, to regard all things as passing away, and to say to one's self: I am here today, but shall be gone tomorrow: at the hour of death, what will honor, fortune, or pleasure avail me? Only in proportion as I have used them as though I used them not.

Happy the Christian who dies thus to the world in affection, before he quits it in reality, who endeavors meritoriously to die daily to some one of those things which he will be forced to relinquish in death! Thus by dying daily, he will best secure for himself a happy departure hence.

We bewail our temporal losses, we incessantly dwell upon them, we are scarcely to be consoled when they happen to us; but when the soul perishes, its loss is soon forgotten, we soon become insensible to it, though this alone should affect a Christian. We cannot suffer the loss of any earthly good without regret, but the loss of Thee, my God, we mourn not, though Thou alone art our sovereign good.

Prayer

Enlighten our minds, we beseech Thee, O Lord, and impress our hearts with the greatness of our loss when we withdraw ourselves from Thee. Grant that we may ever prefer Thee before all things else, and choose rather to lose all worldly goods than relinquish but for one moment Thy grace and love. When, O God, shall I resemble the dead within their graves (that which according to St. Paul is the spirit, the character, and the duty of all true Christians)? When shall I think no more of the world, and be content for the world to think no more of me? From henceforth, O Jesus, I desire to die to all things else, that I may live only to Thee for time and eternity. Amen.

Chapter 45

Credit Is Not to Be Given to All Men, And That Men Are Prone to Offend in Words

Disciple

GRANT me help, O Lord, from trouble, for vain is the salvation of man. (*Ps.* 59:13).

How often have I not failed to find faith there where I thought I might depend upon it.

And how often have I found it where I did not expect it?

Vain, therefore, is all hope in men; but the safety of the just is in Thee, O Lord.

Blessed be Thou, O Lord my God, in all things that befall us.

We are weak and unsettled, we are quickly deceived and changed.

2. Who is the man that is able to keep himself so warily, and with so much circumspection in all things, as not to fall sometimes into some deceit or perplexity?

But he that trusts in Thee, O Lord, and seeks Thee with a simple heart does not so easily fall. (*Wis.* 1:1).

And if he fall into some tribulation, in what manner soever he may be entangled therein, he will quickly be rescued or comforted by Thee; for Thou wilt not forsake forever him that trusts in Thee. (*Ps.* 36:28).

A trusty friend is rarely to be found that continues faithful in all the distresses of his friend. (*Ecclus.* 6:10).

Thou, O Lord, Thou alone art most faithful in all things, and besides Thee, there is no other such.

3. Oh, how wise was that holy soul that said, My mind is strongly settled and grounded upon Christ. (*Eph.* 3:17).

If it were so with me the fear of man would not so easily give me trouble, nor flying words move me.

Who can foresee all things, or who is able to provide against all future evils?

If things foreseen do nevertheless often hurt us, how can things unlooked-for fail of wounding us grievously?

But why did I not provide better for myself, miserable wretch that I am! why also have I so easily given credit to others!

But we are men, and but frail men, though by many we are reputed and called angels.

To whom shall I give credit, O Lord? to whom but to Thee? Thou art the truth which neither canst deceive, nor be deceived. (*John* 14:6).

And on the other side, every man is a liar (*Ps.* 115:11),

infirm, unstable, and subject to fail, especially in words; so that we ought not readily to believe even that which in appearance seems to sound well.

4. How wisely didst Thou forewarn us to beware of men (*Matt.* 10:17), and that a man's enemies are they of his own household (*Matt.* 36); and that we are not to believe, if any-one should say, "Behold here, or behold there." (*Matt.* 24:23).

I have been taught to my cost, and I wish it may serve to make me more cautious, and not to increase my folly.

"Be wary," saith one, "be wary, keep to thyself what I tell thee." And whilst I hold my peace, and believe the matter to be secret, he himself cannot keep the secret which he desires me to keep, but presently betrays both me and himself, and goes his way.

From such tales and such incautious people defend me, O Lord, that I may not fall into their hands, nor ever commit the like.

Give to my mouth truth and constancy in my words, and remove far from me a crafty tongue.

What I am not willing to suffer I ought by all means to shun.

5. Oh, how good a thing and how peaceable it is to be silent of others (*Prov.* 25:9), nor to believe all that is said, nor easily to report what one has heard:

To lay one's self open to few; always to seek Thee, the beholder of the heart;

Not to be carried about with every wind of words; but to wish that all things, both within and without us, may go according to the pleasure of Thy will.

How secure it is for the keeping of heavenly grace to fly

the sight of men; and not to seek those things that seem to cause admiration abroad; but with all diligence to follow that which brings amendment of life and fervor.

To how many hath it been hurtful to have their virtue known and over-hastily praised.

How profitable indeed hath grace been kept with silence in this frail life! all which is a state of temptation and a warfare.

Practical Reflections

What is it to be "strongly settled and grounded upon Christ?" (St. Agatha). It is, first, to rely only upon Him, and trust but little to the promises of men; secondly, it is to prefer His grace and love before the friendship and consideration of all mankind besides; for there is no true good but in being well with God; thirdly, it is to treat with Him with all the earnestness of our souls, confidently to have recourse to Him in all our necessities, and to oblige our hearts to love Him, that at the moment of death, when we shall appear before Him, He may show Himself to us as a Father of mercy, and as a Saviour whom we have long known and loved, and not as a strange God and terribly just Judge, saying to us: You would not endeavor to know Me and love Me in time; now will I not know you for eternity, you shall not be Mine forever.

Prayer

Grant me, O Jesus, to know what Thou art in Thyself, and what Thou art to me, that my heart may be penetrated with Thy holy fear and love. Shall I be so ungrateful and so unjust as to give my heart to any other but Thee, my God, or to rely on any creature in preference to Thee? Were I to act thus, how justly should I deserve to be miserable both for time and eternity! What, Lord! I suffice for Thee, and shouldst not Thou suffice for me? No, blessed Jesus, it shall not be thus; I desire only Thee and the accomplishment of Thy holy will, as my happiness for time and eternity. Amen.

Chapter 46

Of Having Confidence in God When Words Arise against Us

CHRIST

SON, stand firm and trust in Me; for what are words but words: they fly through the air, but hurt not a stone.

If thou art guilty, think that thou wilt willingly amend thyself.

If thy conscience accuse thee not, think that thou wilt willingly suffer this for God's sake. It is a small matter that thou shouldst sometimes bear with words, if thou hast not as yet courage to endure hard stripes.

And why do such small things go to thy heart, but because thou art yet carnal, and regardest men more than thou oughtest!

For because thou art afraid of being despised, thou art not willing to be reprehended for thy faults, and seekest to shelter thyself in excuses.

2. But look better into thyself and thou shalt find that the world is still living in thee, and a vain desire of pleasing men.

For when thou art unwilling to be humbled and confounded for thy defects, it is plain indeed that thou art not truly humble, nor truly dead to the world, nor the world crucified to thee. (*Gal.* 6:14).

But give ear to My word, and thou shalt not value ten thousand words of men.

Behold, if all should be said against thee which the malice of men can invent, what hurt could it do thee if thou wouldst let it pass, and make no account of it? Could it even so much as pluck one hair from thee? (*Luke* 21:18).

3. But he who has not his heart within, nor God before his eyes, is easily moved with a word of censure.

Whereas he that trusts in Me, and desires not to stand by his own judgment, will be free from the fear of men.

For I am the judge and discerner of all secrets, I know how the matter passeth; I know both him that offers the injury, and him that suffers it.

From Me this word went forth: by My permission it happened, that out of many hearts thoughts may be revealed. (*Luke* 2:35).

I shall judge the guilty and the innocent, but by a secret judgment I would beforehand try them both.

4. The testimony of men oftentimes deceives; My judgment is true, it shall stand and not be overthrown. (*Ps.* 18:10).

It is hidden for the most part, and to few laid open in everything; yet it never errs, nor can it err, even though to the eyes of the unwise it seem not right.

To Me, therefore, must thou run in every judgment and not depend upon thine own will.

For the just man will not be troubled whatever happens to him from God. (*Prov.* 12:21). And if anything be wrongfully pronounced against him he will not much care.

Neither will he vainly rejoice if by others he be reasonably excused.

For he considers that I am He that searcheth the heart and the reins (*Ps.* 7:10); who judgeth not according to the face, nor according to human appearance.

For oftentimes that is found culpable in My eyes which in the judgment of men is esteemed commendable.

Disciple

5. O Lord God, the just Judge, strong and patient, Who knowest the frailty and perverseness of men, be Thou my strength and all my confidence, for my own conscience sufficeth me not.

Thou knowest that which I know not, and therefore in every reprehension I ought to humble myself, and bear it with meekness.

Pardon me, I beseech Thee, in Thy mercy, as often as I have done thus, and give me again the grace to suffer still more.

For better to me is Thy plenteous mercy for the obtaining of pardon, than the justice which I imagine in myself for the defense of my hidden conscience.

Although my conscience accuse me not, yet I cannot hereby justify myself (*1 Cor.* 4:4); for setting Thy mercy aside, in Thy sight no man living shall be justified. (*Ps.* 142:2).

Practical Reflections

It is difficult not to be troubled when we are blamed, reprimanded, or condemned. But true Christian humility consists in not entertaining nor expressing the resentment we at first experience; that is, it consists, first, in not indulging ill-natured and contemptuous reflections upon those who despise us; secondly, in stifling the mortification they occasion us, and in offering it as a sacrifice to God; thirdly, in behaving kindly towards them, speaking to them and rendering them services as occasion may occur, and in doing them as much good as we think they have done us harm. But, alas, how few practice this true humility, and make good use of contradictions and contempt, although all believe without true humility it is impossible to be saved!

Prayer

How little, O God, is a true Christian affected, one who fears and loves Thee above all things, how little is he affected by the judgments of men, and how much concerned as to the judgment Thou wilt one day pass upon him! When present before Thee, in the most holy Sacrament, I will ask, how do I stand with Thee? What am I in Thy sight? What will be my eternal lot? With such thoughts let me die to the desire of the esteem and to the fear of the contempt of men, that I may seek only to find favor with Thee. Amen.

Chapter 47

All Grievous Things Are to Be Endured for Eternal Life

CHRIST

SON, be not dismayed with the labors which thou hast undertaken for Me; neither let the tribulations which befall thee quite cast thee down; but let My promise strengthen thee, and comfort thee in every event. (*Ps.* 118:71).

I am sufficient to reward thee beyond all measure. (*Gen.* 15:1).

Thou shalt not labor here long, nor shalt thou be always oppressed with sorrows.

Wait a little while and thou shalt see a speedy end of all thine evils.

The hour will come when labor and trouble shall be no more.

All is little and short which passeth away with time. (*Wis.* 3:9).

2. Do thy part well; mind what thou art about; labor faithfully in My vineyard, I will be thy reward.

Write, read, sing, sigh, keep silence, pray, bear thy crosses manfully; eternal life is worthy of all these, and greater combats.

Peace shall come in one day, which is known to the Lord; and it shall not be a vicissitude of day and night, such as is at present; but everlasting light, infinite brightness, steadfast peace, and secure rest. (*Apoc.* 21:23).

Thou shalt not then say: Who shall deliver me from the body of this death? (*Rom.* 7:24). Nor shalt thou cry out: Woe is me, that my sojourning is prolonged. (*Ps.* 119:5). For death shall be no more, but never-failing health; no anxiety, but blessed delight; and a society sweet and lovely.

Oh, if thou hadst seen the everlasting crown of the saints in Heaven, and in how great glory they now triumph who appeared contemptible heretofore to this world, and in a manner even unworthy of life, doubtless thou wouldst immediately cast thyself down to the very earth, and wouldst rather seek to be under the feet of all, than to have command over so much as one.

Neither wouldst thou covet the pleasant days of this life, but wouldst rather be glad to suffer tribulation for God's sake, and esteem it thy greatest gain to be reputed as nothing amongst men.

3. Ah, if thou didst but relish these things, and suffer them to penetrate deeply into thy heart, how wouldst thou dare so much as once to complain!

Are not all painful labors to be endured for everlasting life?

It is no small matter to lose or gain the Kingdom of God.

Lift up therefore thy face to Heaven. Behold, I, and all My saints with Me, who in this world have had a great conflict, do now rejoice, are now comforted, are now secure, are now at rest, and they shall for all eternity abide with Me in the Kingdom of My Father. (*Wis.* 5:1).

Practical Reflections

How hard is this saying, that salvation is only to be obtained by a life of continual suffering, by constantly fighting against and by ever renouncing and dying to ourselves! But how we are encouraged to submit to such a course by the hope and assurance of eternal happiness, which will be the reward we shall receive in exchange for the disappointments and miseries of this present time! Nothing will afford us such great consolation at the hour of death as the good use we have made of sufferings: then shall we find that we have done nothing purely for God but what we have done contrary to ourselves, and that a truly Christian life must necessarily be a life of crosses and self-denials.

Prayer

As, O God, we believe and hope for the good things of eternity, grant that we may so use the transitory miseries of this life as to obtain the permanent felicity of the next. At the hour of death, what shall we not wish to have done, to have suffered, and renounced for the sake of obtaining Heaven! Instill, O Lord, into our hearts something of the desires we shall then entertain to no purpose, that we may now really renounce and die to ourselves. Grant we may never consider anything as great but what is eternal, and regard all that passes away with time, as little and contemptible. O happiness! O joy! O eternal felicity! console us under the afflictions of our mortal course. And since we must of necessity repent either in time or for all eternity, suffer either in this life or in the next, grant us, we beseech Thee, O Jesus, patiently to endure all present evils, in hopes of obtaining future bliss and happiness. Amen.

Chapter 48

The Day of Eternity, and Of the Miseries of This Life

DISCIPLE

O MOST happy mansion of the city above! O most bright day of eternity, which knows no night, but is always enlightened by the sovereign truth! A day always joyful, always secure, and never changing its state for the contrary!

Oh, that this day would shine upon us, and all those temporal things would come to an end!

It shines indeed upon the saints, resplendent with ever-lasting brightness (*Tob.* 13:13), but to us pilgrims upon earth it is seen only as far off, and through a glass. (*1 Cor.* 13:12).

2. The citizens of Heaven know how joyful that day is; but the banished children of Eve lament that this our day is bitter and tedious.

The days of this life are short and evil (*Gen.* 48:9), full of sorrows and miseries: where man is defiled with many sins, is ensnared with many fears, disquieted with many cares, distracted with many curiosities, entangled with many vanities, encompassed with many errors, broken with many labors, troubled with temptations, weakened with delights, tormented with want.

3. Oh, when will there be an end of these evils? When shall I be set at liberty from the wretched slavery of sin? (*Rom.* 7:24).

When, O Lord, shall I think of Thee alone? When shall I to the full rejoice in Thee? (*Ps.* 69:5).

When shall I be without any impediment in true liberty, without any trouble of mind or body?

When shall I enjoy a solid peace never to be disturbed and always secure, a peace both within and without, a peace every way firm?

O good Jesus, when shall I stand to behold Thee? When shall I contemplate the glory of Thy Kingdom? When wilt Thou be all in all to me?

Oh, when shall I be with Thee in Thy Kingdom, which Thou hast prepared for Thy beloved for all eternity? (*Matt.* 25:34).

I am left a poor and banished man in an enemy's

country, where there are wars every day, and very great misfortunes.

4. Comfort me in my banishment, assuage my sorrow; for all my desire is after Thee, and all that this world offers for my comfort is burdensome to me.

I long to enjoy Thee intimately, but cannot attain to it.

I desire to cleave to heavenly things, but the things of this life and my unmortified passions bear me down.

I am willing in mind to be above all things, but by the flesh am obliged against my will to be subject to them.

Thus, unhappy man that I am, I fight with myself, and am become burdensome to myself, whilst the spirit seeks to tend upwards, and the flesh downwards.

5. Oh, what do I suffer interiorly, whilst in my mind I consider heavenly things, and presently a crowd of carnal thoughts comes to interrupt my prayer? O God, be not Thou far from me (*Ps.* 70:12), and decline not in Thy wrath from Thy servant. (*Ps.* 26:9).

Dart forth lightning, and Thou shalt scatter them; shoot out Thine arrows (*Ps.* 143:6), and let all the phantoms of the enemy be put to flight.

Gather my senses together to Thee; make me forget all worldly things; give me the grace speedily to cast away and to despise all wicked imaginations.

Come to my aid, O eternal Truth, that no vanity may move me.

Come, heavenly sweetness, and let all impurity fly from before Thy face.

Pardon me also, and mercifully forgive me the times that I have thought of anything else in prayer besides Thee.

For I confess truly that I am accustomed to be very much distracted.

For oftentimes I am not there where I am bodily standing or sitting, but am rather where my thoughts carry me.

There I am where my thought is; and there oftentimes are my thoughts where that is which I love.

That thing most readily comes to my mind which naturally delights me, or which through custom is pleasing to me.

6. For this reason Thou who art the Truth hast plainly said, where thy treasure is, there also is thy heart. (*Matt.* 6:21).

If I love Heaven I willingly think on heavenly things.

If I love the world I rejoice in the prosperity of the world, and am troubled at its adversity.

If I love the flesh my imagination is often taken up with things of the flesh.

If I love the spirit I delight to think of spiritual things.

For whatsoever things I love, of the same I willingly speak and hear, and carry home with me the images of them.

But blessed is the man, who for Thee, O Lord, lets go all things created; who offers violence to his nature, and through fervor of spirit crucifies the lusts of the flesh: that so his conscience being cleared up, he may offer to Thee pure prayer, and may be worthy to be admitted among the choirs of angels, having excluded all things of the earth both from without and within.

Practical Reflections

What will it avail us to suffer and to deplore the miseries of this life, and to sigh after the good things of the next, if we do not endeavor to receive our present tribulations with patience, as coming from the hand of God, and with humility, as corresponding with our deserts; if we strive not to obtain that eternal happiness, after which we sigh, by constant fidelity? O happy day! O eternal joy! O infinite, unchangeable happiness! O establishment! O mansion! O plentitude of God in us and of us in God! O transformation of a blessed soul into its God and its all! When shall I possess thee? But when shall I deserve thee? Weary of myself and of the inefficacy of my desires, I ardently long for thee, O Paradise! and yet how little do I do to obtain thine eternal happiness! Let us join, my soul, let us add to the esteem we have of Paradise our exertions to obtain it. Let us regard it as a crown which can only be obtained by offering a holy violence to ourselves, and as a recompense to be earned only by a supernatural life.

Prayer

When, O God, shall I withdraw my heart from all things, visible and terrestrial, and give my whole self to Thee, my sovereign and invisible good? When shalt Thou alone become my consolation and the only happiness of my soul? When shall I see in Thee, my Saviour, what I now believe? When shall I possess what I love? When shall I find what I seek? Comfort me in this exile, support me in my sufferings, strengthen me in my weakness. Come, O Jesus, come into my soul, by Thy grace, Thy presence, and Thy love. Take possession of my heart, that it may never more be separated from Thee. I languish, I sigh, and burn with the desire of beholding Thee face to face in Thy glory. O when shall faith be lost in vision, and hope swallowed up in fruition?

How burdened is this life to a soul that loves only Thee, my Saviour! and how cruel a martyrdom to support it! No, Lord, I can no longer live without loving Thee, nor love Thee as I desire, without seeing Thee! Terminate therefore my anguish by closing my life. Speak, my soul, speak to thy God; but rather, O God, do Thou speak to my heart, that it may die to itself, and live only to Thee. Amen.

Chapter 49

The Desire of Eternal Life, and What Great Things Are Promised to Those who Fight

CHRIST

SON, when thou perceivest a longing after eternal bliss to be infused into thee from above, and that thou desirest to go out of the dwelling of this body, that thou mayest contemplate My brightness, without any shadow of change (*James* 1:17), enlarge thy heart (*Ps.* 118:32), and with all thine affections embrace this holy inspiration.

Return very great thanks to the divine bounty, which deals so favorably with thee, which mercifully visits thee, ardently incites thee, and powerfully raises up; lest by thine own weight thou fall down to the things of the earth.

For it is not by thine own thought or endeavor that thou attainest to this; but only by the favor of heavenly grace and the divine visit: that so thou mayest advance in virtue and greater humility, and prepare thyself for future conflicts, and labor with the whole affection of thy heart to keep close to Me, and serve Me with a fervent will.

2. Son, the fire often burns, but the flame ascends not without smoke.

So also some people's desires are on fire after heavenly things, and yet they are not free from the temptation of carnal affection.

And therefore it is not altogether purely for God's honor that they do what they so earnestly request of Him.

Such also is oftentimes thy desire, which thou hast signified to be so strong.

For that is not pure and perfect which is infected with self-interest.

3. Ask not what is delightful and commodious for thee but what is pleasing and honorable to Me; for if thou judgest rightly, thou oughtest to follow My appointment rather than thine own desire, and prefer it before all that thou desirest.

I know thy desire, and I have often heard thy sighs. (*Ps.* 37:10).

Thou wouldst be glad to be at present in the liberty of the glory of the children of God. (*Rom.* 5:2). Thou wouldst be pleased to be now at thine eternal home, and in thy heavenly country abounding with joy; but that hour is not yet come: for this is yet another time, a time of war, a time of labor and trial.

Thou wishest to be replenished with the sovereign good, but thou canst not at present attain to it.

I am that sovereign good; expect Me, saith the Lord (*Soph.* 3:8), till the Kingdom of God come. (*Luke* 22:18).

4. Thou must yet be tried upon earth and exercised in many things.

Consolation shall sometimes be given thee; but to be fully satisfied shall not be granted thee.

Take courage (*Jos.* 1:6), therefore, and be valiant as well in doing as in suffering things repugnant to thy nature.

Thou must put on the new man (*Eph.* 4:24), and be changed into another man.

Thou must oftentimes do that which is against thine inclination, and forego that to which thou art inclined.

That which is pleasing to others shall go forward; that which thou wouldst have shall not succeed.

That which others say shall be hearkened unto, what thou sayst shall not be regarded.

Others shall ask and shall receive, thou shalt ask and not obtain.

5. Others shall be great in the esteem of men; but of thee no notice shall be taken.

To others this or that shall be committed; but thou shalt be accounted fit for nothing.

At this nature will sometimes repine, and it will be no small matter if thou bear it with silence.

In these and many suchlike things the faithful servant of the Lord is used to be tried, how far he can renounce himself, and break himself in all things.

There is scarcely any one thing in which thou standest so much in need of mortifying thyself as in seeing and suffering the things which are repugnant to thy will, and especially when that is commanded which seems to thee incongruous and to little purpose.

And because being under authority thou darest not resist the higher power, therefore thou art apt to think it hard to walk at the beck of another, and wholly to give up thine own sentiment.

6. But consider, son, the fruit of these labors, how quickly they will end, and their exceeding great reward, and thou wilt not be troubled at them, but strongly comforted in thy suffering. (*Heb.* 6:18).

For, in regard to that little of thy will which thou now willingly forsakest, thou shalt forever have thy will in Heaven.

For there thou shalt find all that thou willest, all that thou canst desire.

There thou shalt enjoy all good without fear of ever losing it.

There thy will, being always one with Mine, shall desire nothing foreign or private.

There no one shall resist thee, no man shall complain of thee, none shall hinder thee, nothing shall stand in thy way: but all that thou desirest shall be there together present, and shall replenish thy whole affection, and satiate it to the full.

There I will give thee glory for the affronts which thou hast suffered; a garment of praise for thy sorrow (*Is.* 61:3), and for thy having been seated here in the lowest place, a royal throne for all eternity.

There will the fruit of obedience appear, there will the labor of penance rejoice, and humble subjection shall be gloriously crowned.

7. Bow down thyself then humbly at present under the hands of all, and heed not who it was that has said or commanded this.

But let it be thy great care that whether thy superior, inferior, or equal, desire anything of thee, or hint at anything, thou take all in good part and labor with a sincere will to perform it.

Let one man seek this, another that; let this man glory in this thing, another in that, and be praised a thousand times; but thou, for thy part, rejoice neither in this, nor in that, but in the contempt of thyself, and in My good pleasure and honor alone.

This is what thou oughtest to wish, that whether in life or death God may be always glorified in thee. (*Phil.* 1:20).

Practical Reflections

We are unwilling to suffer the trials which God sends us, and would receive nothing from Him but continual consolations: these however are only given to support us under dryness and desolation of spirit; He imparts them to us to enable us to support His apparent rigor, which in reality is His goodness towards us, by which He spares not in time, that He may be merciful to us for eternity. Think not therefore that thou art rejected by God, when thou dost experience nothing but disgust in His service; but do faithfully whatever thou wouldst then do to please Him, if thou didst experience the greatest delight in serving Him, and it shall be well with thee. Humble thyself on such occasions, think thyself unworthy of the least consolation or support. The Lord is pleased that thou shouldst serve Him without any sensible comfort, and by this means conquer thy repugnance to good, and thine inclination for evil, through a pure desire of pleasing Him, and a real dread of offending Him. Ah, how abundantly will a happy eternity repay thee for the sufferings and fatigues of this life, if thou wilt but bear them now with confidence, fidelity, and patience! Take courage then, my soul, a moment's suffering is eternal joy.

Prayer

Grant, O Lord, that my whole delight may be to please Thee, and to do and to suffer whatever Thou willest. No, my God, I ask no other consolation than the happiness of being faithful to Thee, because I desire to love Thee more for Thyself than on my own account. May Thy love, O God, triumph over all the pursuits and repugnances of self-love! Mayest Thou be all to me in time, that Thou mayest be my all for eternity. Amen.

Chapter 50

How a Desolate Person Ought to Offer Himself into the Hands of God

DISCIPLE

O LORD God, O holy Father, be Thou now and forever blessed, for as Thou wilt, so it has happened, and what Thou dost is always good.

Let Thy servant rejoice in Thee, not in himself, nor in any other; for Thou alone art true joy, Thou my hope and my crown, Thou my gladness and my honor, O Lord.

What hath Thy servant but what he hath received from Thee (*1 Cor.* 4:7), and this without any merit on his side? All things are Thine which Thou hast given, and which Thou hast made.

I am poor, and in labors from my youth (*Ps.* 87:16), and my soul is grieved even unto tears sometimes, and sometimes is disturbed within herself, by reason of the passions which encompass her.

2. I long for the joy of peace, I implore the peace of Thy children, who are fed by Thee in the light of Thy consolation.

If Thou give peace, if Thou infuse holy joy, the soul of Thy servant shall be full of melody and devout in Thy praise.

But if Thou withdraw Thyself, as Thou art very often accustomed to do, he will not be able to run in the way of Thy commandments; but rather must bow down his knees, and strike his breast, because it is not with him as it was yesterday and the day before, when Thy lamp shined over his head, and he was covered under the shadow of Thy wings from temptations rushing in upon him.

3. O just Father, holy, and always to be praised, the hour is come for Thy servant to be tried.

O Father, worthy of all love, it is fitting that Thy servant should at this hour suffer something for Thee.

O Father, always to be honored, the hour is come which Thou didst foresee from all eternity, that Thy servant for a short time should be oppressed without, but always live within to Thee.

That he should be a little slighted and humbled, and should fall in the sight of men; that he should be severely afflicted with sufferings and diseases, that so he may rise again with Thee in the dawning of a new light, and be glorified in Heaven.

O holy Father, Thou hast so appointed and such is Thy will, and that has come to pass which Thou hast ordained.

4. For this is a favor to Thy friend, that he should suffer and be afflicted in this world for the love of Thee; how

oftensoever, and by whomsoever Thou permittest it to fall upon him.

Without Thy counsel and providence, and without cause, nothing is done upon earth.

It is good for me, O Lord, that Thou hast humbled me that I may learn Thy justifications *(Ps.* 118:71), and that I may cast away from me all pride of heart and presumption.

It is advantageous for me that shame has covered my face, that I may rather seek my comfort from Thee than from men.

I have also learned hereby to fear Thine impenetrable judgments, Who afflictest the just together with the wicked; but not without equity and justice.

5. Thanks be to Thee that Thou hast not spared me in my sufferings, but hast bruised me with bitter stripes, inflicting pain, and sending distress both within and without.

And of all things under Heaven there is none can comfort me but Thou, O Lord, my God, the heavenly physician of souls, who scourgest and savest, leadest down to hell, and bringest up again. (*Tob.* 13:2).

Thy discipline is on me, and Thy rod shall instruct me.

6. Behold, dear Father, I am in Thy hands, I bow myself down under the rod of Thy correction.

Strike Thou my back and my neck, that I may bend my crookedness to Thy will.

Make me a pious and humble disciple of Thine, as Thou art wont well to do, that I may walk at Thy nod at all times.

To Thee I commit myself, and all that is mine, to be corrected by Thee; it is better to be chastised here than hereafter.

Thou knowest everything (*Job* 42:2), and there is nothing in man's conscience hidden from Thee.

Thou knowest things to come before they are done; and Thou hast no need to be taught or admonished by any one of those things that pass upon earth.

Thou knowest what is expedient for my progress, and how serviceable tribulation is to rub away the rust of sin.

Do with me according to Thy good pleasure; it is what I desire; and despise not my sinful life, to no one better or more clearly known than to Thyself alone.

7. Grant, O Lord, that I may know what I ought to know; that I may love what I ought to love; that I may praise that which is most pleasing to Thee; that I may esteem that which is valuable in Thy sight; that I may despise that which is despicable in Thine eyes.

Suffer me not to judge according to the sight of the outward eye, nor to give sentence according to the hearing of the ears of men that know not what they are about; but to determine both of visible and spiritual matters with true judgment, and above all things ever to seek Thy good will and pleasure.

8. The sentiments of men are often wrong in their judgments, and the lovers of this world are deceived in loving visible things alone.

What is man the better for being reputed greater by man?

One deceitful man deceives another; the vain deceives the vain, the blind deceives the blind, the weak the weak, whilst he extols him, and in truth, doth rather confound him, whilst he vainly praises him.

For as much as each one is in Thine eyes, so much is he, and no more, saith the humble St. Francis.

Practical Reflections

As God is the sovereign purity and the essence of sanctity, so He is pleased to purify our souls by the most painful and humiliating sufferings in this life, or by torments the most acute and piercing in Purgatory, to fit them for the possession of Himself in the Kingdom of Heaven. By these means He brings them to that degree of purity which is necessary to qualify them for the eternal happy possession of His sanctity. Hence, that which constitutes the conformity of a faithful soul with the designs of God for its sanctification and salvation is, first, to live in such purity of heart as to avoid all willful sin, all human attachments, and, above all, the pursuits of self-love, habitual faults, and self-will. Secondly, it is to be ready to receive, from Jesus Christ, trials the most humiliating and most contrary to its own inclinations; thirdly, it is to support and to fight without ceasing, against the most violent and importunate temptations, by having perpetual recourse to God, with a firm confidence in His goodness; fourthly, in all sufferings it is to keep up a continual spirit of compunction, mortification, and of a horror for sin, which will preserve us from falling into it; fifthly, it is to be most diligent in keeping a guard over the senses and the heart, that no sensual or merely human satisfaction may enter in; sixthly, it is to be humble, dependent, little, and nothing before God, to desire nothing but His will, and to rejoice in its accomplishment, even under the pressure of the heaviest calamities.

Prayer

Although I am convinced, O God, of the necessity of being humble, faithful, and resigned in affliction, yet to excuse my impatience, how often do I pretend that it is the result of a religious fear and anxiety lest these trials should end in sin, instead of victory. But dost Thou not know better than I do, O Father of mercies, and God of all consolation? dost Thou not see this danger? and is this not sufficient to induce Thee, the best of fathers, to assist me? Alas! O Lord, abandon me not, and deliver me not to the desires of my corrupt heart. Remember, O Jesus, how much I have cost Thee, and suffer not Thy torments and death to plead for me in vain. I ardently desire that peace which Thou givest to Thy children, and I find nothing within me but trouble and agitation. Why am I so averse to good, and so much inclined to evil? Why is my soul so frequently bewildered amidst the irregular demands of my passions, and carried by its first impulse towards everything that is contrary to Thy holy will? I mourn over the corruption of my heart, and from Thee alone do I hope for deliverance. It is just I should suffer on account of my sins; but it is not just I should sin in my sufferings. May I never offend Thee and ruin myself by impatience under afflictions, but, O God, grant that I may sanctify my soul and secure my salvation. Amen.

Chapter 51

We Must Exercise Ourselves in Humble Works When We Cannot Attain to the Highest

CHRIST

SON, thou canst not always continue in the most fervent desire of virtue, nor stand in the highest degree of contemplation; but it must needs be that thou sometimes descend to lower things, by reason of original corruption, and that thou bear the burden of this corruptible life, even against thy will, and with irksomeness.

As long as thou carriest about with thee thy mortal body, thou shalt feel trouble and heaviness of heart.

Thou oughtest, therefore, as long as thou art in the flesh, oftentimes to bewail the burden of the flesh, for that thou canst not without intermission be employed in spiritual exercises and divine contemplation.

2. At these times it is expedient for thee to fly to humble and exterior works, and to recreate thyself in good actions, to look for My coming and My heavenly visitation with an assured hope; to bear with patience thy banishment, and the aridity of thy mind, till thou be visited again by Me, and delivered from all anguish.

For I will make thee forget thy pains and enjoy internal rest.

I will lay open before thee the pleasant fields of the Scriptures, that thy heart being enlarged thou mayest begin to run in the way of My Commandments. (*Ps.* 118:32).

And then thou shalt say that the sufferings of this time are not worthy to be compared with the glory to come which shall be revealed in us. (*Rom.* 8:18).

Practical Reflections

How great is the difference between the sanctity of the blessed in Heaven, and of men upon earth! The one is exempt from pain and full of sweetness, the other is replete with bitterness and misery; the one belongs to that delightful abode, our true country, the other is our portion in this vale of tears.

In eternity, we shall love God in possessing Him, and enjoying His felicity; in time, we must love Him by suffering for His sake, and patiently carrying the Cross of Jesus Christ. There, we shall be happy in God, and secure of His love forever; here, we know not whether we be worthy of love or hatred. In the time of spiritual dryness and desolation let us employ ourselves in doing something exteriorly for God, since we find nothing within that sensibly calls us to Him; but at the same time let us not neglect any of the interior exercises of prayer, recollection, and continual recourse to God for His support and assistance.

Prayer

O my God! how long shall my sorrowful and rigorous exile keep me at a distance from Thee, uncertain as to my eternal happiness, and even in danger of losing it? How am I ashamed of appearing in Thy presence, miserable, weak, and defiled with sin! Turn not, O Lord, Thy face away from me; for there is no consolation but in Thy presence. Recall me, O God, recall me to Thyself by interior recollection; and may it supply the want of Thy glorious presence, and console me when I think of Thee, and of the misery of not being able to see and to possess Thee. Amen.

Chapter 52

A Man Ought Not to Esteem Himself Worthy of Consolation, But Rather Deserving of Stripes

DISCIPLE

LORD, I am not worthy of Thy consolation or any spiritual visitation; and therefore Thou dealest justly with me when Thou leavest me poor and desolate.

For if I could shed tears like a sea, yet should I not be worthy of Thy comfort.

Since I have deserved nothing but stripes and punishment, because I have grievously and often offended Thee, and in very many things sinned against Thee.

Therefore, according to all just reason I have not deserved the least of Thy comforts.

But Thou, Who art a good and merciful God, Who wilt not have Thy works perish, to show the richness of Thy goodness towards the vessels of mercy (*Rom.* 9:23), vouchsafest beyond all his deserts to comfort Thy servant above human measure.

For Thy consolations are not like the consolations of men.

2. What have I done, O Lord, that Thou shouldst impart Thy heavenly comfort to me?

I can remember nothing of good that I have ever done: but that I was always prone to vice and very slothful to amend.

It is the truth, and I cannot deny it. If I should say otherwise Thou wouldst stand against me, and there would be none to defend me.

What have I deserved for my sins but Hell and everlasting fire?

In truth I confess that I am worthy of all scorn and contempt, neither is it fitting that I should be named among Thy devout servants. And though I would fain not hear this, yet for truth's sake I will condemn myself for my sins, that so I may the easier obtain Thy mercy.

3. What shall I say who am guilty and full of all confusion?

I have not the face to say anything but this one word: I have sinned, O Lord, I have sinned; have mercy on me, and pardon me.

"Suffer me, therefore, that I may lament my sorrow a little before I go to a land that is covered with the mist of death." (*Job* 10:20).

What dost Thou chiefly require of a guilty and wretched sinner but that he should heartily repent and humble himself for his sins?

In true contrition and humility of heart is brought forth hope of forgiveness; a troubled conscience is reconciled; grace that was lost is recovered; a man is secured from the wrath to come, and God meets the penitent soul in the holy kiss of peace.

4. Humble contrition for sins is an acceptable sacrifice to Thee, O Lord (*Ps.* 1:19), of far sweeter odor in Thy sight than the burning of frankincense.

This is also that pleasing ointment which Thou wouldst have to be poured upon Thy sacred feet, for Thou never yet hast despised a contrite and humbled heart. (*Ps.* 1:19).

Here is a sure place of refuge from the face of the wrath

of the enemy. Here whatever has been elsewhere contracted of uncleanness is amended and washed away.

Practical Reflections

Although we should consider ourselves in all our sufferings, as most unworthy of receiving consolation from God, and as deserving of the heaviest chastisements, having so often merited Hell, it is good, nevertheless, to bewail our exile, and to sigh, in the sense of our miseries, for the Father of mercy, and the God of all consolation; for a cry of lamentation from a soul penetrated with gratitude to God, for His goodness, and with a deep sorrow for having offended Him, is capable of disarming His anger, and of inclining Him to mercy and pardon.

How is a soul, when loaded with the weight of its iniquities, consoled by the certainty of meeting with mercy from God, when it returns to Him with sincere sorrow for sin, and a firm and effectual resolution of renouncing it, and leading a better life for the future! Then God, who is more desirous to pardon us than we are to crave His mercy, ceases to be our Judge and becomes our Father. Forgetting what we were, He remembers only what we now are, and treats us with as much bounty as though we had never offended Him.

Prayer

Give me, O God, that sincere sorrow and contrition which may purge away all my offenses. I can commit sin of myself, but I cannot repent nor free myself from it without Thy grace and assistance. Yes, Father, I have sinned and have offended Thy goodness; and this fills me with grief and confusion. Chastise me, but forgive me, and let my punishment be to hate myself that I may love Thee. I have sinned against Heaven and before

Thee; I am not worthy to be numbered amongst Thy children; receive me as one of Thy servants. Then, happy shall I be, if, feeding upon the bread of tears, living in labor, in a reverential fear of Thee, and in an exact obedience to Thy will, I pass my life in mourning and sighing, in punishing myself and avenging Thee, endeavoring never to pardon in myself what Thou art so willing to forgive me! Take away my life from me, O my Saviour, or keep me from sin, for I can no longer live to offend Thee. Grant that I may frequently recollect this my desire, and that the remembrance of it may ever withhold me from displeasing Thee. Amen.

Chapter 53

The Grace of God is Not Communicated to the Worldly-Minded

CHRIST

SON, My grace is precious; it suffers not itself to be mingled with external things, or earthly consolations.

Thou must, therefore, cast away every obstacle to grace if thou desire to have it infused into thee.

Choose a secret place to thyself; love to dwell with thyself alone; seek not to be talking with anyone; but rather pour forth devout prayers to God, that thou mayest keep thy mind in compunction, and thy conscience clean.

Esteem the whole world as nothing; prefer the attendance on God before all external things.

For thou canst not both attend to Me and at the same time delight thyself in transitory things.

Thou must withdraw from thine acquaintance, and those dear to thee, and keep thy mind disengaged from all temporal comfort.

So the blessed Apostle Peter beseeches the faithful of Christ to keep themselves as strangers and pilgrims in this world. (*1 Ptr.* 2:11).

2. Oh, what great confidence shall he have at the hour of his death who is not detained by an affection to anything in the world.

But an infirm soul is not yet capable of having a heart thus perfectly disengaged from all things, neither doth the sensual man understand the liberty of an internal man. (*1 Cor.* 2:14).

But if he will be spiritual indeed he must renounce as well those that are near him, as those that are afar off, and beware of none more than of himself.

If thou perfectly overcome thyself thou shalt with more ease subdue all things else.

The perfect victory is to triumph over one's self.

For he that keeps himself in subjection, so that his sensuality is ever subject to reason, and reason in all things obedient to Me, he is indeed a conqueror of himself, and lord of all the world.

3. If thou desire to mount thus high, thou must begin manfully, and set the axe to the root (*Matt.* 3:10), that thou mayest root out and destroy thy secret inordinate inclination to thyself, and to all selfish and earthly goods.

This vice, by which a man inordinately loves himself, is at the bottom of all that which is to be rooted out and overcome in thee; which evil being once conquered and brought under, a great peace and tranquillity will presently ensue.

But because there are few that labor to die perfectly to themselves and that fully aim beyond themselves, therefore do they remain entangled in themselves, nor can they be elevated in spirit above themselves.

But he that desires to walk freely with Me must mortify all his wicked and irregular affections, and must not cleave to anything created with any concupiscence or private love.

Practical Reflections

To withdraw the heart from ourselves and all created things, we should, first, frequently raise our affections to God, and endeavor to love Him in and above all things; secondly, we should renounce all voluntary attachments to creatures and to self-seeking; thirdly, we should separate and wean ourselves from all that is naturally pleasing to us, by regarding all things as passing away, and ourselves as pilgrims and strangers in a foreign land, who must allow themselves no delay in their journey, but pass forward on their way.

When thoroughly impressed with these words of the Apostle: We have not a permanent dwelling place here, but we look for one above, how little does a Christian feel attached to the goods, the vanities, and pleasures of this world, knowing that all these things pass away, and must finally end in death! It is easy, says St. Jerome, to despise all earthly things, when we reflect that we must die and leave them all behind us.

Why then does the figure of this world, which passes away and escapes from our sight, make so deep an impression upon our hearts, and the good things of eternity, which alone never fade, affect us so little! Why should we be so strongly attached to what we possess but for a moment and hold only in trust, and so little attracted by that which is destined to be ours, and forever an eternity of happiness?

Prayer

Grant, O Lord, that my heart may loathe all earthly things, and cleave to those alone which are eternal, which will be given to me in exchange for the little I renounce in this world for the love of Thee. Grant me, O God, to love only that which I shall love forever, and to esteem everything as unworthy of a Christian soul which is not the Eternal and Sovereign Good.

"How little does this world appear," said St. Ignatius, "when I view the heavens! and how little do the material heavens and this immense universe appear when I think of Thee, my God!" Grant that in like manner, when impressed with the idea of Thine immensity, I also may yield my whole soul to Thee. Amen.

Chapter 54

The Different Motions of Nature and Grace

CHRIST

SON, observe diligently the motions of nature and grace; for they move very opposite ways, and very subtlely, and can hardly be distinguished but by a spiritual man, and one that is internally illuminated.

All men indeed aim at good, and pretend to something good in what they do and say: therefore, under the appearance of good, many are deceived.

2. Nature is crafty and draws away many; she ensnares and deceives them, and always intends herself for her end.

But grace walks with simplicity, declines from all appearance of evil, offers no deceits, and does all things purely for God, in whom also she rests as in her last end.

3. Nature is not willing to be mortified, or to be restrained, or to be overcome, or to be subject; neither will she of her own accord be brought under.

But grace studies the mortification of her own self, resists sensuality, seeks to be subject, covets to be overcome, aims not at enjoying her own liberty, loves to be kept under discipline, and desires not to have the command over anyone; but under God ever to live, stand, and be; and for God's sake is ever ready humbly to bow down herself under all human creatures. (*1 Ptr.* 2:13).

4. Nature labors for her own interest, and considers what gain she may reap from another.

But grace considers not what may be advantageous and profitable to herself, but rather what may be profitable to many. (*1 Cor.* 10:33).

5. Nature willingly receives honor and respect: But grace faithfully attributes all honor and glory to God.

6. Nature is afraid of being put to shame and despised: But grace is glad to suffer reproach for the name of Jesus. (*Acts* 5:41).

7. Nature loves idleness and bodily rest: But grace cannot be idle and willingly embraces labor. (*1 Cor.* 15:10).

8. Nature seeks to have things that are curious and fine, and does not care for things that are cheap and coarse: But grace is pleased with that which is plain and humble, rejects not coarse things, nor refuses to be clad in old clothes.

9. Nature has regard to temporal things, rejoices at

earthly gain, is troubled at losses, and is provoked at every slight injurious word:

But grace attends to things eternal, and cleaves not to those which pass with time; neither is she disturbed at the loss of things, nor exasperated with hard words, for she places her treasure and her joy in Heaven, where nothing is lost.

10. Nature is covetous, and is more willing to take than to give, and loves to have things to herself:

But grace is bountiful and openhearted, avoids selfishness, is contented with little, and judges it a more blessed thing to give rather than to receive. (*Acts* 20:35).

11. Nature inclines to creatures, to her own flesh, to vanities, and to gadding abroad:

But grace draws to God and to virtue, renounces creatures, flies the world, hates the desires of the flesh, restrains wandering about, and is ashamed to appear in public.

12. Nature willingly receives exterior comfort, in which she may be sensibly delighted:

But grace seeks to be comforted in God alone, and beyond all things visible to be delighted in the Sovereign Good.

13. Nature doth all for her own lucre and interest; she can do nothing gratis, but hopes to gain something equal, or better, or praise, or favor for her good deeds; and covets to have her actions and gifts much valued:

But grace seeks nothing temporal, nor requires any other recompense but God alone for her reward, nor desires anything more of the necessaries of this life than may be serviceable in attaining a happy eternity.

14. Nature rejoices in a multitude of friends and kindred; she glories in the nobility of her stock and descent; she fawns on them that are in power, flatters the rich, and applauds such as are like herself:

But grace loves even her enemies, and is not puffed up with having a great many friends, nor esteems family or birth, unless when joined with greater virtue.

She rather favors the poor than the rich; she has more compassion for the innocent than the powerful; she rejoices with him that loves the truth, and not with the deceitful.

She ever exhorts the good to be zealous for better gifts, and to become like unto the Son of God by the exercise of virtues.

15. Nature easily complains of want and of trouble:

But grace bears poverty with constancy.

16. Nature turns all things to herself and for herself she labors and disputes:

But grace refers all things to God, from whom all originally proceed; she attributes no good to herself, nor does she arrogantly presume of herself; she does not contend, nor prefer her own opinion to others, but in every sense and understanding she submits herself to the eternal wisdom, and to the divine examination.

17. Nature covets to know secrets, and to hear news: is willing to appear abroad, and to have experience of many things by the senses; desires to be taken notice of, and to do such things as may procure praise and admiration.

But grace cares not for the hearing of new and curious things, because all this springs from the old corruption, since nothing is new or lasting upon earth.

She teaches, therefore, to restrain the senses, to avoid vain complacency and ostentation, humbly to hide those things which are worthy of praise and admiration, and from everything and in every knowledge to seek the fruit of spiritual profit, and the praise and honor of God.

She desires not to have herself or what belongs to her extolled; but wishes that God may be blessed in His gifts, who bestows all through mere love.

18. This grace is a supernatural light and a certain special gift of God, and the proper mark of the elect, and pledge of eternal salvation, which elevates a man from the things of the earth to the love of heavenly things, and from carnal makes him spiritual.

Wherefore, the more nature is kept down and subdued, the greater abundance of grace is infused; and the inward man, by new visitations, is daily more reformed according to the image of God. (*Col.* 3:10).

Practical Reflections

What is it to repose in God as in our last end? It is to desire, to seek, and to love only Him; it is to do and to suffer all things for His sake; it is to acquiesce without any reserve in His holy designs; it is to will only what He wills; it is never to go astray, nor turn aside from the way of His ordinances; it is, in fine, to place our whole happiness in pleasing Him, and in not gratifying ourselves; but to do this, is contrary to nature; grace alone can accomplish it.

I. Nature has always for its object self-satisfaction; but grace leads us to do violence to ourselves, that is, to deny and renounce ourselves in all things.

II.   Nature is unwilling to die, to captivate itself, or to be made subject; but grace captivates the soul, restrains and subjects it to what is most hard and contrary to its inclinations; so that it gives up its own liberty on all occasions; fights against its own humors, and yields itself to God; and to honor His sovereign dominion, it rejoices in humiliations, restraint, and subjection.

III.   Nature ever wishes to rule over others; but grace humbles us under the all-powerful hand of God, and makes us obedient for His love to those whom He has appointed in His place over us.

IV.   Nature labors always for its own interest, to please and to establish itself; but grace labors only for God's sake, and watches incessantly over the motions of the heart, to preserve it from sin, and to enable it to seek only its establishment in Jesus Christ.

V.   Nature is pleased with the esteem and praises of men, presuming on its own deserts: but grace makes us think ourselves unworthy of them, and refers all honor to God, and is so nice on this head, that it will not permit the humble and faithful soul to make the least voluntary reference of vanity towards itself, lest it should take some degree of complacency in the good which it performs.

VI.   Nature is afraid of disappointments, and flies from contempt; but grace receives these, and willingly endures them as justly inflicted upon us as sinners, and even makes us grateful to Jesus Christ for allowing us to share with Him what was wont to be the delight of His Heart.

VII. Nature loves the repose of a soft, indolent, and useless life; but grace seeks only labor; she dreads and avoids all useless thoughts, words, and actions; and not being able to endure indolence, either of the heart or mind, she leads the one to be impressed with a sense of the presence of God, and the other to live for His love.

VIII. Nature is attracted by everything that is great, beautiful, splendid, or commodious; but grace despises and shuns all these, and thinks nothing great but what is divine, supernatural, and eternal.

The more, however, nature is repressed, the more abundantly does grace communicate itself to the soul, renew it in the interior spirit, and establish it perfectly in God.

Prayer

It is time, O Lord, I should cast myself on Thy mercy, to obtain the pardon of my sins, and on Thy love, to follow all its attractions. Support me, O Lord, and strengthen me by Thy grace against the inclinations of nature and self-love; for, of myself, it is impossible to resist and conquer the motions of corrupt nature, which is ever seeking its own gratification, in direct opposition to Thy holy will. Grant us Thy grace to rise superior to nature, to correspond faithfully with the inspirations of the Holy Spirit, to conquer and renounce ourselves, that we may be renewed and established in the possession of Thy love. Amen.

Chapter 55

The Corruption of Nature, And the Efficacy of Divine Grace

DISCIPLE

O LORD, my God, Who hast created me to Thine own image and likeness, grant me this grace, which Thou hast declared to be so great, and so necessary to salvation, that I may overcome my corrupt nature, which draws me to sin and perdition.

For I perceive in my flesh the law of sin contradicting the law of my mind (*Rom.* 7:23), and leading me captive to obey sensuality in many things; neither can I resist the passions thereof unless assisted by Thy most holy grace, infused copiously into my heart.

2. I stand in need of Thy grace, and of a great grace, to overcome nature, which is always prone to evil from her youth.

For the first man, Adam, being corrupted by sin, the punishment of his sin has descended upon all mankind: so that nature itself, which by Thee was created good and right, is now put for the vice and infirmity of corrupt nature; because the motion thereof, left to itself, draws to evil, and to things below.

For the little strength which remains is but like a spark hidden in the ashes.

This is our natural reason, which is surrounded with a great mist, having yet the judgment of good and evil, and of the distance of truth and falsehood, though it be unable to fulfill all that it approves; neither does it now enjoy the full light of truth, nor the former purity of its affections.

3. Hence it is, O my God, that according to the inward man, I am delighted with Thy law (*Rom.* 7:22), knowing Thy command to be good, just, and holy, and reproving all evil and sin, as what ought to be shunned.

And yet in the flesh I serve the law of sin, whilst I rather obey sensuality than reason.

Hence it is, that to will is present with me, but to accomplish that which is good, I find not. (*Rom.* 7:18).

Hence I often make many good purposes: but because I

want grace to help my weakness, through a slight resistance I recoil and fall off.

Hence it comes to pass, that I know the way to perfection, and see clearly enough what it is I ought to do.

But being pressed down with the weight of my own corruption I rise not to those things which are more perfect.

4. Oh, how exceedingly necessary is Thy grace for me, O Lord, to begin that which is good, to go forward with it, and to accomplish it!

For without it I can do nothing; but I can do all things in Thee, when Thy grace strengthens me. (*Phil.* 4:13).

O truly heavenly grace, without which we have no merits of our own, neither are any of the gifts of nature to be valued.

No arts, no riches, no beauty or strength, no wit or eloquence, are of any worth with Thee, O Lord, without grace.

For the gifts of nature are common to the good and bad; but grace or divine love is the proper gift of the elect, and they that are adorned with it are esteemed worthy of eternal life.

This grace is so excellent that neither the gift of prophecy, nor the working of miracles, nor any speculation, how sublime soever, is of any value without it.

Nor even faith, nor hope, nor any other virtues, are acceptable to Thee without charity and grace.

5. O most blessed grace, which makest the poor in spirit rich in virtues, and renderest him who is rich in many good things humble of heart.

Come, descend upon me, replenish me betimes with

Thy consolation, lest my soul faint through weariness and dryness of mind.

I beseech Thee, O Lord, that I may find grace in Thy sight (*Gen.* 18:3), for Thy grace is enough for me (*2 Cor.* 12:9), though I obtain none of those other things which nature desires.

If I be tempted and afflicted with many tribulations I will fear no evil whilst Thy grace is with me.

She is my strength; she gives counsel and help.

She is mightier than all my enemies, and wiser than all the wise.

6. She is the mistress of truth, the teacher of discipline, the light of the heart, the comforter of affliction, the banisher of sorrow, the expeller of fears, the nurse of devotion, the producer of tears.

What am I without her but a piece of dry wood, and an unprofitable stock, fit for nothing but to be cast away?

Let Thy grace, therefore, O Lord, always both go before me and follow me and make me ever intent upon good works, through Jesus Christ Thy Son. Amen.

Practical Reflections

We do justice to ourselves when we mistrust our own strength, and to God, when we confide in the assistance of His grace. This is never wanting to us; but we are often wanting in our correspondence with it, though the only means of ensuring salvation is to be faithful to its attractions, for they would lead us to the practice of every virtue.

Human nature having been corrupted by the first man's sin, the effect of this corruption, as well as the stain of sin, descended to all mankind; hence are we constrained to fight incessantly against the motions of nature, and to follow those of grace. Without offering this holy violence to ourselves, by which we subdue and renounce our own inclinations, it would be impossible to be saved. In the state of innocence, all in man being orderly and subject to God on account of original justice, the passions did not revolt against reason; but in our present state of sin, concupiscence continually rebels against the soul: this we must never cease to resist until we cease to live.

Prayer

When, O God, shall Thy grace reign in our hearts, and subject them to the influence of Thy love? He who knows how to estimate the value and excellence of Thy grace, O Lord, which is a participation of Thy divine nature, and a holy infusion of Thy goodness into our souls, will suffer the loss of all things else, rather than be deprived of such a treasure; and will not hesitate to make any sacrifice, however great, to preserve it.

When I consider, O Lord, that those graces which I reject, or neglect, have been purchased for me at the price of Thy suffering and Precious Blood, how I am covered with confusion, for having made so bad a use of them, and for having preferred even trifles before them! Well may the account I must one day give of all the inspirations which I have neglected, as of so many drops of Thy sacred Blood dissipated or profaned, fill me with alarm and terror, and induce me henceforth to correspond with them most faithfully, that I may not forfeit my salvation. Amen.

Chapter 56

We Ought to Deny Ourselves, and Imitate Christ by the Cross

CHRIST

SON, as much as thou canst go out of thyself, so much wilt thou be able to enter into Me.

As desiring nothing abroad brings peace at home, so relinquishing thyself joins thee interiorly to God.

I will have thee learn the perfect renunciation of thyself, according to My will, without contradiction or complaint.

Follow Me (*John* 21:19): I am the way, the truth, and the life. (*John* 14:6). Without the way there is no going; without the truth there is no knowing; without the life there is no living.

I am the way which thou must follow; the truth which thou must believe; the life for which thou must hope.

I am the way inviolable, the truth infallible, and the life interminable.

I am the straightest way, the sovereign truth, the true life, the blessed life, and uncreated life.

If thou continue in My way thou shalt know the truth, and the truth shall deliver thee (*John* 8:32), and thou shalt attain to life everlasting. (*Matt.* 19:29).

2. If thou wilt enter into life, keep the Commandments. (*Matt.* 19:17).

If thou wilt know the truth, believe Me. (*John* 14:17).

If thou wilt be perfect, sell all things. (*Matt.* 19:21).

If thou wilt be My disciple, deny thyself. (*Matt.* 16:24).

If thou wilt possess a blessed life, despise this present life. (*Matt.* 16:25).

If thou wilt be exalted in Heaven, humble thyself in this world. (*Matt.* 18:4).

If thou wilt reign with Me, bear the cross with Me.

For none but the servants of the cross find the way of bliss and true light.

DISCIPLE

3. Lord Jesus, forasmuch as Thy way is narrow, and despised by the world, grant that I may follow Thee, and be despised by the world.

For the servant is not greater than his lord, neither is the disciple above his master. *(Matt.* 10:24).

Let Thy servant meditate on Thy life, for there is my salvation and true holiness.

Whatever I read or hear besides does not recreate nor fully delight me.

CHRIST

4. Son, now thou knowest these things and hast read them all, happy shalt thou be if thou fulfill them.

"He that hath my commandments, and keepeth them, he it is that loveth me; and I will love him, and will manifest myself unto him" (*John* 14:21), and "I will make him sit with me in the kingdom of my Father." (*Matt.* 19:28).

DISCIPLE

5. Lord Jesus, as Thou hast said and hast promised, so may it be indeed, and may it be my lot to merit it.

I have received the cross, I have received it from Thy hand; I will bear it, yea, I will bear it until death, as Thou hast laid it upon me.

Indeed the life of a good religious man is a cross, but it is a cross that conducts him to Paradise.

We have now begun, it is not lawful to go back, nor may we leave off. (*Luke* 9:62).

6. Take courage, my brethren, let us go forward together, Jesus will be with us. (*Heb.* 12:1).

For the sake of Jesus we took up His cross; for the sake of Jesus let us persevere on the cross.

He will be our helper, who is our captain and our leader.

Behold our King marches before us, who will fight for us.

Let us follow Him manfully; let no one shrink through fear; let us be ready to die valiantly in battle, and not stain our glory by flying from the standard of the cross. (*1 Mach.* 9:10).

Practical Reflections

If any man will come after Me, says our Divine Redeemer, let him deny himself, and let him take up his cross daily, and follow Me. In this is included the whole practice of a Christian life, and the way marked out by which we may securely go to eternal salvation, for Jesus is the way, the truth, and the life; the way we must follow, the truth we must believe, and the life we must hope for. To live as Christians, and to secure salvation, we must begin by renouncing and dying to ourselves; for this renunciation—this spirit of self-denial, is the first principle of the Gospel, the fundamental law of Christianity, our most essential duty, and the most effectual means of obtaining salvation. It is this interior mortification, this circumcision of the heart, this retrenchment of all criminal, dangerous, or useless indulgences, which constitutes the difference between the elect and the reprobate. The character of our present sinful state should be that of penance, which is the end of Christianity and the assurance of salvation.

To carry our cross with Jesus Christ is to suffer from all, while we are careful not to become the cause of suffering in others; it is to receive all pains of body and mind as coming from above; it is to endure with patience all the evils which happen to us from the justice of God or the injustice of man; it is to accept of contempt as our due, and to consider it our greatest misfortune to suffer nothing for God, but our sovereign happiness to suffer always for His love.

Prayer

O Divine Saviour, how few are willing to be with Thee on Calvary, yet how gladly would all accompany Thee on Thabor and in Heaven! While each one desires and seeks exemption from the cross, to live in tranquillity and ease, no one chooses to suffer for Thee; although the only sure proof we can give Thee of our love is to be willing to suffer with Thee, and to copy Thy painful example.

O cross of Jesus! how patiently do we bear Thy sorrows in our hearts! How shall I be able to behold Thee with confidence at the last day, if now I look upon Thee with horror? How shall I be able to give up my soul in the embraces of the crucifix, if now I live an enemy to that emblem of mercy? Permit it not, O Jesus, and since Thou hast saved me by the cross, grant that I may be ever willing to live in its practice, that I may die in its salvation. Amen.

Chapter 57

A Man Should Not Be Too Much Dejected When He Falls into Some Defects

CHRIST

SON, patience and humility in adversity are more pleasing to Me than much consolation and devotion in prosperity.

Why art thou disturbed at a little thing said against thee? If it had been more thou oughtest not to have been moved.

But now let it pass, it is not the first, or anything new, nor will it be the last, if thou live long.

Thou art valiant enough so long as no adversity or opposition comes in thy way.

Thou canst also give good advice, and encourage others with thy words; but when any unexpected trouble comes to knock at thy door then thy counsel and thy courage fail thee.

Consider thy great frailty which thou dost often experience in small difficulties; yet it is intended for thy good as often as these or such like things befall thee.

2. Put it from thy heart the best thou canst; and if it has touched thee, yet let it not cast thee down, nor keep thee a long time entangled. At least bear it patiently, if thou canst not receive it with joy.

And though thou be not willing to bear it, and perceivest an indignation arising within thyself, yet repress thyself, and suffer no inordinate word to come out of thy mouth, which may scandalize the weak.

The commotion which is stirred up in thee will quickly be allayed, and thine inward pain will be sweetened by the return of grace.

I am still living, saith the Lord, ready to help thee, and comfort thee more than before, if thou put thy trust in Me, and devoutly call upon Me.

3. Keep thy mind calm and even (*Mark* 10:49), and prepare thyself for bearing still more.

All is not lost if thou feel thyself often afflicted, or grievously tempted.

Thou art man and not a god; thou art flesh, and not an angel.

How canst thou think to continue ever in the same state of virtue, when this was not found in the angels of heaven, nor in the first man in paradise?

I am He who raises up and saves those who mourn; and those who know their own infirmity I advance to My divinity.

DISCIPLE

4. O Lord, blessed be this Thy word, it is more sweet to my mouth than honey and the honeycomb. (*Ps.* 18:11).

What should I do in such great tribulation and anguish if Thou didst not encourage me with Thy holy words?

What matter is it how much or what I suffer, so I come at length to the haven of salvation? Grant me a good end, grant me a happy passage out of this world.

Remember me, O my God, and direct me by the straight road to Thy Kingdom.

Practical Reflections

When languishing under great and long-continued sufferings, let us remember that humble submission to the cross is incomparably more pleasing to God than the enjoyment of consolation; and hence, that the greatest consolation of the soul should be to be deprived of every other consolation but that of being ever faithful to its crucified Redeemer.

When tempted and inclined to sin, let us turn away from our evil inclinations, and resist them with all the strength and courage possible; let us have recourse to Our Lord for His assistance, and to the Blessed Virgin for her prayers. The sense of evil must not deject or discourage us, but elevate us to God. In Him let us place all our confidence, and, with an extreme horror for sin, withdraw our minds, as far as we are able, from the sinful objects which affect them, and our hearts from the criminal pleasures which allure them. That we may remain faithful under contradictions let us endeavor, when the heart is moved, to keep silence, and to sacrifice to God all those ill-natured reflections and excited feelings which proceed from resentment against those who have been the cause of our uneasiness; knowing that whatever we think or desire, or say against our neighbor, we think, desire, and say against Jesus Christ.

Let us remember, in our interior afflictions, that all is not lost because we are in trouble and violent temptation. Let us resist temptation, submit to humiliation, and believe that before we can be elevated to a union with God we must first descend into the depth of our own miseries.

Prayer

Permit not, O Lord, my afflictions to become unavailable to salvation; and if I do not suffer them with joy, grant at least that I may endure them with patience. It is good for me to be humbled, that I may learn to keep Thy holy ordinances. Doubly wretched should I be, to make the miseries of this life serve only to consign me to eternal torments and despair! May then the sufferings which Thou sendest me, O God, become the pledges of my salvation. Amen.

Chapter 58

Of Not Searching into High Matters, Nor into the Secret Judgments of God

CHRIST

SON, see thou dispute not of high matters, nor of the hidden judgments of God: why this man is left thus, and this other is raised to so great a grace, or why this person is so much afflicted and that other so highly exalted.

These things are above the reach of man, neither can any reason or discourse penetrate into the judgments of God.

When, therefore, the enemy suggests to thee such things as these, or thou hearest curious men inquiring into them, answer with the Prophet: "Thou art just, O Lord: and thy judgment is right." (*Ps.* 118:137).

And again: "The judgments of the Lord are true, justified in themselves." (*Ps.* 18:10).

My judgments are to be feared, not to be searched into; for they are incomprehensible to human understanding. (*Rom.* 11:23).

2. In like manner do not inquire nor dispute concerning the merits of the saints, which of them is more holy than the other, or which greater in the Kingdom of

Heaven. (*Matt.* 18:1).

These things oftentimes breed strife and unprofitable contentions, and nourish pride and vainglory; whence arise envy and dissensions, this man proudly seeking to prefer this saint, and another man preferring another.

To desire to know and to search into such things as these is of no profit, but rather displeaseth the saints; for I am not the God of dissension but of peace (*1 Cor.* 14:33), which peace consists more in true humility than in exalting oneself.

3. Some are carried by a zeal of love towards these or those, with greater affection, but this affection is rather human than divine.

I am He who made all the saints; I gave them grace; I have brought them to glory.

I know the merits of each of them; I have prevented them with blessings of My sweetness. (*Ps.* 20:4).

I foreknew My beloved ones before the creation; I chose them out of the world; they were not beforehand to choose Me. (*John* 15:16).

I called them by My grace, and drew them by My mercy; I led them safe through many temptations.

I imparted to them extraordinary comforts, I gave them perseverance, I have crowned their patience.

4. I know the first and the last: I embrace them all with an inestimable love.

I am to be praised in all My saints (*Ps.* 67:36), I am to be blessed above all things (*Dan.* 3:52), and to be honored in every one of them whom I have thus gloriously magnified and eternally chosen, without any foregoing merits of their own.

He, therefore, that despises one of the least of My saints, honors not the greatest, for both little and great I have made. (*Wis.* 6:7).

And he that derogates from any one of the saints derogates also from Me, and from all the rest of them in the Kingdom of Heaven.

They are all one through the bond of love; they have the same sentiments, the same will, and all mutually love one another. (*John* 17:21).

5. And yet, which is much higher, they all love Me more than themselves and their own merits.

For being elevated above themselves, and drawn out of the love of themselves, they are wholly absorbed in the love of Me, in whom also they rest by an eternal enjoyment.

Nor is there anything which can divert them from Me, or depress them; for being full of the eternal truth, they burn with the fire of charity that cannot be extinguished.

Therefore, let carnal and sensual men, who know not how to love anything but their private satisfactions, forbear to dispute of the state of the saints. They add and take away according to their own inclinations, not according to what is pleasing to the everlasting truth.

6. In many there is ignorance, especially in such as, being but little enlightened, seldom know how to love anyone with a perfect spiritual love.

They are as yet much inclined to these or those by a natural affection, and human friendship; and as they are affected with regard to things below they conceive the like imaginations of the things of Heaven.

But there is an incomparable distance between what the

imperfect imagine and what the illuminated contemplate by revelation from above.

7. Take heed, therefore, My son, that thou treat not curiously of these things which exceed thy knowledge, but rather make it thy business and thine aim that thou be found even the least amongst those who inherit the Kingdom of God.

And if anyone should know who were more holy or greater in the Kingdom of Heaven, what would this knowledge profit him unless he would take occasion from knowing this, to humble himself in My sight, and to praise My name with greater fervor?

It is much more acceptable to God for a man to think of the greatness of his own sins, and how little he is advanced in virtue, and at how great a distance he is from the perfection of the saints, than to dispute which of them is greater or less.

It is better to invoke the saints with devout prayers and tears, and to implore their glorious suffrages with an humble mind, than by a vain inquiry to search into their secrets.

8. They are well and perfectly contented, if men would but be contented and refrain from their vain discourses.

They glory not in their own merits, for they ascribe nothing of goodness to themselves, but all to Me, because I bestowed all upon them out of My infinite charity.

They are filled with so great a love of the Deity, and such overflowing joy, that there is nothing wanting to their glory, nor can any happiness be wanting to them.

All the saints, the higher they are in glory the more humble are they in themselves, and nearer to Me, and better beloved by Me.

Therefore, thou hast it written, that they cast down their crowns before God, and fell upon their faces before the Lamb, and adored Him that liveth forever and ever. (*Apoc.* 4:10; 5:14).

9. Many examine who is greatest in the Kingdom of God, who know not whether they shall be worthy to be numbered among the least.

It is a great matter to be even the least in Heaven, where all are great, because all shall be called, and shall be the children of God. (*Matt.* 5:9).

The least shall be as a thousand, and the sinner of a hundred years shall die. (*Is.* 60:22; 65:20).

For when the disciples asked who was the greatest in the Kingdom of Heaven they received this answer:

"Unless you be converted, and become as little children, you shall not enter into the kingdom of heaven. Whosoever therefore shall humble himself as this little child, he is the greater in the kingdom of heaven." (*Matt.* 18:3).

10. Woe to those who disdain to humble themselves willingly with little children; for the low gates of the heavenly Kingdom will not suffer them to enter therein.

Woe also to the rich, who have their consolation here (*Luke* 6:24), for when the poor shall go into the Kingdom of God they shall stand lamenting without.

Rejoice you that are humble, and be glad you that are poor, for yours is the Kingdom of God (*Matt.* 5:3): yet so, if you walk in truth.

Practical Reflections

If we would honor the saints as they deserve, we should invoke and imitate them, rather than dispute about their degrees of heavenly glory. We should endeavor to copy their bright example; for this is really to honor the saints, to become saints like themselves.

God hath formed all the saints upon the model of His Son, the Word incarnate; so that we cannot become the objects of God's love, if we make not Jesus Christ the object of our imitation. He has willed, said St. Cyprian, that there should be saints in all states and conditions of life, to make known to all men that each one in his own state may sanctify his soul, and obtain salvation, by living a holy and Christian life. He has constituted saints for our protectors and our models, that we may gain Heaven by walking in their footsteps; they hear our prayers, and, being secure of their own happiness, are solicitous only for ours.

Let us then endeavor to live and to suffer with them here, that we may live and reign with them hereafter; and let us remember that, according to the Gospel, there is but one way of arriving at the happy term which they have reached, which is the way of penance, mortification, and disengagement from the world; every other way leads to perdition.

Prayer

Thou desirest, O Lord, our sanctification and our salvation, and Thou givest us the most efficacious means of attaining them, but we have hitherto miserably neglected them. Grant that henceforth we may really honor the saints by forming ourselves upon their example, and rendering ourselves worthy of the eternal happiness which they possess by copying their endeavors to obtain it. Suffer us not to be idle admirers of their felicity, but doers of these good deeds by which they obtained it, that thus we may be assured that ours also shall be the Kingdom of Heaven. Amen.

Chapter 59

All Hope and Confidence Is to Be Fixed in God Alone

DISCIPLE

LORD, what is my confidence which I have in this life? or what is my greatest comfort amongst all things that appear under Heaven? Is it not Thou, my Lord God, Whose mercies are without number?

Where was I ever well without Thee? or when could things go ill with me when Thou wast present?

I had rather be poor for Thee than rich without Thee.

I choose rather to sojourn upon earth with Thee than to possess Heaven without Thee. Where Thou art there is Heaven; and there is death and Hell where Thou art not.

After Thee I have a longing desire, and therefore must needs sigh after Thee, and cry and pray.

In fine, I cannot fully trust to anyone to bring me seasonable help in my necessities, save only to Thee, my God.

Thou art my hope, Thou art my confidence, Thou art my comforter, and most faithful above all.

2. All seek their own interest; Thou aimest only at my salvation and profit, and turnest all things to my good. (*Rom.* 8:28).

And although Thou expose me to various temptations

and adversities, yet all this Thou ordainest for my good, Who art wont to prove Thy beloved servants a thousand ways.

Under which proofs Thou oughtest not less to be loved and praised, than if Thou wert to fill me with heavenly comforts.

3. In Thee, therefore, O Lord God, I put all my hope and refuge; to Thee I make known all my tribulations and anguish (*Ps.* 31:7); for I find all to be infirm and unstable whatever I behold out of Thee.

For neither will a multitude of friends be of any service to me; nor can strong auxiliaries bring me any succor, nor wise counsellors give me a profitable answer, nor the books of the learned comfort me, nor any wealth deliver me, nor any secret and pleasant place secure me, if Thou Thyself do not assist, help, strengthen, comfort, instruct, and defend me.

4. For all things which seem to be for our peace and for our happiness, when Thou art absent, are nothing; and in truth contribute nothing to our felicity.

Thou, therefore, art the foundation of all good, the height of life, and the depth of wisdom; and to trust in Thee above all things is the greatest comfort of Thy servant.

To Thee I lift up mine eyes; in Thee, O my God, the Father of mercies, I put my trust. (*Ps.* 140:8).

Bless and sanctify my soul with Thy heavenly blessings, that it may be made Thy holy habitation, and the seat of Thine eternal glory; and let nothing be found in the temple of Thy dignity that may offend the eyes of Thy majesty.

According to the greatness of Thy goodness, and the multitude of Thy tender mercies, look down upon me

(*Ps.* 68:17), and give ear to the prayer of Thy poor servant, who is in banishment afar off from Thee in the region of the shadow of death.

Protect and defend the soul of Thy poor servant, amidst the many dangers of this corruptible life, and direct him in the company of Thy grace, through the way of peace, to the country of everlasting light. Amen.

Practical Reflections

When afflicted and loaded with interior troubles, or exterior trials and contradictions, or with all these at the same time, let us confidently have recourse to God, who alone can aid and assist us, and let us say to Him: Lord, Thou knowest the designs of our enemies against our souls; how shall we be able to escape them if Thou assist us not? We raise up our eyes and our hearts towards Thee, Who alone art able to protect us; Thou art our God engaged to help us; Thou art our Redeemer, and wilt deliver us: Thou art our Father, and with Thine assistance we shall not yield nor be in danger of perishing.

Prayer

Thou hast said, O Lord, that to become Thy disciples we must deny ourselves, and take up our cross and follow Thee. Thou knowest our extreme repugnance to both one and the other. Suffer not our faith on this point to condemn us for not practicing what we believe to be necessary for salvation, but grant that as we believe so may we ever live as becometh Christians. Amen.

Book IV

Of the
Blessed Sacrament

"COME to me all you that labour and are burdened and I will refresh you." (*Matt.* 11:28). "The bread that I will give is my flesh, for the life of the world." (*John* 6:52).

"Take ye and eat; this is my body, which shall be delivered for you; this do for the commemoration of me." (*1 Cor.* 11:24).

"He that eateth my flesh, and drinketh my blood, abideth in me, and I in him." (*John* 6:57).

"The words that I have spoken to you are spirit and life." (*John* 6:64).

Chapter 1

With How Great Reverence Christ Is to Be Received

DISCIPLE

THESE are Thy words, O Christ, the eternal truth, though not all delivered at one time, nor written in one place.

Since, therefore, they are Thy words, and true, they are all to be received by me with thanks and with faith.

They are Thine, and Thou hast spoken them; and they are also mine because Thou hast delivered them for my salvation.

I willingly received them from Thy mouth, that they may

319

be more inseparably ingrafted in my heart.

These words of such great tenderness, full of sweetness and love, encourage me; but my sins terrify me, and my unclean conscience keeps me back from approaching such great mysteries. The sweetness of Thy words invites me, but the multitude of my offenses weighs me down.

2. Thou commandest me to approach to Thee with confidence if I would have part with Thee; and to receive the food of immortality if I desire to obtain life and glory everlasting.

"Come," sayest Thou to me, "all you that labor and are burdened, and I will refresh you." (*Matt.* 11:28).

O sweet and amiable word in the ear of a sinner, that Thou, O Lord my God, shouldst invite the poor and needy to the Communion of Thy most sacred Body!

But who am I, O Lord, that I should presume to come to Thee?

Behold, the Heaven of heavens cannot contain Thee (*3 Kgs.* 8:27); and Thou sayest, "Come you all to Me."

3. What means this most loving condescension, and so friendly invitation?

How shall I dare to approach, who am conscious to myself of no good on which I can presume?

How shall I introduce Thee into my house, who have oftentimes provoked Thine indignation?

The angels and the archangels stand with a reverential awe; the saints and the just are afraid; and Thou sayest, "Come you all to Me." Unless Thou, O Lord, didst say it, who could believe it to be true?

And unless Thou didst command it, who would dare attempt to approach?

4. Behold Noe, a just man (*Gen.* 6:9), labored a hundred years in building the ark, that he with a few might be preserved; and how shall I be able in the space of one hour to prepare myself to receive with reverence the Maker of the world?

Moses Thy servant, Thy great and special friend, made an ark of incorruptible wood, which he also covered with the most pure gold, that he might deposit therein the tables of the law; and shall I, a rotten creature, presume so easily to receive Thee, the Maker of the law, and the Giver of life?

Solomon, the wisest of the kings of Israel, employed seven years in building a magnificent temple for the praise of Thy name:

And for eight days together celebrated the feast of the dedication thereof; he offered a thousand victims as peace offerings, and brought the Ark of the Covenant in a solemn manner into the place prepared for it, with sound of trumpet and jubilee. (*3 Kgs.* 8:6).

And I, a wretch, and the vilest of men, how shall I bring Thee into my house, who can hardly spend one half hour devoutly? And would I had even once spent one half hour itself as I ought!

5. O my God, how much did they endeavor to do to please Thee!

Alas! how little is what I do! How short a time do I spend when I prepare myself to communicate, being seldom wholly recollected, very seldom free from all distraction!

And yet, surely in the life-giving presence of Thy Deity, no unbecoming thought should occur, nor anything created take up my mind; for it is not an angel, but the Lord of angels that I am to entertain.

6. And yet there is a very great difference between the Ark of the Covenant with its relics, and Thy most pure Body, with its unspeakable virtues; between those sacrifices of the law, which were figures of things to come, and the true sacrifice of Thy Body, which is the accomplishing of all those ancient sacrifices.

7. Why then am I not more inflamed, considering Thy venerable presence?

Why do I not prepare myself with greater care to receive Thy sacred gifts, seeing that these ancient holy patriarchs and prophets, yea kings also and princes, with the whole people, have shown so great an affection of devotion towards Thy divine worship?

8. The most devout King David danced before the ark of God with all his might (*2 Kgs.* 6:14), commemorating the benefits bestowed in times past on the fathers. He made musical instruments of sundry kinds; he published psalms, and appointed them to be sung with joy; he himself likewise often sang them, playing upon his harp, inspired with the grace of the Holy Ghost. He taught the people of Israel to praise God with their whole heart, and to join their voices in blessing and magnifying Him every day.

If such great devotion was then used, and such remembrance of the praise of God before the Ark of the Covenant, how great ought to be the reverence and devotion which I and all Christian people should have in the presence of this Sacrament, and in receiving the most excellent Body of Christ!

9. Many run to sundry places to visit the relics of the

saints, and are astonished to hear their wonderful works; they behold the noble church buildings and kiss their sacred bones, wrapt up in silk and gold.

And behold I have Thee here present on the altar, my God, the Saint of saints, the Creator of men, and the Lord of angels.

Oftentimes in seeing these things men are moved with curiosity, and the novelty of the sight, and but little fruit of amendment is reaped thereby; especially when persons lightly run hither and thither, without true contrition for their sins.

But here, in the Sacrament of the Altar, Thou art wholly present, my God, the man Christ Jesus; where also the fruit of eternal salvation is plentifully reaped, as often as Thou art worthily and devoutly received.

And to this we are not drawn by any levity, curiosity, or sensuality; but by a firm faith, a devout hope, and a sincere charity.

10. O God, the invisible Maker of the world, how wonderfully dost Thou deal with us! How sweetly and graciously dost Thou order all things in favor of Thine elect, to whom Thou offerest Thyself to be received in this Sacrament!

For this exceeds all understanding of man; this in a particular manner engages the hearts of the devout, and enkindles their love.

For Thy true faithful, who dispose their whole life to amendment, by this most worthy Sacrament, frequently receive a great grace of devotion and love of virtue.

11. Oh, the wonderful and hidden grace of this Sacrament, which only the faithful of Christ know; but unbelievers

and such as are slaves to sin cannot experience.

In this Sacrament is conferred spiritual grace; lost virtue is repaired in the soul; and beauty disfigured by sin returns again.

And so great sometimes is this grace that from the abundance of the devotion that is bestowed, not only the mind, but the frail body also feels a great increase of strength.

12. Yet it is much to be lamented and pitied that we should be so lukewarm and negligent as not to be drawn with greater affection to the receiving of Christ, in whom consists all the hope and merit of those that shall be saved.

For He is our sanctification and our redemption; He is our comfort in our pilgrimage, and the eternal beatitude of the saints.

It is therefore much to be lamented that many esteem so lightly this saving mystery which rejoices Heaven and preserves the whole world.

Oh, the blindness and hardness of the heart of man that doth not more highly prize so unspeakable a gift; and from daily use falls into a disregard of it.

13. For if this most holy Sacrament were only celebrated in one place, and consecrated by only one priest in the world, how great a desire would men have to go to that place, and to such a priest of God; that they might see the divine mysteries celebrated?

But now there are made many priests, and Christ is offered up in many places, that the grace and love of God to man may appear the greater, the more this sacred Communion is spread throughout the world.

Thanks be to Thee, O good Jesus, our eternal Shepherd,

Who hast vouchsafed to feed us poor exiles with Thy precious Body and Blood, and to invite us to the receiving these mysteries with the very words of Thine Own mouth, saying, "Come to me all you that labour and are burdened, and I will refresh you." (*Matt.* 11:28).

Practical Reflections

Who can conceive or explain the excellence of the all-divine gift which Jesus Christ bestows upon us in giving us His blessed Body and Blood in the Holy Eucharist, in which we receive God with all His perfections, the plenitude of His divinity, all the virtues and grace of His humanity, and all the merits of a Man-God? We may say, with St. Augustine, that God, though all-powerful, cannot bestow upon us anything greater than Himself, whom He here gives us; though most rich and liberal, yet He cannot dispense to us anything more from the treasures of His bounty than this one gift of His Body and Blood, His whole self; and though the uncreated and incarnate Wisdom of the Father, yet He cannot invent a more efficacious means of gaining our hearts than to enter into them by the Holy Communion, and thus unite and transform us into Himself.

But what should delight our minds and hearts is that in the sacred Host which we receive, and even in its smallest part (that we may lose nothing of so precious a gift), He has included all the riches of His bounty, wisdom, and love, to communicate them all to us, and by communicating them to us, to enable us to live in a supernatural and divine life by feeding and nourishing us with God; for it is to this end that He assumes a new life upon our altars, to impart it to us in the Holy Communion by which, says the Council of Trent, He infuses into our souls all the riches of His love. Yes, my Saviour, after having bestowed upon us all the goods of nature and of grace Thou addest still more to Thy gifts—Thy whole self in the blessed Eucharist. After having been liberal of Thy gifts in our regard, which, although most precious, are still much less than Thyself, in this adorable Sacrament Thou art prodigal even of Thy very self. Who then can refuse and withhold his heart from God, who comes thus to take possession of it, as belonging to Him upon so many titles?

Prayer

What return can I make Thee, O Lord, for all Thy gifts and favors? What can I give Thee in exchange for Thyself, Whom Thou bestowest upon my soul, to become to me the principle of a truly Christian life and the pledge of my salvation? As often as I have the honor of receiving Thee, my most amiable Saviour, I may say that Thou art all mine, and yet, alas! after having received Thee so frequently, I cannot as yet say that I am all Thine. Come, O Jesus, and take full possession of my ungrateful and unfaithful heart, which is so little devoted to Thee, and so much given to the world and to itself. Conquer its perversity, O Lord, and oblige it to love Thee, that it may hate itself, and, recalling its affections, devote them entirely to Thee. It is Thine, O God, as the work of Thy hands and the price of Thy blood; it is Thy purchased inheritance, which Thou comest to take possession of. Permit it not to depart from Thee to become the slave of its passions, but, being come to me, establish Thy reign entirely and forever over me.

Suffer me not, O Jesus, when I receive Thee, Who art my all, both now and forever, to be so unhappy, like many Christians, as to be Thine only in appearance and exteriorly, only in desires and wishes, or to be but half Thine, so as to wish to reconcile God and the world, vanity and devotion; which Thou declarest in the Gospel is impossible and incompatible with salvation. Suffer me not to be so miserable as to belong to Thee only for a time, by almost immediately after Communion falling again into voluntary habitual faults, which Thy presence should correct, or at least diminish; for the fruit of a good Communion is strength, courage, and constancy to resist and conquer ourselves.

Receive, O Jesus, my most humble thanks for Thine institution of this adorable Sacrament, in which Thy love triumphs over all Thine other attributes, to feed and nourish me with Thine own Body and Blood. In gratitude for so great a favor, for so wonderful and divine a benefit, I beseech Thee to accept of the sincere, perfect, and irrevocable offering which I now make of my whole self to Thee, for time and eternity. Amen.

Chapter 2

God's Great Goodness and Charity Are Shown to Man in This Sacrament

DISCIPLE

O LORD, trusting in Thy goodness, and in Thy great mercy, I come sick to my Saviour, hungry and thirsty to the fountain of life, needy to the King of Heaven, a servant to his lord, a creature to his Creator, and one in desolation to his tender comforter.

But whence is this to me, that Thou shouldst come to me? Who am I that Thou shouldst give Thyself to me?

How dare such a sinner appear before Thee? And Thou, how dost Thou vouchsafe to come to a sinner?

Thou knowest Thy servant, and Thou knowest that he has nothing of good in him that can entitle him to this favor.

I confess therefore my unworthiness, I acknowledge Thy bounty, I praise Thy goodness, and I give Thee thanks for Thine excessive charity.

For out of Thine own mercy Thou dost this, not for my merits, that Thy goodness may be better known to me; that greater charity may be imparted, and humility more perfectly recommended.

Since, therefore, this pleaseth Thee, and Thou hast commanded it should be so, Thy merciful condescension pleaseth me also but, oh! that my iniquity may be no obstacle.

2. O most sweet and most bountiful Jesus, what great reverence and thanks, with perpetual praise, are due to Thee for the receiving of Thy sacred Body, whose dignity no man can sufficiently express!

But what shall I think on in this communion, when I am approaching to my Lord, whom I can never reverence so much as I ought, and yet long to receive with devotion.

What can I think on better or more wholesome to my soul than to humble myself entirely in Thy presence, and extol Thine infinite goodness above me?

I praise Thee, O my God, and I extol Thee forever; I despise myself and subject myself to Thee, casting myself down to the depth of my unworthiness.

3. Behold Thou art the Saint of saints, and I am the greatest of sinners.

Behold Thou bowest Thyself down to me, who am not worthy to look up to Thee.

Behold Thou comest to me; Thou art willing to be with me; Thou invitest me to Thy banquet.

Thou wilt give me Thy heavenly food, and the bread of angels to eat (*Ps.* 77:25); no other, verily, than Thyself, the Living Bread, Who didst come down from Heaven, and Who givest life to the world. (*John* 6:33,41).

4. Behold whence love proceeds; what a bounty shines forth! What great thanks and praises are due to Thee for these things!

Oh, how wholesome and profitable was Thy design in this institution! how sweet and delightful this banquet, in which Thou givest Thyself to be our food!

Oh, how admirable is Thy work, O Lord! how powerful Thy virtue! how ineffable Thy truth!

For Thou hast spoken, and all things were made; and that has been done which Thou didst command.

5. A wonderful thing it is, and worthy of faith, and exceeding all human understanding, that Thou, O Lord my God, true God, and true man, art contained whole and entire under a small form of bread and wine, and without being consumed, art eaten by the receiver.

Thou the Lord of all things, Who standest in need of no one, hast been pleased by this Sacrament to dwell in us.

Preserve my heart and my body without stain, that with a joyful and clean conscience I may be able often to celebrate Thy sacred mysteries, and to receive for my eternal salvation what Thou hast principally ordained and instituted for Thine honor and perpetual remembrance.

6. Rejoice, O my soul, and give thanks to thy God for so noble a gift, and so singular a comfort left to thee in this vale of tears.

For as often as thou repeatest this mystery, and receivest

the Body of Christ, so often dost thou celebrate the work of thy redemption, and art made partaker of all the merits of Christ.

For the charity of Christ is never diminished, and the greatness of His propitiation is never exhausted.

Therefore oughtest thou to dispose thyself for this, by perpetually renewing the vigor of thy mind, and to weigh with attentive consideration this great mystery of thy salvation.

And as often as thou sayest or hearest Mass, it ought to seem to thee as great, new, and delightful as if Christ that same day, first descending into the Virgin's womb, had been made man; or hanging on the cross, was suffering and dying for the salvation of mankind.

Practical Reflections

1. When thou approachest the Holy Communion, consider the greatness and majesty of God, whom thou art going to receive, and the baseness and unworthiness of thyself, a vile and sinful creature, who art about to receive Him. Humble thyself in His presence, and say to Him: Who am I, Lord, that I should dare to approach Thee; and who art Thou, that Thou shouldst debase Thyself so low as to come to me! When I consider, on the one hand, the excellence of Thy sanctity and purity, and, on the other, the corruption and disorders of my soul, I am forced to acknowledge that I am most unworthy to receive Thee, and that I cannot, without rashness, permit Thee to enter into my heart. But, knowing the excess of Thy goodness, and the need which I have of Thee for my sanctification and salvation, I will approach to Thee, my Saviour, with a holy confidence, for Thou hast said that those who are well stand not in need of a physician, but only those who are sick; to Thee, Who comest to

seek and to save those who are gone astray, and are in danger of perishing: to Thee Who art the "Word made flesh for love of man;" to Thee Whose desire is that we be converted and live. I am indeed a grievous sinner, but I will no longer remain such. I feel neither consolation nor delight in Thy holy presence, but sensible of my many miseries, I come to lay them all at Thy sacred feet; here I will rest.

2. Whence comes this honor and this happiness, that my God should so far conceal His sovereign majesty as to become the food and nourishment of my soul? Ah! it is the profound humility of a Man-God, who would carry His abjection not only so far as not to appear as God, but not even as man, and thus eclipse all the splendors of His majesty, to evince the excess of His bounty and the charms of His love for us. O my Saviour, while Thou concealest Thy divine perfections from our sight, that we may not be dazzled by their glory, Thou dost disclose to us the depth of Thy humility, that we may be induced to copy it in our conduct. O my soul, canst thou desire to be known by others, when thou beholdest thy God concealed and hidden in the Holy Eucharist! How shall such a miserable worm of the earth as I am dare to exalt myself when I reflect that my God annihilates Himself in this mystery, to impress upon me the character of His humility?

3. Say not, Christian soul, that thou dost not dare to approach frequently to a God so great and awful. Thou art indeed unworthy, and thou wilt not cease to be so if thou dost not endeavor to attend diligently to thy correction; but, says St. Augustine, this bread of angels is not a poison; it is a nourishment given for thy use, and necessary for thy salvation. Receive it therefore, and frequently nourish thy soul with it; but let not habit deprive thee of all relish for this heavenly food, as it generally does for all worldly dainties. The holy dispositions in

which thou shouldst receive the God of Holiness ought to increase with the frequency of thine approach to the Holy Table. It is not for thee to know this increase; but there is always advancement when thou dost strive with greater earnestness to become more holy by means of recollection and humility.

Prayer

I believe, O Lord, that Thou art my God, and the sovereign Judge Who will decide my eternal doom. With what respect, therefore, ought I to approach Thee! Alas! who am I, that I should dare even so much as to lift up my eyes towards Thee? How then shall I dare to receive Thee into my heart, which is so miserable, so corrupt, and so unworthy of Thee? Supply, O Lord, my great unworthiness by the excess of Thy merciful goodness, which does not suppose, but constitutes, the merit of Thy creatures.

O infinite greatness! O sovereign Majesty! O immensity of my God, concealed and annihilated in the sacred Host which I am going to receive! to Thee do I give all glory, and to myself all possible contempt, which alone is my due. Come, O Jesus, come and fill my empty and depraved heart with the plenitude of Thy love. Come, and do Thou take the place of self within me, and raise me, who am poor, from the dust and from nothing, and elevate me to the possession of Thy love. But am I nothing? I am worse, I am a sinner and deserve Hell. Ah, I would willingly say with St. Peter: Depart from me, O Lord; but fearing lest Thou shouldst say to me, as Thou didst to him, that I shall have no part in Thy glory if I do not honor Thy humility, I consent to Thy being born in my soul, although a thousand times poorer than the crib, that henceforth I may live only by and for Thee. Amen.

Chapter 3

That It Is Profitable to Communicate Often

DISCIPLE

BEHOLD, I come to Thee, O Lord, that it may be well with me by Thy gift, and that I may be delighted in Thy holy banquet, which "in Thy sweetness, O God, thou hast provided for the poor." (*Ps.* 67:11).

Behold, in Thee is all whatsoever I can or ought to desire; Thou art my salvation and redemption, my hope and my strength, my honor and my glory.

Therefore, "Give joy to the soul of thy servant, for to thee, this day, O Lord Jesus, I have lifted up my soul." (*Ps.* 85:4).

I desire at this time to receive Thee devoutly and reverently; I would gladly bring Thee into my house, that, like Zacheus, I may receive Thy blessing, and be numbered among the children of Abraham. (*Luke* 19:9).

My soul longs to be nourished with Thy Body; my heart desires to be united with Thee.

2. Give Thyself to me and it is enough; for without Thee no comfort is available.

Without Thee I cannot subsist; and without Thy visitation I cannot live.

And, therefore, I must come often to Thee, and receive Thee for the remedy, and for the health and strength of my soul; lest perhaps I faint in the way, if I be deprived of this heavenly food.

For so, O most merciful Jesus, Thou wast pleased once to say, when Thou hadst been preaching to the people, and curing sundry diseases: "I will not send them away fasting, lest they faint in the way." (*Matt.* 15:32).

Deal now in like manner with me, Who hast left Thyself in the Sacrament for the comfort of Thy faithful.

For Thou art the most sweet refection of the soul; and he that shall eat Thee worthily shall be partaker and heir of everlasting glory.

It is indeed necessary for me, who so often fall and commit sin, and so quickly grow slack and faint, by frequent prayers and confessions, and by the holy communion of Thy Body, to repair my strength, to cleanse and inflame my soul, lest perhaps by abstaining for a longer time, I fall away from my holy purpose.

3. For the imaginations of man are prone to evil from his youth (*Gen.* 8:21); and unless Thy divine medicine succor him man quickly becomes worse.

The Holy Communion, therefore, withdraws him from evil, and strengthens him in good.

But if I am so often negligent and lukewarm now when I communicate, or celebrate, how would it be were I not to take this remedy, and seek so great a help?

And although I am not every day fit nor well disposed to celebrate, yet I will endeavor, at proper times, to receive the divine mysteries, and to make myself partaker of so great a grace.

For this is the one main comfort of a faithful soul, so long as she sojourns afar off from Thee in this mortal body; being mindful often of her God, to receive her beloved with a devout mind.

4. O wonderful condescension of Thy tender love

towards us, that Thou, O Lord God, the Creator and enlivener of all spirits, shouldst vouchsafe to come to a poor soul, and with Thy whole divinity and humanity, satisfy her hunger!

O happy mind, and blessed soul, which deserves to receive Thee, her Lord God, devoutly; and in receiving Thee, to be filled with spiritual joy!

Oh, how great a lord does she entertain! how beloved a guest does she bring into her house! how sweet a companion does she receive! how faithful a friend does she accept of! how beautiful and how noble a spouse does she embrace, beloved above all, and to be loved beyond all that she can desire!

Let Heaven and earth, with all their attire, be silent in Thy presence, O my dearest beloved (*Hab.* 2:20); for whatever praise or beauty they have is all the gift of Thy bounty; nor can they equal the beauty of Thy name, of whose wisdom there is no end.

Practical Reflections

*That we ought ardently to desire to receive the
Holy Communion, or at least be sensible of the need
we have of it, and should frequently receive it.*

We have great reason to be humbled and confounded before Our Lord Jesus Christ, when we feel ourselves cold and indifferent in approaching to Him, and are induced to receive Him in the Holy Communion only through obedience, and not by the ardor of our desires. For how can we know Thee, O Jesus, and not love Thee, and how can we love Thee and not desire to receive Thee, and to be transformed into Thee, by worthily and frequently receiving Thee in the Holy Communion? And yet, O God, how often does insensibility towards Thee desolate my soul, and would discourage me, were I not assured that, although I am deficient of that love which I desire to have for Thee, which I cannot acquire of myself, but which I ask of Thee, Thou wouldst still have me receive Thee through obedience and with humility. What, O God, would become of me, in the dryness which I experience, were I not assured that the great miseries of my soul draw down Thy mercies upon me, and that Thy delight is to dwell in a heart which, conscious of its own unworthiness, does all in its power to prepare itself for Thee? In truth, the humble acknowledgment of our unworthiness, after a confession the most entire of which a Christian is capable, supplies the place of ardent desire for the Holy Communion; and we cannot either honor or please God more than by debasing ourselves for His love before His sacred majesty. We should not therefore abstain from the Holy Communion because we feel no devotion nor any desire of approaching; but we should communicate as often as a wise and discreet director advises us, and receive Jesus Christ in obedience to him at whose voice Jesus Himself descends upon the altar.

Is there anything more easy or more consoling than to reflect, when we are preparing ourselves in the best manner we are able for the Holy Communion, that Jesus Christ has said that those who are well need not a physician, but only such as are sick?

Prayer

O Jesus! it is with full confidence in those words which Thou speakest to me, and which I have just read, that I prepare myself to receive Thee, not because I deserve such a favor, but because I have need of Thee, and my soul cannot live without Thee. It is afflicted with many maladies and infirmities which Thou alone, its sovereign and charitable physician, canst heal. Come, then, my Saviour, and apply a remedy to my wounds, heal the pride of my heart with Thy humility, and consume all self-love with the fire of Thy divine charity. Come and invest me with Thy strength, that I may conquer my passions; animate me with Thy spirit, that I may seek only to please Thee and live that supernatural and divine life which is characteristic of the life which Thou livest, and which Thou bringest to me in the holy Sacrament of the Eucharist. Amen.

Chapter 4
Many Benefits Are Bestowed on Them Who Communicate Devoutly

DISCIPLE

O LORD, my God, anticipate Thy servant with blessings of Thy sweetness (*Ps.* 20:4), that I may approach worthily and devoutly to Thy magnificent Sacrament.

Raise up my heart towards Thee, and deliver me from this heavy sluggishness. Visit me with Thy grace, that I may taste in spirit Thy sweetness (*Ps.* 33:9), which plentifully lies hid in this Sacrament (*Apoc.* 2:17), as in its fountain.

Illuminate also my eyes (*Ps.* 12:4), to behold so great a mystery, and strengthen me to believe it with an undoubting faith.

For it is Thy work, not the power of man; Thy sacred institution, not man's invention.

For no man can be found able of himself to know and

understand these things, which surpass even the subtlety of angels.

What shall I, therefore, an unworthy sinner, who am but dust and ashes (*Gen.* 18:27), be able to search into or conceive of so high and sacred a mystery?

2. O Lord, in the simplicity of my heart, with a good and firm faith, and in obedience to Thy command, I come to Thee with hope and reverence; and I do verily believe that Thou art here present in the Sacrament, God and man.

It is then Thy will that I should receive Thee, and through love unite myself to Thee.

Wherefore, I implore Thy mercy; and I beg of Thee to give me for this a special grace, that I may be wholly melted away in Thee and overflow with Thy love, and never more seek comfort in aught else.

For this most high and most excellent Sacrament is the health of soul and body, the remedy of all spiritual diseases, by which my vices are cured, my passions are restrained, temptations are overcome or lessened, a greater grace is infused, virtue receives an increase, faith is confirmed, hope strengthened, and charity inflamed and extended.

3. For Thou hast bestowed, and still oftentimes dost bestow, many good things in this Sacrament on Thy beloved, who communicate devoutly, O my God, Thou support of my soul, Who art the repairer of human infirmity, and the giver of all interior consolations.

For Thou impartest unto them much consolation to support them in their many troubles; and Thou liftest them up from the depth of their own dejection to the hope of Thy protection; and Thou dost recreate and enlighten them interiorly with a certain new grace, so that they who before communion were anxious, and felt no affection in themselves, after being fed with this heavenly meat and drink, find themselves changed for the better.

And Thou art pleased thus to deal with Thine elect, to the end that they may truly acknowledge and plainly experience how great is their infirmity when left to themselves, and how much they receive from Thy bounty and grace.

For of themselves they are cold, dry, and in-devout; but by Thee they are made fervent, cheerful, and devout.

For who is he that, approaching humbly to the fountain of sweetness, does not carry away with him some little sweetness?

Or who, standing by a great fire, does not receive from it some little heat?

Now, Thou art the fountain always full and overflowing; Thou art a fire always burning and never decaying. (*John* 4:14; *Heb.* 12:29).

4. Wherefore, if I cannot draw out of the fullness of the fountain, nor drink my fill, I will at least set my mouth to the orifice of this heavenly pipe, that so I may draw from it some small drop to refresh my thirst, to the end that I may not wholly be dried up.

And if I cannot as yet be all heavenly, and all on fire, like the cherubim and seraphim, I will, however, endeavor to apply myself to devotion, and to prepare my heart for acquiring some small flame of divine fire, by humbly receiving this life-giving Sacrament.

And whatever is wanting to me, O good Jesus, most

blessed Saviour, do Thou in Thy bounty and goodness supply for me, Who hast vouchsafed to call all unto Thee, saying, "Come to Me, all you that labor and are burdened, and I will refresh you."

I labor indeed in the sweat of my brow, I am tormented with grief of heart, I am burdened with sins, I am troubled with temptations, and am entangled and oppressed with many evil passions; and there is no one to help me (*Ps.* 21:12), no one to deliver and save me, but Thou, O Lord God, my Saviour (*Ps.* 24:5), to Whom I commit myself and all that is mine, that Thou mayest keep me, and bring me to everlasting life.

Receive me for the praise and glory of Thy name, Who hast prepared Thy Body and Blood for my meat and drink.

Grant, O Lord God, my Saviour, that with the frequenting of this Thy mystery, the affection of my devotion may increase.

Practical Reflections

*Ask of Jesus Christ a lively faith
in His real presence, and an ardent love for Him,
in the most holy Sacrament of the Altar.*

I believe, O Lord, that Thou art present, both body and soul, in the adorable Sacrament which I am about to receive. Thou wilt there make me partaker of the merits of Thy blessed humanity, and wilt inebriate me with the plenitude of Thy divinity. Change then, O Lord, change the indifference of my heart into an ardent desire of loving Thee, of pleasing and possessing Thee. Permit me not to regard or to receive Thee with coldness, Who comest to inflame my heart with the fire of Thy love. Supply in me whatever is wanting of faith in a mystery so incomprehensible to all human understanding; enliven me with a lively sense of Thy presence, and grant that my heart may receive Thee as its God with reverence, as its Saviour with confidence, and as its Father with love.

Is it possible, my soul, that, surrounded and replenished with all the ardor of God's love for thee, thou shouldst still remain all ice in the midst of so much fire! Alas! O Jesus! how miserable am I to feel so much eagerness to please myself, and so much indifference about pleasing Thee! Lord, if Thou wilt, Thou canst heal me; say then to me, as Thou didst say to the leper: I will—be thou healed of thy tepidity and insensibility.

PRAYER

To Thee do I address myself, O my most amiable Saviour, that I may obtain fervor and fidelity in Thy love. Thou knowest that, full of myself and self-love, I am most unworthy and incapable of Thy love; but I beseech Thee, the God of my heart, to inspire me to copy Thy virtues, to follow Thine inclinations, and to rely on Thy merits; instill into my soul Thy meekness, humility, and patience, that so I may be animated with Thy spirit, and live by Thee. Amen.

Chapter 5

Of the Dignity of the Sacrament And of the Priestly State

CHRIST

IF THOU hadst the purity of an angel, and the sanctity of St. John the Baptist, thou wouldst not be worthy to receive or handle the Sacrament.

For this is not due to any merits of men, that a man should consecrate and handle the Sacrament of Christ, and receive for his food the bread of angels. (*Ps.* 77:25).

Great is this mystery, and great the dignity of priests, to whom that is given which is not granted to angels:

For priests alone, rightly ordained in the Church, have power to celebrate and to consecrate the Body of Christ.

The priest indeed is the minister of God, using the word of God, and by the command and institution of God: but God Himself is there, the principal author and invisible worker, to whom is subject all that He wills, and to whose command everything is obedient.

2. Thou must, therefore, give more credit to an omnipotent God, in everything relating to this most excellent Sacrament, than to thine own sense or any visible sign; and, therefore, thou art to approach to this work with fear and reverence.

Take heed to thyself (*1 Tim.* 4:16) and see what kind of ministry has been delivered to thee by the imposition of the bishop's hands.

Lo, thou art made a priest, and art consecrated to say Mass; see now that in due time thou faithfully and devoutly offer up sacrifice to God, and that thou behave thyself in such manner as to be without reproof.

Thou hast not lightened thy burden, but art now bound with a stricter band of discipline, and art obliged to a greater perfection of sanctity.

A priest ought to be adorned with all virtues, and to give example of a good life to others. (*Titus* 2:7).

His conversation should not be with the ordinary and common ways of men but with the angels in Heaven (*Phil.* 3:20), or with perfect men upon earth.

3. A priest clad in his sacred vestments is Christ's vicegerent, to pray to God for himself, and for all the people, in a suppliant and humble manner.

He has before him and behind him the Sign of the Cross of the Lord that he may always remember the passion of Christ.

He bears the cross before him in his vestment that he may diligently behold the footsteps of Christ, and fervently endeavor to follow them.

He is marked with the cross behind that he may mildly suffer, for God's sake, whatsoever adversities shall befall him from others.

He wears the cross before him that he may bewail his own sins; behind him, that through compassion he may lament the sins of others, and know that he is placed, as it were a mediator between God and the sinner. Neither ought he to cease from prayer and holy oblation until he be favored with the grace and mercy which he implores.

When a priest celebrates he honors God, he rejoices the angels, he edifies the Church, he helps the living, he obtains rest for the dead, and makes himself partaker of all that is good.

Practical Reflections

*Of the holy dispositions with which
the priest should celebrate Mass,
and with which a Christian should assist at it,
in order to hear it with advantage.*

The priest, by his ordination, has received the power of con-secration, so that, according to St. Augustine, God as it were becomes again incarnate, and takes upon Himself a new life, in the hands of the priest by virtue of his word. It is this power which, in some sense, makes him superior to the angels, and exalts him in dignity above all other creatures.

Such being thine exalted dignity, O priest of the Lord, how great must thine obligations be! Thine endeavor should be to cherish within thee, throughout the day, the same dispositions with which thou shouldst approach the altar. Keep thyself closely united to God, recollected in His presence, faithful to His graces, and diligent in all duties; cherish continually within thy soul, and offer to Jesus Christ, the sentiments and, as it were, the condition of a victim entirely devoted to His glory, and the salvation of souls.

When thou celebratest this adorable Sacrifice, endeavor, first, to effect within thine own interior what Jesus accomplishes upon the altar, to humble thyself most profoundly, and immo-late thyself and thy petitions to God. Secondly, unite the sacri-fice of thy soul to that of the Body and Blood of Christ; enter into His sentiments and dispositions, as the minister of the Sac-rifice which He offers to His eternal Father, by thy means, for the salvation of men; offer thyself a victim of love for that God who Himself becomes the victim of His love for thee. Cease to be thine own, and become entirely His, as He becomes entirely thine upon the altar, that He may live sacramentally in thy heart and consummate the great work of thy salvation.

The priest, who feeds upon God and is every day nourished with His Body and Blood, should live only for God, says St. Augustine; and if the priests of the Old Law were required to live holily, because they offered bread and incense to the Lord, how much more perfect should the sanctity of the priests of the New Law be, who every day offer God to God Himself! How pure, exclaims St. Chrysostom, should that hand be which immolates the Body of the Word incarnate! how spotless that tongue which is purpled with the Blood of Jesus! and how clean that heart into which the infinite purity of a Man-God is received together with all His other attributes.

Reflect then, O priest of the Lord, that Jesus Christ, the great High Priest, celebrates Mass in thy person, and that as thou art invested with His power to consecrate upon the altar, so thou shouldst also be animated with His spirit, and conform thy life to His divine example. When thou dost pronounce the words of Consecration, give thine all, thy heart, and thy whole self, together with the sacred words which thou utterest.

Whilst thou art putting on thy vestments, meditate on the mysteries of Christ's passion, which they represent, and beg pardon for thy sins, which were the cause of all His sufferings.

When going to the altar, reflect that thou art accompanying Jesus Christ in spirit to Calvary, and that thou art going to behold Him, with the eyes of faith, mystically die by thy hands.

At the foot of the altar, ask pardon for thy sins and for those of the faithful whose place thou holdest as their agent and mediator.

At the *Gloria in Excelsis*, beseech God to bestow upon thee, and upon all who assist at the holy Sacrifice, an efficacious will to be saved.

At the *Epistle*, conceive a holy desire that Christ may be born on the altar, and in the souls of all: such a desire as the Prophets had for the coming of the Messias, and the Apostles to establish Jesus Christ in the hearts of all mankind.

At the *Gospel*, enliven thy faith and animate thy zeal: thy faith, to believe and to practice the Gospel, and thy zeal to instill its maxims into others.

At the *Credo*, beseech the Lord that thy life may be conformable to thy faith.

At the *Offertory*, offer the Sacrifice of the holy Mass to the honor of God, in thanksgiving for His blessings, in atonement for thy sins, to obtain all those virtues necessary for salvation, and for the relief and consolation of the souls in Purgatory.

At the *Canon*, transport thyself in spirit into Heaven: and endeavor there to enter into the dispositions of the Blessed Virgin and of the Apostles, that through thee He may be born again upon the altar, and in the hearts of all the faithful.

At the *Consecration*, let all yield to God, who comes upon the altar at thy word, and takes upon Himself as it were a new life.

Join thyself to His intentions, pray through His merits, immolate thy whole self to Him; and, overflowing with His love, present Him to His eternal Father for the living and for the dead.

At the *Pater Noster*, enter into the sentiments of perfect confidence in Jesus Christ.

At the dividing of the Host, which mystically represents the death of Jesus Christ, beseech Him to assist thee in perfectly dying to thyself, in giving thy whole heart and affections to Him, and to bring thee to a holy life, and a good death.

At the *Communion*, renew thy faith in the God whom thou receivest, thy confidence in thy Saviour, and thy love for thy Father, who comes to take possession of thy heart, and to give thee Himself as thine inheritance. Say to Him with thy whole soul and all thy power: Be Thou the God of my heart, and my portion forever.

After the *Communion*, return thanks to Jesus Christ for having given Himself entirely to thee, and beseech Him that nothing may anymore separate thee from Him.

In a word, let both priests and people, after having celebrated or after having heard Mass, endeavor, by a life of separation from the vanities and pleasures of the world, by mortifying their passions, and by wholly applying themselves to their duties, to make themselves, as St. Augustine says, the one, priests of the Lord according to the spirit, and His victims according to the flesh; the other, priests not in character and in power, but in intention, by entering into the views of Jesus Christ upon the altar. Remember how the pagans returned from Calvary, penetrated with a lively faith in Jesus Christ, overwhelmed with sorrow for their sins, and truly changed and converted; and reflect how much more you ought, after having celebrated Mass, which is the same sacrifice as that of Calvary, or, after having heard it, to be filled with contrition for your offenses, and resolved to live henceforth by faith and by hope, and as victims of the love of Christ Jesus Our Lord.

Prayer

To obtain from God the grace of saying and of hearing Mass well.

O Lord, Who in the adorable Sacrifice of the Mass art Thyself both Priest and Victim, immolating Thyself, by the priest's ministry, to the justice of Thy Father for the salvation of men, grant that we may sacrifice our hearts in union with the sacrifice of Thy Body and Blood, and endeavoring to produce in our souls the same that Thou effectest upon the altar, employ ourselves, during the holy Mass, in the exercise of profound humility and prayer, and offer ourselves as victims for Thy people in and by Thee.

We offer up this adorable Sacrifice, which is the same as that of Calvary, to Thine honor and glory, in thanksgiving for all Thy benefits, to obtain the virtues necessary for salvation, and to bring down Thy mercy upon us in forgiveness of our manifold offenses. Grant, O Jesus, that the sacramental life which Thou assumest on the altar may become for us, by real or spiritual communion, the source of a new life. As Thou takest the place of the substances of bread and wine, by their destruction, so do Thou take the place of our self-love in our hearts, and, destroying all that is estranged from Thee, establish Thy love in place of our self-love, and let everything give way to Thee.

O adorable Victim of our salvation and love! as Thou makest choice of our hearts for the consummation of Thy sacramental life, be pleased to complete in us the sacrifice of self, which would separate us from Thee; suffer us not, whilst we feed upon the Lamb of God, to live only as men, but enable us to imitate Thee in the practice of those virtues which in the Holy Communion Thou comest to imprint in our souls. Amen.

Chapter 6

A Petition Concerning the Exercise Proper before Communion

DISCIPLE

WHEN I consider Thy greatness, O Lord, and my own vileness, I tremble very much, and am confounded in myself.

For if I come not to Thee I fly from life; and if I intrude

myself unworthily I incur Thy displeasure.

What then shall I do, O my God, my helper, my counsellor in necessities?

2. Do Thou teach me the right way: appoint me some short exercise proper for the Holy Communion.

For it is necessary to know in what manner I should reverently and devoutly prepare my heart for Thee, for the profitable receiving of Thy Sacrament, or for celebrating so great and divine a sacrifice.

Practical Reflections

One of the best dispositions for worthily receiving the Holy Communion is to be resolved that Jesus shall reign forever the God of our hearts, that is, that we will obey Him in all things, and refuse Him nothing that He demands of us, for it is in quality of king that He comes, and as the King of all bounty; He comes into our souls to be again born there, and to reign over our passions and affections.

Prayer

Yes, my Saviour, when I communicate, I indeed make Thee the Master, the King, and the God of my heart; I then protest sincerely that I am entirely Thine; but, after receiving Thee, I become again the slave of my own humor, and shaking off the sweet yoke of Thine empire, I subject myself to the servitude of concupiscence. At the time of Communion I am all Thine, but soon, alas! do I again become wholly devoted to myself. What an injustice to Thy dominion! what an outrage on Thy bounty! thus to rob Thee of a heart which upon so many titles belongs only to Thee! No, I will never again withdraw myself from the empire of Thy love; secure to Thyself Thine own conquest, and suffer me not to escape from Thee, or evermore to be separated from Thee. Amen.

Chapter 7

Of the Examination of One's Own Conscience, and of a Resolution of Amendment

CHRIST

ABOVE all things it behooves the priest of God to come to the celebrating, handling, and receiving this Sacrament with very great humility of heart, and lowly reverence; with an entire faith, and a pious intention of the honor of God.

Diligently examine thy conscience, and to the best of thy power cleanse and purify it by true contrition and humble confession: so that there be nothing weighty to give thee remorse and hinder thy free access.

Repent thee of all thy sins in general, and in particular lament and grieve for thy daily offenses.

And if thou hast time confess to thy God, in the secret of thy heart, all the miseries of thy passions.

2. Sigh and grieve that thou art yet so carnal and worldly, so unmortified in thy passions, so full of the motions of concupiscence;

So unguarded in thine outward senses, so often entangled with many vain imaginations;

So much inclined to exterior things, so negligent as to the interior;

So easy to laughter and dissipation, so hard to tears and compunction;

So prone to relaxation and to the pleasures of the flesh, so sluggish to austerity and fervor;

So curious to hear news, and to see fine sights, so remiss to embrace things humble and abject;

So covetous to possess much, so sparing in giving, so close in retaining;

So inconsiderate in speech, so little able to hold thy peace;

So disorderly in thy carriage, so over-eager in thine actions;

So greedy at meat, so deaf to the word of God;

So hasty for rest, so slow to labor;

So wakeful to hear idle tales, so drowsy to watch in the service of God;

So hasty to make an end of thy prayers, so wandering as to attention;

So negligent in saying thine office, so tepid in celebrating, so dry at the time of receiving;

So quickly distracted, so seldom quite recollected within thyself;

So easily moved to anger, so apt to take offense at others;

So prone to judge, so severe in reprehending;

So joyful in prosperity, so weak in adversity;

So often proposing many good things, and effecting little.

3. Having confessed and bewailed these and thine other defects with sorrow and a great dislike of thine own weakness, make a strong resolution always to amend thy life and to advance in virtue.

Then with a full resignation and with thy whole will,

offer thyself up to the honor of My name, on the altar of thy heart, as a perpetual holocaust, by committing faithfully to Me both thy soul and body.

That so thou mayest be worthy to approach to offer up sacrifice to God, and to receive for thy salvation the Sacrament of My Body.

4. For there is no oblation more worthy, nor satisfaction greater for washing away sins, than with the oblation of the Body of Christ, in the Mass and in the Communion, to offer up thyself purely and entirely to God.

If a man does what lies in him, and is truly penitent, as often as he shall come to Me for pardon and grace, "As I live, saith the Lord God, I desire not the death of the sinner, but that he should be converted from his ways and live" (*Ezech.* 33:11; 18:23), I will no longer remember his iniquities (*Ibid.* 22), but all shall be forgiven him.

Practical Reflections

1. The first disposition for a worthy Communion is purity of heart, which consists in detachment from all willful sin, and from all affection to it. It is in this sense that St. Augustine, speaking to priests and those who communicate, says that we must come to the altar innocent. You should therefore, before Communion, carefully examine your conscience in detail upon your ordinary faults. See before God if there be not some considerable sin upon your soul, and if so confess it with sincere sorrow; for in this case it is not sufficient, says the Council of Trent, to make an act of contrition, you must also go to confession before you approach to the Holy Communion. In this manner it explains those words of St. Paul, "Let a man prove

himself," that so he may be prepared to receive worthily this heavenly bread, and may not eat it to his own condemnation.

2. Be not satisfied with examining whether your conscience reproaches you with any considerable sin; but examine also before God and detest even the smallest sins which you so easily commit, especially such as are knowingly committed against the inspirations of grace; sins of habit, of attachment, and of indisposition, that is, those which are most consonant with your natural inclinations; the sins which you may have occasioned in others, or in which you have participated; hidden sins, etc. Ask pardon for them of Jesus Christ, before you receive Him, and pray for grace to correct them, and to punish yourself for having committed them.

Prayer

An Act of Contrition before Communion.

I come to Thee, O Jesus, as a sick man to his physician, in hopes of obtaining a cure. Thou hast said that those who are afflicted with disease should approach to him who is able and willing to heal them; wherefore do I desire to approach to Thee and to receive Thee frequently, the true Physician and Saviour of my soul, for I have need of Thee to heal my many maladies. To Thee do I cry with the leper in the Gospel: "Lord, if Thou wilt, Thou canst make me clean."

Inspire me with the same holy confidence with which the sick, during Thy lifetime, presented themselves before Thee. Grant that, like them, I may say within myself: If I shall but touch the hem of His garment, that is, the appearances under which Thou art concealed, I shall be healed. With like confidence, I approach and prostrate myself at Thy sacred feet, and beg pardon for all the sins of my whole life, which I detest from my heart, for the love of Thee.

Pardon, O Jesus, pardon me all that is displeasing to Thee. Suffer me not to receive Thee unworthily. I truly regret having wounded Thy heart, insulted Thy goodness, provoked Thine anger, resisted Thy grace and the allurements of Thy love. I have offended all Thy divine perfections; forgive and chastise me, and let my punishment be to hate myself, that I may love Thee. To Thee alone do I address my grief; I have grievously offended Thee, and for this will I live and die in the sorrows of repentance. Take from me life, or take away sin, for I can no longer live and offend Thee; I desire to avoid everything that is displeasing to Thee, or can in any degree remove or separate me from Thee. Amen.

Chapter 8

Of the Oblation of Christ on the Cross, And of our own Resignation

CHRIST

AS I willingly offered myself to God My Father, for thy sins, with My hands stretched out upon the cross, and My body naked, so that nothing remained in Me which was not turned into a sacrifice, to appease the divine wrath:

Even so must thou willingly offer thyself to Me daily in the Mass, for a pure and holy oblation, together with all thy powers and affections, as heartily as thou art able.

What do I require more of thee, than that thou endeavor to resign thyself entirely to Me?

Whatsoever thou givest besides thyself I regard not; for I seek not thy gift, but thyself.

2. As it would not suffice thee if thou hadst all things but

Me, so neither can it please Me whatever thou givest, as long as thou offerest not thyself.

Offer thyself to Me, and give thy whole self for God, and thine offering will be accepted.

Behold, I offered My whole self to the Father for thee, and have given My whole Body and Blood for thy food, that I might be all thine, and thou mightest be always Mine.

But if thou wilt stand upon thine own self, and wilt not offer thyself freely to My will, thine offering is not perfect, nor will there be an entire union between us.

Therefore, before all thy works, thou must make a free oblation of thyself into the hands of God, if thou desire to obtain liberty and grace.

For the reason why so few become illuminated and internally free is because they do not wholly renounce themselves.

My sentence stands firm: "Unless a man renounce all he cannot be my disciple." (*Luke* 14:33). If, therefore, thou desire to be My disciple, offer up thyself to Me with all thine affections.

Practical Reflections

Be not of the number of those who, when they communicate, give themselves entirely to God, and immediately after return to themselves; whose lives, being a constant succession of good desires and frail relapses, are never firmly established either in the fear or love of God. It is of such souls, who are thus mean and ungenerous towards a God who is so prodigal of Himself towards them, that the Prophet speaks when he says: "On account of the iniquity of his covetousness I was angry, and

I struck him; I hid my face from thee, and was angry; and he went away wandering, in the way of his own heart." (*Is.* 57:17).

Prayer

Yes, O Lord, Thou art now the God of my heart, for Thou comest to take possession of it, and to give me Thyself to repose within it. Mayest Thou be such in all things and forever; mayest Thou alone be the God of my soul in time, that Thou mayest be my portion for eternity. Unite me to Thyself, by making me like to Thee, meek, humble, patient, and charitable. Suffer not the union with which I am now honored to remain ineffective, like that of a dry branch with the sap of the vine, or languid, like that of a paralyzed arm with a vigorous body; but grant that it may become lively, vivifying and perpetual, like that of food with the body which it cherishes. Amen.

Chapter 9

That We Must Offer Ourselves and All That Is Ours to God, and Pray for All

DISCIPLE

LORD, all things are Thine that are in Heaven and earth. I desire to offer myself up to Thee as a voluntary oblation, and to remain forever Thine.

Lord, in the sincerity of my heart I offer myself to Thee this day to be Thy servant evermore, to serve Thee, and to become a sacrifice of perpetual praise to Thee.

Receive me with this sacred oblation of Thy precious Body, which I offer to Thee this day, in the presence of Thine angels invisibly standing by, that it may be for mine and all the people's salvation.

2. Lord, I offer to Thee all my sins and offenses which I have committed in Thy sight and that of Thy holy angels, from the day that I was first capable of sin until this hour, upon Thy propitiatory altar, that Thou mayest burn and consume them all with the fire of Thy charity, and remove all the stains of my sins, and cleanse my conscience from all offenses, andrestore to me Thy grace, which I have lost by sin, by fully pardoning me all, and mercifully receiving me to the kiss of peace. (*Heb.* 9:13, 14).

3. What can I do for my sins but humbly confess, them, and lament them, and incessantly implore Thy mercy for them.

Hear me, I beseech Thee, in Thy mercy, where I stand before Thee, O my God.

All my sins displease me exceedingly, I will never commit them anymore; I am sorry for them, and will be sorry for them as long as I live; I am willing to do penance for them, and to make satisfaction to the utmost of my power.

Forgive, O my God, forgive me my sins for Thy holy name's sake; save my soul, which Thou hast redeemed with Thy precious Blood. (*1 Ptr.* 1:19).

Behold, I commit myself to Thy mercy; I resign myself into Thy hands.

Deal with me according to Thy goodness (*Ps.* 118:124), not according to my wickedness and iniquity. (*Ps.* 102:10).

4. I offer also to Thee all the good I have, though very little and imperfect; that Thou mayest make it better and sanctify it; that Thou mayest be pleased with it, and make it acceptable to Thee, and perfect it more and more; and

mayest moreover bring me, who am a slothful and unprofitable wretch, to a good and happy end.

5. I offer to Thee also all the godly desires of Thy devout servants, the necessities of my parents, friends, brethren, sisters, and all of those that are dear to me; and of all such as, for the love of Thee, have been benefactors to me or others; or who have desired and begged of me to offer up prayers and Masses for themselves and all that belonged to them; whether they live as yet in the flesh, or whether they are now departed out of this world!

That they all may be sensible of the assistance of Thy grace, of the benefit of Thy comfort, of Thy protection from dangers, and of a deliverance from their pains, and that being freed from all evils they may with joy give worthy thanks to Thee.

6. I offer up also to Thee my prayers and this sacrifice of propitiation for those in particular who have in anything wronged, grieved, or abused me, or have done me any damage or displeasure.

And for all those likewise whom I have at any time grieved, troubled, injured, or scandalized, by word or deed, knowingly or unknowingly; that it may please Thee to forgive us all our sins and offenses one against another.

Take, O Lord, from our hearts all jealousy, indignation, wrath, and contention, and whatsoever may hurt charity, and lessen brotherly love.

Have mercy, O Lord, have mercy on those that crave Thy mercy; give grace to them that stand in need thereof, and grant that we may be worthy to enjoy Thy grace, and that we may attain to life everlasting. Amen.

Practical Reflections

Weary of the servitude of our passions, and fatigued with the inefficacy of our desires, by which we promise God what we never perform, and pretend to be His, without ceasing to be our own or weaning ourselves from the world and vanity, let us now at least, after having received Him, make a firm resolution of giving ourselves really to Him, and of dedicating and consecrating ourselves to His love. It is time, O my Saviour, that this heart, which was made for Thy love, and redeemed by Thy blood, should forever cease to be devoted to itself, and become wholly and irrevocably Thine; and I protest at Thy sacred feet that such is my ardent desire. This heart has received Thee, my Jesus, and Thou desirest to consummate within it that new life which Thou hast assumed on the altar, to make it a victim of Thy love. Sacrifice then to Thy Father Thy holy life together with my life of sin; and never suffer me to recall that heart which on this day I wholly give to Thee.

Prayer

I adore Thee, O Jesus, with reverence as my God, with confidence as my Saviour, with love as my Father, and with humble fear as my Judge. When Thou shalt come to judge me, Thou Who hast now come to enter into my soul to sanctify and to save it, condemn me not. I offer Thee the holy Mass which I have heard, and the Communion which I have received, to obtain the pardon of all my sins, for the conversion of sinners, and the sanctification of all the just. Enlighten my understanding, change my heart, regulate my life, suppress my passions, and, as an absolute master, reign Thou entirely over me. Would that I could make Thee known and loved by all the world! I would willingly give my life to procure for Thee the glory and the delight of beholding all mankind subjected to Thine empire. Grant, O Jesus, that I may seek only to please Thee in all things, and that detached from all things I may unite myself to Thy love, and thus commence in time what I hope in Thy great mercy to continue throughout eternity. Amen.

Chapter 10

That the Holy Communion Is Not Lightly to be Omitted

CHRIST

THOU oughtest often to have recourse to the fountain of grace, and of divine mercy, to the fountain of all goodness and all purity, that thou mayest be healed of thy passions and vices, and be made more strong and vigilant against all the temptations and deceits of the devil.

The enemy, knowing the very great advantage and remedy which is in the Holy Communion, strives by all means and occasions, as much as he is able, to withdraw and hinder faithful and devout persons from it.

2. For when some are preparing themselves for the sacred Communion, they suffer the greater assaults of Satan.

This wicked spirit, as it is written in Job (1:6), cometh amongst the sons of God, to trouble them with his accustomed malice, or to make them overfearful and perplexed, that so he may diminish their devotion, or, by his assaults, take away their faith: so that perhaps, they may altogether omit the Communion, or at least approach it with tepidity.

But there is no regard to be paid to his wiles and suggestions, be they ever so filthy and abominable; but all his attempts are to be turned back upon his own head.

The wretch is to be condemned and scorned, nor is the Holy Communion to be omitted for his assaults, and the commotions which he causes.

3. Oftentimes also a person is hindered by too great a solicitude for obtaining devotion, and a certain anxiety about making his confession.

Follow herein the counsel of the wise, and put away all anxiety and scruple, for it hindereth the grace of God, and destroyeth devotion.

Leave not the Holy Communion for every small trouble and vexation, but go quickly to confession, and willingly forgive others their offenses against thee.

And if thou hast offended anyone, humbly crave pardon, and God will readily forgive thee.

4. What doth it avail thee to delay thy confession for a long time, or to put off the Holy Communion?

Purge thyself with speed, spit out the venom presently, make haste to take this remedy, and thou shalt find it to be better for thee than if thou hadst deferred it for a long time.

If thou deferrest it today, for this cause, perhaps tomorrow a greater will occur and so thou mayest be hindered a long time from Communion, and become more unfit.

With all possible speed shake off this heaviness and sloth, for it is to no purpose to continue long in uneasiness, to pass a long time in trouble, and for these daily impediments to withdraw thyself from the divine mysteries.

Yea, it is very hurtful to delay the Communion long; for this usually causeth a great lukewarmness and numbness.

5. Alas! some tepid and dissolute people are willing to put off their confession, and desire that their Communion should be deferred, lest they should be obliged thereby to keep a strict watch over themselves.

6. Ah! how little is their love of God; how weak is their devotion, who so easily put off the sacred Communion!

How happy is he, and acceptable to God, who so liveth, and keepeth his conscience in such purity, as to be ready and well disposed to communicate every day, if it were permitted, and he might do it without being singular.

If sometimes a person abstains out of humility, or by reason of some lawful impediment, he is to be commended for his reverence.

But if sloth steal upon him, he must stir up himself, and do what lieth in him; and God will assist his desire for his good will, which He chiefly regards.

7. And when he is lawfully hindered, he must yet always have a good will and pious intentions to communicate, and so he shall not lose the fruit of the Sacrament.

For every devout man may every day, and every hour, receive Christ spiritually without any prohibition, and with great profit to his soul.

And yet on certain days, and at the times appointed, he ought, with an affectionate reverence, to receive sacramentally the Body of his Redeemer, and rather aim at the praise and honor of God than seek his own comfort.

For he communicates mystically, and is invisibly fed, as often as he devoutly calleth to mind the mystery of the Incarnation and Passion of Christ, and is inflamed with the love of Him.

8. He that prepareth not himself but when a festival draweth near, or when custom compelleth him thereunto, shall often be unprepared.

Blessed is he that offereth himself up as a holocaust to the Lord as often as he celebrates or communicates.

Be neither too long nor too hasty in celebrating, but observe the good common manner of those with whom thou livest.

Thou oughtest not to be too tedious and troublesome to others, but to keep the common way according to the appointment of superiors, and rather consult the profit of others than thine own inclination or devotion.

Practical Reflections

1. The ardent desire which Jesus Christ evinces to come and take possession of our hearts, that He may reign there as God, should convince us that we afford Him a real pleasure by worthy and frequent Communion; and that, by staying away from the Holy Table, apparently from respect, but in reality from sloth, as is the case with many Christians, we deprive Jesus Christ of the satisfaction He would have in remaining with us, testified in these words: "My delight is to be with the children of men." To abstain through our own fault from the Holy Communion is to oppose the designs of His wisdom; it is to interrupt the connecting links of our predestination, because it is to deprive ourselves of one of the most effectual means of securing the salvation of our souls, a worthy and frequent participation of the Holy Communion (for these two should never be separated), and it is to expose ourselves to the danger of losing those graces upon which depends our eternity.

2. Now the most essential dispositions for good and frequent

Communion are, first, a fixed resolution never to commit any willful sin; secondly, to be determined, after confession, to amend our faults and to lead a truly Christian life; thirdly, to trust and hope that the real presence of Jesus Christ in our souls, and the efficacy of His grace, will preserve us in this twofold resolution. Hence, habitual sinners who communicate but seldom, on account of their unworthiness, must renounce their bad habits, and prove themselves beforehand that they may not receive to their own condemnation. Worldly souls who excuse themselves from frequent Communion, under the specious pretext of their attachment to the world, must wean themselves from the vanities, amusements, and engagements of a worldly life, that they may be properly disposed to communicate frequently and worthily: and pious persons who would approach but seldom, for fear of an unworthy Communion, must not absent themselves through false humility, but, as the author says, humble themselves and approach.

Prayer

Truly, Lord, I do not deserve to be admitted at Thy Holy Table, as a child in his father's house, because I have rendered myself unworthy of this honor by my sins and infidelities; but as Thou invitest all to come to Thee who labor and are heavy laden with the weight of their miseries, promising to refresh and to comfort them, I will pay more regard to Thy mercy than to my own unworthiness.

Thou sayest in the Gospel, O Jesus, that those who are sick stand in need of a physician; I will therefore frequently approach Thee, for I have great need of the abundance of Thy graces, and of the multitude of Thy mercies, to keep me in Thy love, to preserve me from sin, and to defend me against the enemies of my salvation.

I feel no devotion when I go to Communion; but it is not necessary sensibly to experience Thy consolations and graces, but only to be faithful to them; and frequent Communion is the means of inspiring me with this fidelity, since the fruit of a good Communion is not always spiritual sweetness, but strength to conquer ourselves, and fidelity in the discharge of our duties.

I am indeed subject to many faults, weak, slothful, and inconstant in Thy service; but who is so able to correct me of my weaknesses, and to alleviate my miseries, as Thou, my Jesus, Who art the God of mercy and the Bread of the strong.

I beseech Thee, therefore, O my most amiable Saviour, to grant me the dispositions necessary for frequent and worthy Communion. Come, my Jesus, come often into my heart, Thou Who art the life of my soul, for I desire to live only for and by Thee. Amen.

Chapter 11

That the Body of Christ and the Holy Scriptures are Most Necessary To a Faithful Soul

DISCIPLE

O SWEETEST Lord Jesus, what great sweetness hath a devout soul that feasteth with Thee in Thy banquet; where there is no other meat set before her to be eaten but Thyself, her only beloved, and most to be desired, above all the desires of her heart.

And to me indeed it would be delightful to pour out tears in Thy presence, with the whole affection of my heart, and like the devout Magdalen to wash Thy feet with my tears. (*Luke* 7:38).

But where is this devotion, where is this plentiful shedding of holy tears?

Surely in the sight of Thee, and of Thy holy angels, my whole heart ought to be inflamed and to weep for joy.

For I have Thee in the Sacrament truly present, though hidden under another form.

2. For to behold Thee in Thine own divine brightness is what mine eyes would not be able to endure, neither could the whole world subsist in the splendor of the glory of Thy majesty.

In this, therefore, Thou condescendest to my weakness, that Thou hidest Thyself under the Sacrament.

I truly have and adore Him whom the angels adore in Heaven; but I as yet in faith, they by sight, and without a veil. (*1 Cor.* 13:12).

I must be content with the light of true faith, and walk therein till the day of eternal brightness breaks forth, and the shades of figures pass away. (*Cant.* 2:17).

But when that which is perfect shall come (*1 Cor.* 13:10), the use of Sacraments shall cease; for the blessed in heavenly glory stand not in need of the medicine of the Sacraments.

For they rejoice without end in the presence of God, beholding His glory face to face (*1 Cor.* 13:12): and being transformed from glory into the glory (*2 Cor.* 3:18) of the incomprehensible Deity, they taste the Word of God made flesh (*John* 1:14), as He was from the beginning, and as He remaineth forever.

3. When I call to mind these wonders, even every spiri-

tual comfort becomes grievously tedious to me; because as long as I behold not my Lord openly in His glory I make no account of anything I see and hear in the world.

Thou art my witness, O God, that not one thing can comfort me, nor anything created give me rest, but only Thou, my God, whom I desire forever to contemplate.

But this is not possible whilst I remain in this mortal life.

And, therefore, I must endeavor to acquire much patience and submit myself to Thee in all my desires.

For Thy saints also, O Lord, who now rejoice with Thee in the Kingdom of Heaven, whilst they were living expected in faith and great patience the coming of Thy glory. What they believed I believe; what they hoped for I hope for; and whither they are gone I trust that I also, through Thy grace, shall go.

In the meantime I will walk in faith (*2 Cor.* 5:7), strengthened by the examples of Thy saints.

I shall have moreover for my comfort, and the direction of my life, the holy books (*1 Mach.* 12:9); and above all these things Thy most holy Body for a singular remedy and refuge.

4. For in this life I find there are two things especially necessary for me, without which this miserable life would be insupportable.

Whilst I am kept in the prison of this body I acknowledge myself to need two things, namely, food and light.

Thou hast therefore given to me, weak as I am, Thy sacred Body, for the nourishment of my soul and body, and Thou hast set "thy word as a lamp to my feet." (*Ps.* 118:105).

Without these two I could not well live, for the word of

God is the light of my soul and Thy Sacrament is the bread of life. (*John* 6:35).

These also may be called the two tables set on either side in the storehouse of Thy holy Church.

One is the table of the holy altar having the holy bread, that is, the precious Body of Christ;

The other is that of the divine law, containing Thy holy doctrine, teaching the right faith, and firmly leading even within the veil, where is the holy of holies.

Thanks be to Thee, O Lord Jesus, Light of eternal Light, for the table of holy doctrine which Thou hast afforded us by the ministry of Thy servants, the Prophets and Apostles, and other teachers.

5. Thanks be to Thee, O Thou Creator and Redeemer of men, Who to manifest Thy love to the whole world hast prepared a great supper (*Luke* 14:16), wherein Thou hast set before us to be eaten, not the typical lamb, but Thy most sacred Body and Blood; rejoicing all the faithful with Thy holy banquet, and inebriating them with the cup of salvation (*Ps.* 22:5), in which are all the delights of Paradise; and the holy angels feast with us, but with a more happy sweetness.

6. Oh, how great and honorable is the office of priests, to whom it is given to consecrate with sacred words the Lord of majesty; to bless Him with their lips, to hold Him with their hands, to receive Him with their own mouths, and to administer Him to others!

Oh, how clean ought those hands to be, how pure that mouth, how holy that body, how unspotted the heart of a priest, into whom the Author of purity so often enters!

From the mouth of a priest nothing but what is holy, no

word but what is good and profitable ought to proceed, who so often receives the Sacrament of Christ.

7. His eyes ought to be simple and chaste, which are used to behold the Body of Christ: his hands pure and lifted up to Heaven, which are used to handle the Creator of Heaven and earth.

Unto the priests especially it is said in the law: Be ye holy, because I the Lord your God am holy. (*Lev.* 19:2).

8. Let Thy grace, O Almighty God, assist us, that we, who have undertaken the office of priesthood, may serve Thee worthily and devoutly in all purity and good conscience. (*1 Tim.* 1:5).

And if we cannot live in such great innocence as we ought, grant us at least duly to bewail the sins which we have committed; and in the spirit of humility, and the resolution of a good will, to serve Thee more fervently for the time to come.

Practical Reflections

The reading of pious books is a means of attaining the dispositions of Communion, and of preserving the fruit thereof in the soul.

God heretofore gave the Israelites in the desert a pillar of fire to light and to guide them, and manna to support them in their journey to the promised land. In like manner has Our Lord given us pious books to enlighten us, and the adorable Sacrament of His Body and Blood to nourish us in our way to Heaven. We should therefore make frequent use of both, in order to arrive there; of good books that we may not go astray, and of the Divine Eucharist that we may be strengthened to walk in that narrow path which leads to Paradise.

On this account it is proper, on the eve and on the day of Communion, to read some pious book, which treats of the Blessed Sacrament, in order to keep up in the soul that spirit of fervor, fidelity, and love towards God, and that sacred fire which Jesus Christ Himself comes to enkindle within us. That all-divine discourse which Jesus made to His Apostles, after the institution of the Most Holy Sacrament, may be read; but we should read the Scriptures in those sentiments in which the Holy Spirit composed them; we should read them with that faith, respect, and docility, which they merit, and with which they inspire those who read them fervently and in a proper manner; we should read them with all the attention due to the presence of God, with an ardent desire to profit by them, and to derive nourishment from them, confidently having recourse to the Holy Spirit, who dictated them.

Prayer

O my Saviour! Who hast so abundantly provided us with pious books, to serve us as a bright shining light, to withdraw or to preserve us from those wanderings which are so dangerous to our souls, enlighten our minds with the truths we read, and move our hearts to practice them. Grant that they may be our consolation in trouble, our support in difficulties, and the rule of our whole conduct. But grant also, O Word incarnate, that we may hear Thy voice speaking to our hearts, when we read Thy Gospel with our lips, and that through the respect we owe to Thy divine word, we may endeavor to put it in practice on those occasions when we have need of it, since it is not less necessary to practice the holy maxims of the Gospel than it is to believe them. Amen.

Chapter 12

That He who is to Communicate Ought to Prepare Himself for Christ With Great Diligence

CHRIST

I AM the lover of purity and the giver of all holiness. I seek a pure heart, and there is the place of My rest. (*Is.* 66:1).

Make ready for Me "a large upper room furnished, and I will eat the pasch with thee, together with My disciples." (*Mark* 14:14, 15).

If thou wilt have Me come to thee, and remain with thee, purge out the old leaven (*1 Cor.* 5:7), and make clean the habitation of thy heart.

Shut out the whole world, and all the tumult of vices: sit like a sparrow solitary on the housetop (*Ps.* 101:8), and think of thine excesses in the bitterness of thy soul. (*Is.* 38:15).

For every lover prepareth the best and fairest room for his dearly beloved; and hereby is known the affection of him that entertaineth his beloved.

2. Know, nevertheless, that thou canst not sufficiently prepare thyself by the merit of any action of thine although thou shouldst prepare thyself a whole year together, and think of nothing else.

But it is of My mere goodness and grace that thou art suffered to come to My table; as if a beggar should be invited to dinner by a rich man, who hath nothing else to return him for his benefits but to humble himself and give him thanks.

Do what lieth in thee, and do it diligently; not out of custom, nor for necessity, but with fear, reverence, and affection, receive the Body of thy beloved Lord, thy God, who vouchsafes to come to thee.

I am He that hath invited thee, I have commanded it to be done, I will supply what is wanting in thee; come and receive Me.

3. When I bestow the grace of devotion give thanks to thy God, not for that thou art worthy, but because I have had mercy on thee. (*Luke* 18:10, 13).

If thou hast it not, but rather findest thyself dry, continue in prayer, sigh and knock at the gate of divine mercy; and give not over till thou receive some crumb or drop of divine grace.

Thou hast need of Me, not I of thee.

Neither dost thou come to sanctify Me, but I come to sanctify and make thee better.

Thou comest that thou mayest be sanctified by Me, and united to Me; that thou mayest receive new grace, and be inflamed anew to amendment.

Neglect not this grace, but prepare thy heart with all diligence, and bring thy beloved into thy heart.

4. But thou oughtest not only to prepare thyself by devotion before Communion, but carefully also to keep thyself therein after receiving the Sacrament; neither is carefully guarding thyself afterwards less required than devoutly preparing thyself before; for a good guard afterwards is the best preparation for again obtaining greater grace.

For what renders a man very much indisposed is presently turning himself to seek exterior consolation.

Beware of much talk, remain in secret and enjoy thy God; for thou hast Him whom all the world cannot take from thee.

I am He to whom thou oughtest to give thy whole self; so that thou mayest henceforward live, without any solicitude, not in thyself but in Me. (*Gal.* 2:20).

Practical Reflections

That it is necessary to nourish ourselves with the Body and Blood of Jesus Christ.

As the Blessed Eucharist is a Sacrament in which we find a heaven upon earth, and God Himself in us, as it is the greatest prodigy of God's love for man, so to profit by it we must endeavor to approach it with a lively faith, a firm hope, and an ardent love of Jesus Christ, trusting that He will supply our deficiency in these three virtues, and increase them within us in proportion as we communicate frequently, and as far as we are able, worthily. Hence those who would stay away from the Holy Communion because they do not sensibly experience the holy impression of these virtues, nor an ardent desire to receive Jesus Christ, should not on this account deprive themselves of it; because it is necessary to enable them to practice the virtues of Christianity, and the duties of their state of life; they should therefore receive their Blessed Saviour on account of the need they have of Him.

The holy martyrs of the primitive Church, before they appeared at the tribunals of their judges, there to confess their faith, were accustomed to receive the Holy Communion; for they did not think themselves, says St. Cyprian, in a fit state without it, or as having sufficient strength to undergo the torments of martyrdom. In like manner should Christians, in order to fight against their passions, and to resist the temptations of the devil, clothe and nourish themselves with the virtue of the Body and Blood of Jesus Christ; without which they must be in danger of falling and of being lost.

Prayer

O Jesus, the Bread of angels! the divine and necessary nourishment of my soul! what should I be without Thee? How truly might I exclaim with the Psalmist, "I am smitten like grass and my heart is withered because I forgot to eat my bread!" Thou hast said in the Gospel that if Thou shouldst suffer the people, who had followed Thee into the desert, to return fasting to their homes, they would faint in the way. This evil would surely befall me, my Saviour, were I not to be nourished with Thy Body and Blood. Weak as I am of myself, and becoming still weaker from the neglect of that divine food which is my strength and my spiritual life, I should soon grow feeble and unequal to contend with my passions.

How, O Jesus, wilt Thou be the God of my heart, and my portion for eternity, if Thou dost not now take possession of it in the Holy Communion, and commence within it that holy alliance which Thou desirest to perfect in Heaven? Come then, my Saviour, come to me often, that I may never be separated from Thee. Amen.

Chapter 13

That a Devout Soul Ought to Desire, With Her Whole Heart, to Be United to Christ in This Sacrament

DISCIPLE

WHO will give me, O Lord, that I may find Thee alone, that I may open my whole heart to Thee and enjoy Thee as my soul desireth; and that now no man may despise me (*Cant.* 8:1), nor anything created move me or regard me, but that Thou alone speak to me, and I to Thee; as the beloved is wont to speak to his beloved, and a friend to entertain himself with his friend. (*Ex.* 33:11).

This I pray for, this I desire, that I may be wholly united to Thee, and may withdraw my heart from all created things, and by the Holy Communion, and often celebrating, may more and more learn to relish heavenly and eternal things.

Ah! Lord God, when shall I be wholly united to Thee, and absorbed in Thee, and altogether forgetful of myself.

Thou in me, and I in Thee; and so grant us both to continue in one. (*John* 15:5).

2. Verily Thou art my beloved, the choicest amongst thousands (*Cant.* 5:10), in whom my soul is well pleased to dwell all the days of her life.

Verily Thou art my peacemaker (*Cant.* 8:10), in Whom is sovereign peace and true rest; out of Whom is labor and sorrow and endless misery.

Thou art, in truth, a hidden God (*Is.* 45:15), and Thy

counsel is not with the wicked; but Thy conversation is with the humble and the simple. (*Prov.* 3:32).

Oh, how sweet is Thy spirit, O Lord, Who, to show Thy sweetness towards Thy children, vouchsafest to feed them with the most delicious bread which cometh down from Heaven! (*John* 6:50).

Surely, there is no other nation so great, that hath gods so nigh them as Thou our God art present (*Deut.* 4:7) to all Thy faithful; to whom, for their daily comfort, and for the raising up of their hearts to Heaven, Thou givest Thyself to be eaten and enjoyed.

3. For what other nation is there so honored as the Christian people?

Or what creature under Heaven so beloved as a devout soul, into whom God cometh, that He may feed her with His glorious Flesh?

O unspeakable grace! O wonderful condescension! O infinite love, singularly bestowed upon man!

But what return shall I make to the Lord for this grace, and for so extraordinary a charity? (*Ps.* 115:12).

There is nothing that I can give Him that will please Him better than if I give up my heart entirely to God, and unite it closely to Him. (*Prov.* 23:26).

Then all that is within me shall rejoice exceedingly when my soul shall be perfectly united to my God; then will He say to me: If thou wilt be with Me, I will be with thee: and I will answer Him: Vouchsafe, O Lord, to remain with me, and I will willingly be with Thee.

This is my whole desire, that my heart may be united to Thee.

Practical Reflections

*Of the ends for which Jesus Christ is present
upon our altars, and the pious dispositions
with which we should visit the Blessed Sacrament,
and assist at Mass and Benediction.*

The Son of God remains upon our altars not only during Mass, but likewise at other times, first to hear and favorably to receive our prayers, and to continue the same mediation between God and man which He exercised upon the cross; secondly, to receive our visits, our homage, and adorations; hence, those Christians who visit Him seldom, coldly, through custom, or with indifference, are highly blameable for thus appearing before their God, their Saviour, and their Judge, without either reverence, love, or fear; thirdly, to console us under afflictions, to support us in difficulties, and to resolve and dissipate our doubts, according to what is written. Let us go to the Son of Joseph, and He will console us;* and as a prophet said to a prince, who sent to consult a false god: Is it because there is no God in Israel? fourthly, to be our nourishment during life, and our viaticum at the hour of death.

How should a Christian who has recourse to Jesus Christ in the Blessed Sacrament with assiduity, respect, and gratitude, as to his King, his God, and his Saviour, who never omits hearing Mass but from necessity, and when he assists at it, or at Benediction, endeavors to attend with a spirit of religion, that he may depart affected, converted, and a better man—how, I say, should a Christian, who is faithful in the discharge of all pious duties towards Jesus Christ immolated for him on the altar, repose his

---

*St. Joseph passed for the father of Jesus Christ, but was only His foster parent.

confident hope in His bounty and mercies, both in life and in death? Will not, however, the Son of God have reason one day to reproach multitudes of Christians who either neglect to visit Him in the Most Holy Sacrament, or do so with very little devotion; will He not have reason to reproach them with their irreverence and want of faith; saying to them, "There hath stood one in the midst of you whom ye knew not"? You have neglected to know and visit God, who was in the midst of you. In vain have I performed prodigies of power, wisdom, and bounty in the blessed Eucharist, that I might gain your hearts; you would not interrupt your employments, nor even your pleasure to come and pay Me your homage.

To answer the ends therefore for which Jesus Christ is always present in the Most Holy Sacrament, we should visit Him, hear Mass, and attend at Benediction with all the respect and submission of courtiers before their king, with the recollection and fervor of angels before their God, with the humble fear of criminals before their judge, and with the confidence and love of children before their father.

Prayer

Which may be recited either during Mass or at the Benediction, or when visiting the Blessed Sacrament.

1. I adore Thee, O Sovereign Majesty, Who residest upon our altars, to receive our homage, and dost there annihilate and immolate Thyself in honor of Thine eternal Father, to come and reign in our hearts. I profoundly pay Thee all the homage due to a God who is to decide my eternal doom. I prostrate myself before Thee. I desire to join in the profound adorations of the seraphim who assist around the altar, and I beseech Thee to

accept their recollection and their love to supply the wanderings of my mind, and the indifference of my heart.

2. Penetrated with sorrow and confusion for the irreverences and indecencies which I have dared to commit in Thy presence, and for those also of all other Christians, I most humbly crave pardon for them, and am resolved to make amends for them, by appearing before Thee with all that modesty, all that reserve, all that respect, and all that spirit of religion with which I ought to present myself before Thee. I desire to satisfy Thy justice for all the outrages Thou hast received from impious libertines and heretics in the Most Holy Sacrament. Forgive them, O Lord, for they know Thee not; and cause me to suffer the temporal punishment which they have deserved, rather than abandon and punish them forever.

Grant, O adorable Victim of Thy love and of our salvation, grant that faith may immolate my mind, charity consecrate my heart, and religion sacrifice my whole being to Thee; and that so long as I shall be in Thy house, my eyes may behold only Thee, my heart overflow with Thy love, and my tongue proclaim Thy praise in prayer and supplication.

3. While the angels lie prostrate before Thee, O great God! and, struck with humble fear, fervently pay Thee their tribute of profound respect and ardent love, shall we mortals, who are the works of Thy hands and the price of Thy blood, appear in Thy presence with wandering eyes and dissipated minds, with cold and indifferent hearts, without addressing Thee, and almost without thinking of Thee? O my Saviour, suffer me not to be thus wanting in the respect and love which I owe to Thy greatness, and which Thou dost so much the more deserve as Thou dost the more humble Thyself for the love of me.

4. Inspire me with the sentiments of the publican, who dared not lift up his eyes towards God, penetrated with sorrow

and confusion for his sins, and of the prodigal son, when he returned to his father's house; and grant that, like them, I may be restored through Thy bounty and my sorrow, to Thy grace and favor.

5. O my soul, behold thy God who died for thee, and of whose death thou wert the cause; how canst thou refrain from testifying thy love and gratitude towards Him? O my heart! be thou before Jesus Christ like the lamp* which burns before Him, and be thou in like manner consumed in His presence. No, I desire not to depart from before Thee, my Saviour, without being truly converted and entirely Thine. Amen.

Chapter 14

Of the Ardent Desire of Some Devout Persons to Receive the Body of Christ

DISCIPLE

OH, HOW great is the multitude of Thy sweetness, O Lord, which Thou hast hidden for them that fear Thee! (*Ps.* 30:20). When I remember some devout persons, who came to Thy Sacrament with the greatest devotion and affection, I am often confounded and ashamed within myself, that I approach so tepidly and coldly to Thine altar, and to the table of the Holy Communion; that I remain so dry, and without affection of heart; that I am not wholly set

---

*In Catholic countries a lamp is kept continually burning in the churches, before the altar on which the Blessed Sacrament is kept.

on fire in Thy presence, O my God, nor so earnestly drawn and affected, as many devout persons have been, who, out of a vehement desire of communion, and a sensible love in their hearts, could not contain themselves from weeping; but with their whole souls eagerly thirsted to approach, both with the mouth of their heart and their body, to Thee, O God, the living fountain; being in nowise able to moderate or satisfy their hunger, but by receiving Thy Body with all joy and spiritual eagerness. (*Ps.* 41:3).

2. O true ardent faith of these persons, being a probable argument of Thy sacred presence!

For they truly know their Lord in the breaking of bread, whose heart burneth so mightily within them, from Jesus walking with them. (*Luke* 24:35).

Such affection and devotion as this, so vehement a love and burning, is often far from me.

Be Thou merciful to me, O good Jesus, sweet and gracious Lord, and grant me, Thy poor suppliant, to feel sometimes at least, in the sacred Communion, some little of the cordial affection of Thy love, that my faith may be more strengthened, my hope in Thy goodness increased, and that my charity, being once perfectly enkindled, and having tasted the manna of Heaven, may never decay. (*2 Cor.* 9:8).

3. Moreover, Thy mercy is able to give me the grace I desire, and to visit me in Thy great clemency with the spirit of fervor, when it shall please Thee:

For though I burn not at present with so great a desire as those that are so singularly devoted to Thee; yet, by Thy grace, I desire to have this same greatly inflamed desire; praying and wishing that I may be made partaker with all such Thy fervent lovers and be numbered in their holy company.

Practical Reflections

How to make a good Spiritual Communion.

Spiritual Communion, which the Council of Trent approves of, and so strongly advises and commends as a substitute for the sacramental and corporeal reception of Jesus Christ, may be made at all times and in all places, whether we are in the presence of the Blessed Sacrament or not. We may make it every hour, or after a Hail Mary said in honor of the Blessed Virgin, Mother of God, uniting ourselves to those holy dispositions with which she conceived Jesus Christ in her chaste womb. We should bring our minds to a respectful remembrance of Jesus Christ in the Most Holy Sacrament; we should there adore Him, and direct our hearts towards Him, as Daniel did towards the temple; we should give all to Him, and desire to receive Him sacramentally; as, however, we cannot enjoy that happiness, not being prepared, we should pray to Him for the communication of His holy Spirit, in place of His sacred Body and Blood.

But the most proper time for making a good Spiritual Communion is when we assist at Mass, at the time of the priest's Communion. Then a Christian, animated with a lively and actual faith in the real presence of Jesus Christ in the Blessed Sacrament, and with an ardent desire of being intimately united to Him, should evince such dispositions by humbling himself profoundly in His presence; and, esteeming himself unworthy of really receiving Him, implore Him to come and dwell in his mind by faith, and in his heart by love and gratitude for His goodness, that so he may say with the Apostle, I live, now not I, but Christ liveth in me.

Prayer

O most amiable Saviour! Who wast the perpetual object and reigning desire of the ancient Patriarchs and Prophets, and of all the saints of the Old Testament, who sighed incessantly for Thine Incarnation, come into my soul, which burns with the desire of receiving Thee, and of being united to Thee, as the author of my salvation, and the source of all good. Come and destroy within me the tyranny of sin and self-love, and establish there the reign of Thy grace and charity. I have reason to judge myself unworthy of really partaking of Thy Body and Blood, but in Thy mercy grant me to partake of Thy spirit, and of Thy virtues, through the desire I have of receiving Thee in the most holy Sacrament.

No, my Jesus, I cannot leave Thee, nor live without Thee; Thou only canst satisfy my heart and make me happy. O ye seraphim! who ardently desire to be sacramentally united to Jesus Christ, yet cannot, I unite myself to the ardor and purity of your desires, to be united to the same God whom with me you adore upon the altar. But, O Lord, do Thou come and purify my heart from all attachment to myself or to creatures, my heart which was made but to love and to possess Thee. Thou alone canst satisfy it and all that is not Thee is as nothing. O amiable God! O loving God! can I know Thee and not love Thee, and love Thee and not burn with desire to receive Thee on earth, and to see and to possess Thee forever in Heaven. Amen.

Chapter 15

That the Grace of Devotion Is Obtained by Humility and Self-Denial

CHRIST

T HOU oughtest to seek the grace of devotion earnestly, to ask it fervently, to wait for it patiently and confidently, to receive it thankfully, to keep it humbly, to work with it diligently, and to commit to God the time and manner of heavenly visitation, until it please Him to come unto thee.

Thou oughtest chiefly to humble thyself when thou feelest inwardly little or no devotion; and yet not to be too much dejected, nor to grieve inordinately.

God often giveth in one short moment what He hath a long time denied.

He giveth sometimes in the end that which in the beginning of prayer He deferred to grant.

2. If grace were always presently given, and ever at hand with a wish, it would be more than man's infirmity could well bear.

Therefore the grace of devotion is to be expected with a good hope and humble patience. Yet impute it to thyself and to thy sins, when it is not given thee, or when it is secretly taken away.

It is sometimes a little thing that hinders or hides grace from thee; if that may be called a little, and not rather great, which hindereth so great a good.

But if thou remove this same, be it small or great, and perfectly overcome it, thou shalt have thy desire.

3. For as soon as ever thou hast delivered thyself up to God with thy whole heart, and neither seekest this nor that for thine own pleasure or will, but wholly placest thyself in Him, thou shalt find thyself united to Him, and at peace; for nothing will relish so well and please thee so much as the good pleasure of the divine will.

Whosoever, therefore, with a single heart shall direct his attention upwards to God, and purify himself from all inordinate love or dislike of any created thing, shall be the most fit to receive grace, and worthy of the gift of devotion. (*Matt.* 6:22).

For the Lord bestows His blessing there where He finds the vessels empty.

And the more perfectly one forsakes these things below, and the more he dies to himself by the contempt of himself, the more speedily grace cometh, entereth in more plentifully, and the higher it elevateth the free heart.

4. "Then shall he see and abound; his heart shall wonder and be enlarged" (*Is.* 60:5) within him, because the hand of the Lord is with him, and he has put himself wholly into His hand forever. Behold, thus shall the man be blessed that seeketh God with his whole heart, and taketh not his soul in vain.

Such a one as this, in receiving the Holy Eucharist, obtains a great grace of divine union, because he looks not towards his own devotion and comfort, but, above all devotion and comfort, regards the honor and glory of God.

Practical Reflections

*How we are to dispose ourselves to receive the grace
of the Holy Communion that we may profit by it.*

The end of the Holy Eucharist is to unite us intimately to
Jesus Christ, and to form in our souls a moral incarnation of His
spirit and His virtues; hence the holy Fathers call this adorable
Sacrament an extension of the Incarnation: it is to perpetuate
the reign of His grace and love within us, and to enable us
always to live a divine and supernatural life in and by Him. Thus
the grace which the Holy Communion produces in us is conformable to the end for which it was instituted; and is agreeable
to what Jesus Christ says of it in the Gospel: for, first, it causes
us to remain in Him, forming and imprinting in our souls the
character of His virtues, as a seal makes its impression upon the
wax to which it is applied; secondly, it makes us live by Him and
for Him, that is, act only to please Him and by the influence of
His love; thirdly, it enables us to live always a life of grace. Thus
the grace which Jesus Christ communicates to us in the Holy
Communion is to establish Himself in us, to make us act in all
things and live only in Him and for Him, and to give us eternal
life. We should dispose ourselves to receive and profit by this
grace and these three effects of a good communion; first, by
separating ourselves from all willful sin, and the affection for it;
secondly, by renouncing and dying incessantly to ourselves;
thirdly, by being ever faithful to the grace of God, and in the
exercise of His love.

Prayer

1. What confusion for me, O Jesus, to have communicated
so often, and to have profited so little by my Communions; to
have been so frequently nourished with God, and to have lived

always as man, an idle and sensual life! Pardon, my Saviour, pardon me the evil dispositions with which I have approached the Holy Communion, pardon me for having had so often a dissipated mind, a heart attached to self-love, and to the world, and for having done so little to acquire the dispositions for a good communion, to return Thee thanks after having received it and to reap the fruit of it, which is the re-establishment of myself in fidelity and fervor.

2. How much reason have I to fear, O my Saviour, that Thou wilt one day reproach me with the unfruitfulness of my communion. But ought I less to dread Thy just reproach for neglecting to dispose myself for frequent and worthy communion? How I fear lest I shall be condemned for my sloth, which has kept me away from the Holy Table, and caused me to lose so many communions to which Thou wouldst have attached the grace of my conversion.

3. I will therefore from henceforth dispose myself for worthy communion by detachment from sin and the occasions of it, and by interior acts of those virtues which I ought to exercise before, during, and after the Holy Communion, and I will also spare no pains to profit by my communions, by endeavoring to watch over myself, to avoid all willful faults, to do all with a view to please Thee, to be faithful in my religious exercises, and to be courageous in restraining and conquering myself: for these are the true fruits of a good communion. Grant me grace to execute what now, by Thy grace, Thou dost inspire me to resolve. Amen.

Chapter 16

That We Ought to Lay Open Our Necessities to Christ and Crave His Grace

DISCIPLE

O MOST sweet and loving Lord, whom I now desire to receive with all devotion, Thou knowest my weakness and the necessity which I endure; in what great evils and vices I am immersed; how often I am oppressed, tempted, troubled, and defiled. (*Ps.* 138:16).

To Thee I come for remedy; I pray to Thee for comfort and succor.

I speak to Him that knows all things, to whom all that is within me is manifest, and who alone can perfectly comfort and help me.

Thou knowest what good things I stand most in need of, and how poor I am in virtues.

2. Behold, I stand before Thee poor and naked, begging Thy grace, and imploring Thy mercy.

Feed Thy hungry suppliant, inflame my coldness with the fire of Thy love, enlighten my blindness with the brightness of Thy presence.

Teach me to look upon all earthly things with disgust, to bear all things grievous and afflicting with patience, and to look upon all things created with contempt and disregard.

Lift up my heart to Thee in Heaven, and suffer me not to wander upon earth.

Be Thou only sweet to me from henceforth forevermore; for Thou only art my meat and drink, my love and my joy, my sweetness and all my good.

3. Oh, that with Thy presence Thou wouldst inflame, burn, and transform me into Thyself, that I may be made one spirit with Thee, by the grace of eternal union, and by the melting of ardent love.

Suffer me not to go from Thee hungry and thirsty, but deal with me in Thy mercy as Thou hast often dealt wonderfully with Thy saints.

What marvel if I should be wholly set on fire by Thee, and should die to myself; since Thou art a fire always burning (*Heb.* 12:29), and never decaying; a love purifying the hearts and enlightening the understanding.

Practical Reflections

For this and the next chapter.

1. The Son of God, after having taught us by His word, shown us by His example, and merited for us, by His grace, the necessary and essential virtues for Christian salvation, would institute the adorable Sacrament of the Eucharist, to come Himself and imprint them in our hearts. Of these Christian virtues, humility is the first, of which He gives us a splendid example in the most holy Sacrament: for He is there concealed, annihilated, and unknown to sense. During His mortal life, the perfections of His divinity only were concealed, and as it were annihilated in His humanity; but in the Blessed Sacrament His humanity also lies hid, and nothing appears of a Man-God but what is seen by the eyes of faith. Here we learn how we ought to live in this world, in imitation of the humility and annihilation of Jesus Christ in the most holy Sacrament; first, to love a concealed and abject life; secondly, to fly from praise, esteem, and honor, and to welcome

contempt as due to such sinners as ourselves; thirdly, to endeavor to be good and virtuous, without wishing to display our virtue or to perform our actions for the sake of being seen and esteemed by men, but solely to please God; fourthly, to be persuaded that man cannot honor God in any way so effectually as by abasing and humbling himself before Him; fifthly, to yield to hasty persons for the sake of peace; sixthly, never to act from human respect, but from a reverential fear of God; seventhly, never to speak well of ourselves, nor ill of others.

2. The Son of God gives us in the Holy Eucharist an example of perfect obedience and of patience equal to all the outrages which He there receives, by the exact, continual, and miraculous obedience which He pays to the priest, immediately descending upon the altar when the words of consecration are pronounced, and remaining there until man receives Him into his breast! O great God of independence and sovereignty! what a subject of confusion for us, that although Thou art God, Thou dost nevertheless obey man without delay, while man refuses or defers to obey Thee.

I will henceforth, O my Saviour, in honor and imitation of Thy perfect obedience in the most holy Sacrament, promptly, generously, and constantly obey whatever Thou shalt ordain by Thine inspirations, by my superiors, and by the knowledge of my duties.

3. Jesus Christ teaches and inspires us with patience by His practice of it in the Holy Eucharist, in which He is an object of contempt to some, of neglect to others, and of indifference to many, who are but little devoted to God, much to the world, and wholly to themselves; in which He beholds Himself exposed to the unworthy or fruitless communions of so many, whose lives are either decidedly criminal from being spent in the habit and occasion of mortal sin, or, at least, are of no avail

to salvation. Nevertheless He suffers all these outrages with invincible patience, and He suffers them thus, to teach and to induce us to suffer contradictions and injuries in like manner.

4. O my Jesus, the Victim of our salvation and of our sins! why should we daily renew by our irreverence, dissipation, and indevotion, those outrages Thou didst receive when dying on the cross, and renew them even in that state in which Thou art pleased to continue that all-atoning Sacrifice. Pardon, O Jesus, pardon the insensibility, coldness, and indevotion with which we have approached the Holy Communion; forgive us for not having always followed the injunction which Thou givest us in the Gospel of being reconciled to all mankind before we present ourselves at the foot of Thine altar. Pardon also our impatience and the sallies of passion, which our communions have not corrected in us, because we have not profited by them! Suffer not our tongues, which become the resting places of Thy sacred Body, and which are so often purpled with Thy Blood, to be employed as the instruments of our anger and maledictions. O Lord, Who during Thy mortal life didst heal the most incurable diseases, arrest, I beseech Thee, the impetuosity of my tongue. Yes, my Saviour, that I may reap advantage from my communions, I will never speak when my heart is moved, but sacrifice my utterance to Thee, Who, for my sake, didst sacrifice even the last drop of Thy sacred Blood.

Prayer

To attain the fruit of a good communion.

Give, O Jesus, to all who approach Thee in the Holy Communion, a constant courage to conquer themselves, an exact fidelity in corresponding with Thy graces, a restraint upon their tongue, a recollection of mind, and the plenitude of Thy love in their hearts. For Thy honor and glory, O divine Saviour, subject us to Thy dominion, and immolate us to Thy greatness. Suffer not our hearts, which are the conquest of Thy grace, ever more to be separated from Thee.

Be Thou the ruler of our passions, and the God of our souls; and grant that when we communicate, and after communion, we may establish within us the reign of Thy sovereignty by our submission, the reign of Thy bounty by our confidence, and the reign of Thy grace by our fidelity. Amen.

Chapter 17

Of a Fervent Love and Vehement Desire to Receive Christ

DISCIPLE

WITH the greatest devotion and burning love, with all the affection and fervor of my heart, I desire to receive Thee, O Lord; as many saints and devout persons, who were most pleasing to Thee by holiness of life, and most fervent devotion, have desired Thee, when they communicated.

O my God, my eternal love, my whole good, and never-ending happiness, I would gladly receive Thee with the most vehement desire, and most worthy reverence, that any of the saints have ever had or could experience.

2. And although I am unworthy to have all those feelings of devotion, yet I offer to Thee the whole affection of my heart, as if I alone had all those highly pleasing and inflamed desires.

Yea, and whatsoever a godly mind can conceive and desire, all this with the greatest reverence and most inward affection, I offer and present to Thee.

I desire to reserve nothing to myself, but freely and most willingly to sacrifice myself, and all that is mine, to Thee.

O Lord, my God, my Creator, and my Redeemer, I desire to receive Thee this day with such affection, reverence, praise, and honor; with such gratitude, worthiness, and love; with such faith, hope, and purity, as Thy most holy Mother, the glorious Virgin Mary, received and desired Thee, when she humbly and devoutly answered the angel, who declared to her the mystery of the Incarnation, saying: "Behold the handmaid of the Lord; be it done to me according to thy word." (*Luke* 1:38).

3. And as Thy blessed forerunner, the most excellent among the saints, John the Baptist, in Thy presence leaped for joy through the Holy Ghost, while he was yet shut up in his mother's womb, and afterwards seeing Jesus walking amongst men, humbling himself exceedingly, said, with devout affection: "The friend of the bridegroom, who standeth and heareth him, rejoiceth with joy because of the bridegroom's voice." (*John* 3:29). So I also wish to be inflamed with great and holy desires, and to present myself to Thee with my whole heart.

Wherefore I here offer and present to Thee the excessive joys of all devout hearts, their ardent affections, their ecstasies and supernatural illuminations, and heavenly visions; together with all the virtues and praises which are or shall be celebrated by all creatures in Heaven and on earth; for myself and all such as are recommended to my prayers; that by all Thou mayest be worthily praised and glorified forever.

4. Receive my wishes, O Lord, my God, and my desires of giving Thee infinite praise and immense blessings, which according to the multitude of Thine unspeakable greatness, are most justly due to Thee.

These I render, and desire to render Thee every day and every moment; and I invite and entreat all the heavenly spirits, and all the faithful, with my prayers and affections, to join with me in giving Thee praises and thanks.

5. Let all peoples, tribes, and tongues, praise Thee, and magnify Thy holy and sweet name, with the highest jubilation and ardent devotion. (*Dan.* 7:14).

And let all who reverently and devoutly celebrate Thy most high Sacrament, and receive it with full faith, find grace and mercy at Thy hands, and humbly pray for me, a sinful creature.

And when they shall have obtained their desired devotion and joyful union, and shall depart from Thy sacred heavenly table well comforted and wonderfully nourished, let them vouchsafe to remember my poor soul.

*Practical Reflections and Prayer
as in the preceding chapter.*

Chapter 18

That a Man Be Not a Curious Searcher into This Sacrament, But an Humble Follower of Christ, Submitting His Sense to Holy Faith

CHRIST

THOU must beware of curious and unprofitable searching into this most profound Sacrament, if thou wilt not sink into the depth of doubt.

"He that is a searcher of majesty shall be overwhelmed by glory." (*Prov.* 25:27). God is able to do more than man can understand.

A pious and humble inquiry after truth is tolerable, which is always ready to be taught, and studies to walk in the sound doctrine of the Fathers.

2. Blessed is that simplicity that leaveth the difficult ways of dispute, and goeth on in the plain and sure path of God's commandments. (*Ps.* 118:35).

Many have lost devotion whilst they would search into high things.

Faith is required of thee, and a sincere life, not the height of understanding, nor diving deep into the mysteries of God.

If thou dost not understand nor comprehend those things that are under thee, how shouldst thou comprehend those things that are above thee?

Submit thyself to God, and humble thy senses to faith, and the light of knowledge shall be given thee, as far as shall be profitable and necessary for thee.

3. Some are grievously tempted about faith and the Sacrament; but this is not to be imputed to them, but rather to the enemy.

Be not thou anxious, stand not to dispute with thy thoughts, nor to answer the doubts which the devil suggests; but believe the words of God, believe His saints and prophets, and the wicked enemy will fly from thee. (*James* 4:7).

It is often very profitable to the servants of God to suffer such things.

For the devil tempts not unbelievers and sinners, whom he already surely possesses; but the faithful and devout he many ways tempts and molests.

4. Go forward, therefore, with a sincere and undoubting faith, and with an humble reverence approach this Sacrament: and whatsoever thou art not able to understand commit securely to Almighty God.

God deceiveth thee not; but he is deceived that trusteth too much in himself.

God walketh with the simple, and revealeth Himself to the humble; He giveth understanding to the little ones, openeth the gate of knowledge to pure minds, and hideth His grace from the curious and proud. (*Ps.* 98:130; *Matt.* 11:25).

Human reason is weak, and may be deceived, but true faith cannot be deceived.

5. All reason and natural search ought to follow faith, and not to go before it, nor oppose it.

For faith and love are here predominant, and work by hidden ways in this most holy and superexcellent Sacrament.

God, who is eternal and incomprehensible, and of infinite power, doth great and inscrutable things in Heaven and earth, and there is no searching out His wonderful works. (*Is.* 40:28).

If the works of God were such as might be easily comprehended by human reason, they could not be called wonderful or unspeakable.

Practical Reflections

We must firmly believe in the Real Presence, and humbly receive the Body and Blood of Jesus.

1. Taking it for granted that God can do more than man can comprehend; that human reason may be deceived, but that faith cannot; and that we are bound to believe Jesus Christ when He says to His Apostles, "This is My Body, which shall be delivered for you; this is My Blood which shall be shed for you," we must necessarily believe without hesitation the Real Presence of the Body and Blood of Jesus Christ in the Most Holy Sacrament, without wishing to fathom the depth of this mystery, which is wholly incomprehensible to reason and impenetrable to human understanding, our faith supplying the defects of our senses, and contenting ourselves with thinking that a God was able to accomplish it, and has declared to us that He has done so; we must endeavor only to believe, honor, and receive Jesus Christ in the adorable Eucharist.

2. What a happiness thus to sacrifice in this mystery of faith, as indeed in all other mysteries, the light of human reason to the truth of God's word, and the affection of our hearts to the infinite love evinced by our Redeemer in the institution and use of the Most Holy Sacrament, in which, as St. Bernard says,

He is all love for us; in which, according to the Council of Trent, He replenishes our hearts with all the riches of His love; but of a love infinitely liberal, which induces Him to give Himself entirely to us, and to be even prodigal of Himself; for it is, says the sacred text, in this Sacrament, which He instituted at the close of His life, that He gives us the most tender and sensible marks of His love for us, by uniting Himself intimately to us, and us intimately to Himself, to take possession from henceforth of our hearts, and to give us a pledge of possessing Him for all eternity.

3. Such being the admirable designs of Jesus Christ in the Most Holy Sacrament, it is for us to endeavor to correspond with them by a worthy and frequent use of it. A sincere and reverential faith, a Christian life of detachment from the world, a profound humility, a simple docility of belief, and an effectual obedience in refusing nothing required of us by Jesus Christ, when He descends into our souls in the Holy Eucharist, a dedication of our whole selves to the honor of His annihilated greatness, and in gratitude for the ardor of His love, is the whole He requires of us, and all we have to do to dispose ourselves in a proper manner to receive and to profit by this holy Sacrament. But let us always remember that He does not demand from us as a disposition for communion that which is the effect of communion, and that, provided we approach Him with a real desire of being converted, evinced by a good confession, and by a firm hope that Jesus Christ will confirm us by His presence in His grace and love, we may with confidence frequently receive the Holy Communion, that we may obtain courage to conquer ourselves, fidelity in our exercises of piety, and perseverance in the grace and love of God, which are the real effects of frequent and worthy communion.

Prayer

To Jesus Christ, that He may
in His bounty enable us to practice this book.

Allow me, O my Saviour! to offer Thee, with the most profound reverence, these helps to the practice of this book of Thine imitation, which Thou hast inspired me to add to it, to teach and induce all Christians to apply themselves to know Thee, to love Thee, and to follow Thee, to unite themselves to the holy dispositions of Thy heart in all Thy mysteries, to practice the maxims of Thy Gospel, and to imitate Thy virtues; for it is in this, as Thou tellest us, that consists all the happiness and all the merit of a Christian life.

I beseech thee, O holy Virgin, Mother of my God and Saviour! to obtain this grace for me, and for all who shall read these helps to the practice of this book of the "Following of thy Son," and procure for us, by thy powerful intercession, a good life, a holy death, and a happy eternity. Amen.

Indexes

From

The Imitation of Christ

— Index of Lessons —

from *The Imitation of Christ,* suitable
to the Different States of Life and
Spiritual Necessities of the Faithful

For priests

Bk.   I.   chap.   18, 19, 20, 25.
     II.   chap.   11, 12.
     III.   chap.   3, 10, 31, 56.
     IV.   chap.   5, 7, 10, 11, 12, 18.

For seminarians

Bk.   I.   chap.   17, 18, 19, 20, 21, 25.
     III.   chap.   2, 3, 10, 31, 56.
     IV.   chap.   5, 7, 10, 11, 12, 18.

For students

Bk.   I.   chap.   1, 2, 3, 5.
     II.   chap.   2, 38, 43, 44, 58.
     IV.   chap.   18.

For those who complain of making little progress in their studies

Bk.   III.   chap.   29, 39, 41, 47.

For those who aspire to piety

Bk.   I.   chap.   15, 18, 19, 20, 21, 22, 25.
     II.   chap.   1, 4, 7, 8, 9, 11, 12.
     III.   chap.   5, 6, 7, 11, 27, 31, 32, 33, 53, 54, 55, 56.

For those in affliction and humiliation

Bk. I. chap. 12.
II. chap. 11, 12.
III. chap. 12, 15, 16, 17, 18, 19, 20, 21, 29, 30, 35, 41, 47, 48, 49, 50, 52, 55, 56.

For those who repine at their sufferings

Bk. I. chap. 12.
II. chap. 12.

For those who labor under temptations

Bk. I. chap. 13.
II. chap. 9.
III. chap. 6, 16, 17, 18, 19, 20, 21, 23, 30, 35, 37, 47, 48, 49, 50, 52, 55.

For those who suffer interior trials

Bk. II. chap. 3, 9, 11, 12.
III. chap. 7, 12, 16, 17, 18, 19, 20, 21, 30, 35, 47, 48, 49, 50, 51, 52, 55, 56.

For those who are troubled about the future, their health, their fortune, the success of their undertakings

Bk. III. chap. 39.

For those living in the world, or who are distracted with their employments

Bk. III. chap. 38, 53.

For those who are assailed with calumnies or lies

Bk. II. chap. 2.
III. chap. 6, 11, 28, 36, 46.

For those who are beginning their conversion

For timid, weak, or negligent persons

To obtain interior peace

For hardened sinners

For indolent persons

For those who credit and circulate evil reports

For those who are inclined to pride

For querulous and obstinate persons

For those who take offense at the simplicity or the obscurity of the Holy Scriptures

Bk.　I.　chap. 5.

For those who are inclined to jealousy

Bk. III.　chap. 22, 41.

For a retreat

Preparation.	Bk.	I.	chap. 20, 21.
	Bk.	III.	chap. 53.
Miseries of man.	Bk.	I.	chap. 22.
Death.	Bk.	I.	chap. 23.
Judgment and Hell.	Bk.	I.	chap. 24.
	Bk.	III.	chap. 14.
Heaven.	Bk.	III.	chap. 48.
Conclusion.	Bk.	III.	chap. 59.

— Index of Prayers —

from *The Imitation of Christ*

Before spiritual reading

Bk. III. chap. 2.

To obtain the grace of devotion

Bk. III. chap. 3. par. 6 and 7.

To obtain an increase of the love of God

Bk. III. chap. 5. par. 6.

For those who live in retirement and piety

Bk. III. chap. 10.

For resignation to the will of God

Bk. III. chap. 15. par. 1, verses 3 and 4; par. 2, verse 3 to the end.

Acts of resignation

Bk. III. chap. 16 to the end.
Bk. III. chap. 17, par. 2 and 4.
Bk. III. chap. 18, par. 2.

For patience

Bk. III. chap. 19, par. 5.

For those who think they have received less from God than others, either for body or for soul

Bk. III. chap. 22.

For purity of mind and detachment from creatures

For one who is beginning his conversion, or who is desirous of advancing in virtue

To obtain the spirit of strength and wisdom

For a person in great affliction

Acts of resignation and reliance on Divine Providence

When we receive any grace from God

An act of resignation

Pious sentiments

When attacked with calumny

To obtain grace

For priests and religious to obtain perseverance in their vocations

Bk. III. chap. 56, par. 3, 5, 6.

An act of confidence in God

Bk. III. chap. 57, par. 4.

In the presence of the Blessed Sacrament

Bk. IV. chap. 1, 2, 3, 4, 9, 11 (to par. 6), 13, 14, 16, 17, and part of the prayers above.

The dignity of the priests and the sanctity of their ministry

Bk. IV. chap. 5.

For priests and seminarians

Bk. IV. chap. 11, par. 6, 7, 8.

Before Communion

Acts of abasement in the presence of God

Bk. III. chap. 8.

Acts of humility and contrition

Bk. III. chap. 52.

After Communion

An act of thanksgiving

Bk. III. chap. 21, par. 7.

To excite one's self to the love of God

Bk. III. chap. 34.

— Index of Devotions for Holy Communion —

A Retreat of Three Days

First Day

Morning

Noon

Evening

Second Day

Morning

Noon

Evening

Third Day

Morning

Preparation and exercise of humility.

Bk. IV. chap. 6.   Prayer to obtain the grace of
                     approaching the Sacrament worthily.

Bk. IV. chap. 7.   Examination of conscience, contrition,
                     resolution of amendment, confession,
                     and satisfaction.

(Read also on your knees the 8th chapter of Bk. III.)

Noon

Bk. IV. chap. 18. Faith obedient to the mystery of the
                     Eucharist.

Bk. IV. chap. 10. Advantages of frequent Communion.
                     (Omit from the second part of par. 7 to
                     the end.)

(Read on your knees the 52nd chap. of **Bk.** III.)

Evening

Bk. IV. chap. 12. Preparation for Holy Communion.

Bk. IV. chap. 10. Advantages of frequent Communion.

      IV. chap. 15. Devotion founded on humility and
                     self-renunciation.

Bk. IV. chap. 10. Advantages of frequent Communion.

      IV. chap. 9.   Offering of one's self to God in Holy
                     Communion.

(Read on your knees the 40th chap. of Bk. III).

For the Day of Communion

Morning

Bk.   IV.   chap.   10. Advantages of frequent Communion.
      IV.   chap.   1, 2, 3, 4.

Before and during Mass

Bk. IV, chap. 9, 16, 17

After Mass

Bk.   IV.   chap.   10. Advantages of frequent Communion.
      IV.   chap.   11, 13, 14.

During the day and evening

Bk.   IV.   chap.   10. Advantages of frequent Communion.
      III.   chap.   21, 34, 48.
(Repeat the 9th chapter of Bk. IV, and choose one of the prayers set down before, Bk. IV, chap. 6, and following.)

For Six Days following Holy Communion
First Day

*Return thanks to Jesus Christ
and excite yourself to His love.*

Bk.   III.   chap.   5, 7, 8, 10.

Second Day

*Listen to the voice of Jesus Christ,
speaking to the soul after it has received Him.*

Bk.   II.   chap.   1.
Bk.   III.   chap.   1, 2, 3.

Third Day

Detach the soul from creatures.

Bk. III. chap. 26, 31, 42, 45.

Fourth Day

Renounce thyself, and give thyself entirely to God.

Bk. III. chap. 15, 17, 27, 37.

Fifth Day

*Suffer with patience, and in union
with the sufferings of Jesus Christ.*

Bk. II. chap. 12.
Bk. III. chap. 16, 18, 19.

Sixth Day

*Persevere in fervor, and be constant
in your good resolutions.*

Bk. I. chap. 19, 21.
Bk. III. chap. 23, 55.

If you have enjoyed this book, consider making your next selection from among the following . . .

Prices subject to change.

Prices subject to change.